SKIN IN THE GAME:

Unleashing Your Inner Entrepreneur to Find Love

Neely Steinberg, Ed.M.

neely@thelovetrep.com

www.thelovetrep.com

Skin In the Game: Unleashing Your Inner Entrepreneur to Find Love
A Love TREP Publishing Book | 2013

Published by The Love TREP® Publishing
Boston, MA

The Love TREP is a registered trademark with the USPTO.

Cover design: Avery Managhas

ISBN-13: 978-0989723503 (The Love TREP)
ISBN-10: 098972350X

Printed in the United States of America

www.thelovetrep.com

DEDICATIONS

Dedicated to the following people who helped me on my entrepreneurial journey to find love:

My parents, Nancy and Stephen, and my brother, Randy, for helping shape me into the person I am today. My friends—you know who you are—for giving me the love and support I needed when times were tough. My longtime therapist, Dr. Cohen, for being a sounding board and an empathetic listener, for being a voice of reason, for holding up a mirror when I needed one, and for aiding in my growth as a woman and a human being trying to live a more connected, happy life.

And to Dave, the love of my life, the man to whom my entrepreneurial journey steered me. Your support, advice, encouragement, and all the other wonderful things you've given me that defy description, mean the world to me. Your love has empowered me to write this book and believe so strongly in its contents. I love you.

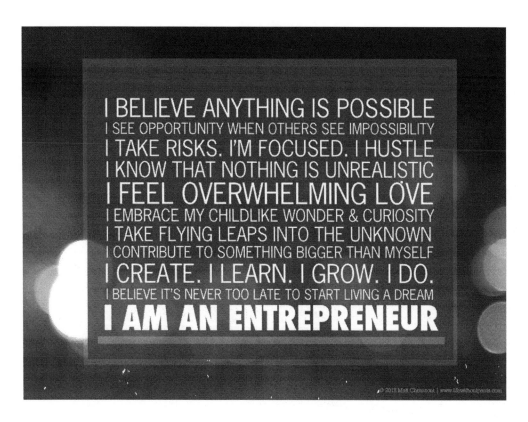

I Am An Entrepreneur Manifesto. Reprinted with permission.

Created by Matt Cheuvront.

- Blog: http://lifewithoutpants.com.
- Company: http://proofbranding.com.
- The above manifesto can be purchased as a poster here: http://store.coolpeoplecare.org/collections/posters/products/i-am-an-entrepreneur-poster

TABLE OF CONTENTS

ATTENTION!
The <u>Preface</u> gives some background on the concepts I present in this book and the <u>Introduction</u> briefly discusses both my personal and professional journey within the world of dating/ relationships. <u>PLEASE NOTE</u>: If you're itching to get started, feel free to skip the Preface and Introduction and go straight to chapter 1.

use reflection and the lessons from your dating
and romantic experiences to your advantage

- Practice makes perfect
  - Discusses the third part of my Date. Learn. Repeat. model
    of entrepreneurial dating: how to harness what you're learn-
    ing from your actions and then incorporate that knowledge
    into future actions you take in the dating world so that you
    date smarter

- If at first you don't succeed...
  - Breaks down the concept of failure and tells you how to
    use it to your advantage in your dating and love life.

- Networking is networking is networking
  - Shows you how to make your dating and love life more
    fruitful by tapping into the power of your networks and by
    creating new networks

- Opportunity awaits
  - Shows you how to identify and seize opportunities to meet
    people

WHO SHOULD READ THIS BOOK?

When you picked up this book, perhaps you were expecting a few anecdotes and touchy-feely catchphrases to start things out, and if this is what you are looking for, there are many, many dating books out there that will appeal to you. But this book espouses a different approach. This book is written for women who are ready for love and willing to work for it. Women who aren't afraid to take a few risks or turn the mirror on themselves and look inside. If you wanted to learn how to renovate your house, would you rely on anecdotal advice, or would you seek out a well-researched, clearly explained, step-by-step guide that gives you all the information you need to leap in and take charge yourself? Renovating your approach to dating can be handled much the same way, and I wrote this book to show you the way, the entrepreneurial way.

As you will soon read, I advocate a trial and error approach to dating. That *is* the entrepreneurial way. This approach may take time. You may need to date entrepreneurially for a year before meeting that special man. For others, it will take longer. And some of you may meet your match within a few months of finishing this book. Everyone is unique, and we're all at different levels of self-awareness and self-growth. I don't believe in dating systems that claim to help you find your partner within a very specific amount of time. I've purchased those books. And while they can be helpful in certain ways, I don't believe in putting an exact timeframe on a person's dating journey. Just know this: If you really make the time and effort to do the Action Steps outlined in this book, I believe you *will* create the results you want in your life in a healthy, measured way that is right for you.

Disclaimers

All names and identifying information pertaining to real-life persons and dating anecdotes have been changed in the pages that follow to protect identities.

All opinions expressed herein are my own and not those of any other person or entity, unless explicitly stated.

HOW TO READ THIS BOOK:

The entrepreneurial way is at its core a method based on action and forward motion. As a dating coach who advocates an action-oriented approach, this is precisely why I believe entrepreneurship is such a worthy field for singles to draw from. I want you to always think of yourself as being in forward motion when it comes to your dating and love life, and that every step you take—be it big or small—is a part of that forward motion (even the ones you feel were mistakes). To that end, there is a section dedicated to Action Steps at the end of each chapter, which you should work on as you progress through these pages. First, though, I encourage you to read the book in its entirety without interruption.

Having lived in the world of entrepreneurship education for so many years, this is an area with which I am well acquainted, but I understand that the majority of readers are new to entrepreneurship and its concepts and will thus benefit from giving the book a once-through read without too much stopping and starting. There's a lot to digest about both dating and entrepreneurship within the pages that follow, so I encourage you first to enjoy the reading process, familiarize yourself with the subject of entrepreneurship, and understand generally how the different components will work in your dating and love life. Once you've finished a first pass, you can dive in, one chapter at a time, and start working on the Action Steps. If you are so inclined, please purchase the workbook for *Skin In the Game*, which is available on Amazon or through my website (www.thelovetrep.com). The 200-page workbook will be an excellent resource for you as you embark on your entrepreneurial journey. It recaps major concepts from this

SIDEBARS!
Don't forget to read these sidebars! They are peppered throughout the book and offer extra tips, suggestions, explanations, definitions, affirmations, pep talks, and much more.

Action Steps.
Use the action steps at the end of each chapter to keep you moving forward.

The Workbook.
You may want to purchase the workbook for Skin In the Game, which is available for purchase on Amazon and my website. The workbook allows you to complete all the Action Steps in one place.

TREP.

Trep = common shorthand for entrepreneur.

Your outlook.

Keep an open, positive mind during this process. Your expectations shape your reality.

book and outlines detailed instructions for all of the Action Steps within each chapter. The workbook allows you to complete all of the Action Steps (exercises, journaling, etc.) in one place.

To be successful in your entrepreneurial journey to find love, it is important that you complete the Action Steps as outlined in each chapter, and do them in sequential order, especially in Parts I and II. For instance, you can't jump into the various exercises in chapter 5 (Part II) if you haven't started the process of removing obstacles, as outlined in chapter 3 (Part I). Part III will help facilitate the work you are doing in Part II.

I strongly encourage you to follow my recommendations, but if you do choose to skip around a bit, it is my sincere hope that you take away something by employing the entrepreneurial mindset and approach in your dating and love life. I truly believe the entrepreneurial way is a force that can transform lives, so much so that I've based my dating coaching business, The Love TREP®, around it. ('Trep' is common shorthand for entrepreneur.) If you take away just one insight that has the power to make a difference in your dating and love life, then I believe I have succeeded as a dating coach.

It is also my hope that this book inspires you to get excited again about dating and the prospect of finding love. As you become a Love TREP, *you* will be building your love story; inevitably, a sense of pride and empowerment will wash over you as you realize *you* have the power to innovate in your life and control your own destiny. Indeed, much of this book is about guiding you to come to your own answers and empowering you to act of your own free will. I can't force you to act. And I won't give you a prescribed set of dating rules to follow. My job as a coach is not to show you how smart I am, but to show you how smart *you can be.*

It is essential that you keep an open mind as you read these pages. Your expectations will shape your reality; in other words, you will experience what you expect to experience. It will therefore be crucial for you to begin this entrepreneurial journey with a positive attitude and the belief that creating change and growth entrepreneurially in your dating and love life is possible.

Finally, I want you to know that this journey won't always be an easy one—quick fixes and answers—because changing the way you think and behave is difficult and never happens overnight. At times, the entrepreneurial way may seem daunting. I am, essentially, asking you to engage in a major mindshift: to see and experience the world of dating and love very differently than the ways in which you have seen and experienced it before. You will need to immerse yourself fully in this world in a variety of ways, some of which may feel uncomfortable for you. I encourage you to hang in there and stick with the process, especially when you feel like giving up.

Entrepreneurs understand that starting a venture is no simple task; it's an unpredictable journey into the unknown, filled with road-blocks, detours, and wrong turns. Despite myriad challenges that in-evitably sprout along the way, successful entrepreneurs find ways to forge ahead, seeing opportunity where others see impossibility. They create their futures, fueled by their entrepreneurial desire to grow and learn, even when the path seems rocky. When you live this way— in both business and love—you will feel tremendously empowered. Your dating and love life can and will change and move forward in

Hold your horses! Finding love, like starting and building a business, takes time. It's not always easy. So stick with it and stay positive.

truly amazing directions. And you'll use the spirit of entrepreneurship and the wisdom of entrepreneurs every step of the way as you create, build, and shape your love story.

I hope you will come to see your entrepreneurial journey as a liberating one, an adventure, full of purposeful motion, illuminating and life-changing a-ha moments, and as a path to self-discovery that allows you to find the happiness you want and deserve in your dating and love life. This book is not just about "putting a ring on it" or "hooking the man"; although your ultimate aim is to find a healthy, happy relationship, much of this book is about encouraging you to enjoy, appreciate, and see the value in the steps along the way. In my experience, the most successful, happiest people in work and life have learned to focus on the journey, instead of concentrating solely on reaching some sort of destination.

So now it is your turn as a love entrepreneur, a Love TREP, to create, build, and shape your future.

Your journey starts today.

Be inTREPid,
Neely

GOALS OF THIS BOOK

By reading this book you will:

- Start seeing your dating and love life as an entrepreneurial venture—one that you have the power to create, build, and shape—and yourself as a Love Entrepreneur, a Love TREP, who thinks and acts like an entrepreneurial leader in your own dating and love life.

- Learn how to apply the lessons from the experiences of traditional entrepreneurs to your dating and love life.

- Learn *how* to think and how to think for yourself, not *what* to think.

- Establish, maintain, and work toward the following vision: *To create a healthy, happy dating life that leads to a healthy, happy relationship.*

- Learn why entrepreneurial qualities such as desire, a problem-solving mindset, and vision are crucial for starting and maintaining your venture.

- Learn how to identify and remove internal and external obstacles that are holding you back and preventing you from thinking and acting more entrepreneurially and creatively in your dating and love life.

- Learn how to ask others for help, advice, and mentoring when it comes to your dating and love life.

- Define and clearly communicate who you are and what you know about your love life and the dating world around you so you can start from a place of knowledge not helplessness, and so that your actions in the dating world are

rooted in a keen understanding of yourself and the environment in which you exist.

- Get a better understanding of the type of person you are looking for while still remaining flexible in your expectations and standards, and be open to different types of men.
- Learn why practice is so important to the entrepreneurial process and *how* to practice *dating*.
- Learn how to take action to move your dating and love life forward.
- Learn how to use reflection to your advantage as you move forward in your dating and love life.
- Learn how to use repetition (iteratively and incrementally) to date smarter and thus move closer to your vision.
- Learn how to reframe failure, mistakes, and wrong turns in your dating and love life so that you see them as assets.
- Learn how to think differently and more rationally about taking risks in your dating and love life.
- Learn how to use your already-established networks to your advantage in your dating and love life.
- Learn how to build and nurture relationships within your networks, thereby increasing your chances of meeting potential dates.
- Learn how to create, identify, and seize your own opportunities through which you can meet potential dates.
- Learn how to use customer feedback—your customers being men—to your advantage in your dating and love life.
- Learn what it means to stay *agile* in your dating and love life.
- Learn about a new field: entrepreneurship.

PREFACE

**(*If you're itching to start your entrepreneurial journey
to find love, feel free to skip this section and
continue straight to chapter 1.*)**

As a dating coach, I am committed to helping women move their dating and love lives forward. At its core, my philosophy is based on a trial and error model of action and reflection: motivating and inspiring women to think deeply about themselves and their love lives, to embrace the unknown, to take action, to reflect some more, and then to act again, but each time in smarter, more empowered ways. My ultimate goal is to help women use this approach to learn how to take charge of their love lives, just as effectively as they take charge in every other area of their lives. I want women to understand that they have a very powerful hand in creating their futures, especially when it comes to dating and love, and that imagining yourself as an entrepreneur creating and building your love story is a very instructive and motivating force.

I am grateful to the field of entrepreneurship and to Babson College, in particular, for indirectly helping to shape my ideas on dating and love into a usable, practical framework for my clients and single women everywhere who seek guidance and direction in dating and love.

Let's briefly explore some of the newest research in the field of entrepreneurship education and how you will be applying some of these exciting concepts to your dating and love life.

Entrepreneurial Thought and Action® (ET&A)

Babson is a prominent leader in shaping the conversation on entrepreneurship education. Building on new research in the field, the school's faculty and leadership have created a valuable methodology for developing entrepreneurial leaders, known as Entrepreneurial Thought and Action® (ET&A), a model that teaches people how to think and act in uncertain, unknowable situations. By providing a bit of background on some of the concepts within this methodology, I hope to give you an understanding of the foundation from which I've shaped and developed some of my ideas with regard to thinking and acting entrepreneurially in one's dating and love life.

Grounded in research. The concepts in ET&A are simple ones, but they are grounded in research.

ET&A® isn't rocket science, nor are its principles limited to the business world. In fact, it's based on simple concepts that humans have been employing for eons in all sorts of different contexts, though its genesis was inspired by studying and understanding entrepreneurs. The genius of ET&A® is that it neatly packages these concepts into an easy-to-understand, tangible framework.

Get excited!

Thinking and acting like an entrepreneur in your dating and love life gets you excited about dating again. And when you're excited about dating, you feel inspired to take more action, to be open to new ideas and possibilities and to look at life differently.

For business leaders, the concept of ET&A® is extremely useful, especially in today's world, because the model offers a framework and mental model when people find themselves in unknowable environments—a logic that allows them to take more timely and intelligent action in these environments. I believe that many of the concepts within the methodology are transferrable to the world of dating and love, especially in the twenty-first century.

Babson faculty members Danna Greenberg and Kate McKone-Sweet, along with H. James Wilson, a senior researcher with Babson

Executive Education, argue in their article "Entrepreneurial Thought and Action®: A Methodology for Developing Entrepreneurial Leaders," that we need to embrace entrepreneurship in contexts outside of where it is traditionally employed. They write: "Entrepreneurial leaders are needed in spaces far beyond the traditional boundaries of business organizations and the discipline of entrepreneurship."

Perhaps they never imagined the space of dating and love when they wrote about "expanding boundaries," but that's, of course, where I come in.

The truth is many of the concepts outlined in ET&A® and many of the ones I espouse as a dating coach are eerily similar. Packaging my concepts in the context of thinking and acting like an entrepreneur has been incredibly inspiring, both for me as a coach and for the singles with whom I work. In particular, two of the three principles that underlie ET&A® can have great value for singles looking to find a healthy, happy relationship.

One of these principles is called "Cognitive Ambidexterity," a way of using both *prediction* ("prediction logic") and *action* ("creation logic") to make decisions. It teaches when to use one approach rather than the other, and how both can be used together to create meaningful change. For a businessperson, using prediction typically means relying either on an examination of the past or on standard analytical approaches, such as marketing research and statistical tools, to solve problems. However, when the future is unknowable, a businessperson looks to action and experimentation to create the future. Greenberg and her co-authors write: "All entrepreneurial leaders will need to employ both creation and prediction approaches and become

Prediction vs. Action. I will show you when to use prediction and analysis of the past to make smarter choices but also when to use action and experimentation to create your future. Typically, prediction works well in situations in which information and knowledge is relevant and accessible. Action and experimenting with new ideas makes sense in more unknowable situations in which the future does not resemble the past.

adept at cycling between the two as they try to introduce new ideas and initiatives."

When it comes to your love life, I will show you how to use prediction that is based on analysis and understanding of yourself and your current and past experiences to make better decisions as you move forward in the dating world. And I will also show you how action, discovery, and experimentation will help you to create your future. You will eventually become adept at moving back and forth between these two approaches, all the while feeling like a true entrepreneur.

One of the other principles of ET&A® is called "Self and Social Identification." In effect, this principle encourages businesspeople to have better self-knowledge. Greenberg and her co-authors write: "Through an authentic and insightful understanding of their own sense of purpose and identity, and how they are affected by the context around them, entrepreneurial leaders make more effective decisions in uncertain and unknowable situations."

Self-awareness.
Creating your future starts with becoming self-aware so that you can leverage this knowledge to guide your actions more effectively.

I will guide you, as a dater, in coming to a better understanding about who you are, what you know from your past and current experiences in the context of dating, love, and relationships, and what and who you are looking for so that you can make smarter decisions in the often ambiguous, uncertain world of dating and love. Your tastes and preferences may evolve over time, and you will learn how to make mindful, informed changes when necessary (also known in the land of entrepreneurship as pivots—more on this to come). Ultimately, you will be creating your future rather than being a slave to what comes your way. Given the unpredictable dating times we live in and the unknowable nature of dating and relationships,

self-knowledge will be an essential asset in your entrepreneurial journey to find love.

Effectual Reasoning

In her pioneering research, Saras D. Sarasvathy, now a tenured professor at the University of Virginia's Darden School of Business, found that the entrepreneurs she studied preferred to use "effectual reasoning"—a logic that begins with a given set of means and allows goals to emerge over time from the "varied imagination and diverse aspirations of the founders and the people they interact with"— over "causal reasoning," defined by Sarasvathy as beginning with "a pre-determined goal and a given set of means, and seeks to identify the optimal—fastest, cheapest, most efficient, etc.—alternative to achieve the given goal."

Effectual reasoning.
Treps like to use effectual reasoning. They achieve a vision by using experimentation and improvisation.

To highlight effectual reasoning in action, Sarasvathy offers the following example:

> The simple task of cooking dinner may be used to contrast the two types of reasoning. A chef who is given a specific menu and has only to pick out his or her favorite recipes for the items on the menu, shop for ingredients and cook the meal in their own well-equipped kitchens is an example of causal reasoning. An example of effectual reasoning would involve a chef who is not given a menu in advance, and is escorted to a strange kitchen where he or she has to explore the cupboards for unspecified ingredients and cook a meal with them. While both causal and effectual reasoning call

Be flexible.

Throw out your preconceived beliefs about dating and men. Entrepreneurs are flexible in their ideas and how they achieve their visions.

for domain-specific skills and training, effectual reasoning demands something more—imagination, spontaneity, risk-taking, and salesmanship.

Let's consider this example in a dating context. You could go the causal reasoning route in which you have a very long and specific list of all the qualities and physical specifications you want in a mate (otherwise you just know you won't be attracted or interested) and follow a very prescribed, linear list of rules to use and places to go to find a man who fits that bill. Or you can think of your journey to find love in terms of *effectual reasoning.* This means you have a more open-minded, creative approach to what and who you are looking for (and how you go about finding him) as you go out into the dating world to explore your metaphorical cupboards, experimenting, meeting, and dating all types of different people, reflecting and learning about yourself and the world around you as you go, eventually narrowing in on a compatible, loving partner.

As Sarasvathy explains, using effectual reasoning means that "plans are made and unmade and revised and recast through action and in-teraction with others on a daily basis. Yet at any given moment, there is always a meaningful picture that keeps the team together, a com-pelling story …" That meaningful picture, that compelling story, will be your vision of creating *a healthy, happy dating life that leads to a healthy, happy relationship.* How you get there and the people you meet along the way and what you learn will help shape and mold how you achieve this vision.

Throughout this book, I will ask you to look at your love life through the lens of effectual reasoning, and not to limit immediately your

ideas of who will make a great partner for you or how you can go about finding that person. I am asking you to be fluid and flexible in your beliefs about finding love, to open yourself to surprises and twists and turns in your dating life, to throw out your preconceived expectations about dating and men. I am asking you to discover many new things about yourself along the way through reflection and experimentation in the dating world.

As Sarasvathy writes: "Entrepreneurs choose to view the future through effectual logic. Consciously, or unconsciously, they act as if they believe that the future is not 'out there' to be discovered, but that it gets created through the very strategies of the players." In this journey to find love, you are creating your future; your fate is what you make of it as you stumble across and respond and adapt to all that is unknowable and uncertain in the dating world. You are not some slave to your past or to predetermined events; *you* are creating your love story, not waiting for some fairytale prince charming to sweep you off into a storybook ending.

You have the power to bring your future into existence.

Create, build, and shape.

Create, build, and shape your entrepreneurial love story. What will your story be?

INTRODUCTION

(*If you're itching to start your entrepreneurial journey to find love, feel free to skip this section and continue straight to chapter 1.*)

I was sitting at my desk at Babson College on a Monday morning when I got an email from a colleague, Professor Joel Shulman, Associate Professor of Entrepreneurship. Joel had read my 750-word essay in the previous day's *Boston Globe Magazine* and thought it had potential for something grander. He wanted to meet with me to discuss how I might expand the themes I had written about into a book. Coincidentally, it was a project I had been thinking a lot about.

Eureka!
The idea for my book came to me years ago. It took three years to see it come to fruition.

I'd seen plenty of writers land book deals after their personal essays were published. Exhibit A: Amy Sutherland. Her 2006 essay, "What Shamu Taught Me About a Happy Marriage," featured in the *New York Times* "Modern Love" column, described her experiments using animal-training tactics on her husband, which she had learned when writing a book about a school for exotic animal trainers. It was one of the most widely read columns in that paper the year it was published. Book publishers were hungry for more, wanting, of course, to capitalize on Sutherland's success by having her turn the concept into a book. A year later, *What Shamu Taught Me about Life, Love, and Marriage: Lessons for People from Animals and Their Trainers* was published and instantly a bestseller. Exhibit B: Lori Gotlieb. Gotlieb, a prominent journalist, was able to capitalize on the success of her controversial personal essay published in the *Atlantic* in 2011. "Marry Him" was Gotlieb's account of her love life regrets and an admonishment

to single women everywhere to "stop chasing the elusive Prince Charming and instead go for Mr. Good Enough." In 2012, she published a book by the same name (with an added subtitle: *The Case for Settling for Mr. Good Enough*) that expanded on her original essay. It became a *New York Times* bestseller and Editor's Choice selection.

For many months prior to it being published, I thought there might be enough material to turn my essay "Dating Like an Entrepreneur," which describes the parallels between entrepreneurship and relationships and was set to be published in the August 1, 2010 issue of the *Boston Globe Magazine*'s "Coupling" column, into a dating and relationship self-help book. (See Appendix for a copy of this essay.) I daydreamed about a flurry of publishers and agents hunting me down after its publication. Unfortunately, other than a bunch of comments beneath the online version and some congratulatory emails from friends, family, and acquaintances, the essay did not send the publishing industry into a frenzy as I fantasized it would. But it did catch the eye of Joel, who gave me hope that despite any lack of initial interest from the publishing world maybe I was onto something.

Skin in the game.

Being invested in something through emotional, financial, or bodily commitment.

We ended up meeting for about an hour or so and chatted about the idea. The original concept we threw around was to interview various entrepreneurs—young and old, men and women, novices and veterans—and transfer the lessons they learned about starting and maintaining a business venture to starting and maintaining a romantic relationship. He offered me a book title suggestion: *Skin In the Game*. It was a brilliant double entendre.

As you will surely learn from this book, be it in traditional business or the business of romance, people must have some "skin in the game"

if they want to move something of value forward; in other words, they must be personally invested in the venture they are building (or why would they care?). They must be willing to take risks and be vulnerable in various ways—emotionally, mentally, financially, psychologically, even bodily. When it comes to dating, you have to have this kind of skin in the dating game if you want to move forward. And because one of the interpretations of a double entendre is typically sexually suggestive, the title worked well for a book about dating and relationships (i.e., skin alludes to sex.)

Joel and I never moved forward together with the idea we discussed, but I am certainly grateful to him for the title suggestion and for giving me the initial support to believe that I could take my idea to the next level.

I remember leaving Joel's office after meeting that day feeling excited about the opportunity, but the truth was I wasn't in any position to undertake such a huge project at the time. My own love life, though active, was still figuring itself out, and I worried about writing a book on how to find love when I was still working to find it myself. Moreover, I just flat-out didn't have the desire to write a book. And, of course, there was that ugly beast I knew all too well: fear. What if I failed? What if I couldn't do it? Why waste my time and energy if I wasn't even sure it could be done? So, like most people paralyzed by fear and doubt, I created every excuse in the book as to why my idea was nothing more than a pipe dream.

For the next two years, though, I secretly fantasized about its possibilities. I was working in the Graduate Programs and Student Affairs office as a program manager and academic advisor for the Two-Year

and One-Year MBA programs and was approaching my ten-year employee anniversary with the school. For almost a decade, I worked closely with Babson students, faculty, and staff. During my tenure, I became well acquainted with the business curricula and specifically many of the principles of entrepreneurship education. I attended countless forums and guest lectures and alumni panels and workshops. I wrote for the school's website and alumni magazine on a freelance basis.

The entrepreneurial spirit at Babson is contagious, like none other in the world. The school has been ranked #1 in entrepreneurship education by *US News and World Report* for the past twenty years in a row and has received countless other honors and awards throughout the years for its dedication to and support of entrepreneurship education nationally and globally. Entrepreneurship is at the heart of everything Babson does as an institution. The students, faculty, and staff live and breathe entrepreneurship.

Connecting the dots. My past prepared me well for this present moment.

When you spend so much time in this kind of an environment, you can't help but catch the entrepreneur bug.

Concurrently with my time at Babson, for about ten years I had been writing and speaking about dating, love, and relationships. My side career as a writer began when I was twenty-five, after a roller coaster relationship ended for the final time. Like many before me, love gone awry—or at least what I deluded myself into thinking was love—inspired me to action. One day, in my anger over our failed union, I wrote an essay on dating—part tough love, part call to arms—and sent it around to a bunch of my girlfriends. "This is great," one friend opined. "Publish this," another replied. I sent it to a woman I knew

who worked for the Boston *Metro*, a free, daily newspaper distributed in the Boston area, and, in turn, she sent it to the editor of the opinion column. A few days later, the editor got in touch and said to send a picture because he was going to publish the piece the next day. Five columns later, I was hooked. Expressing my thoughts about dating and relationships to the world felt great, empowering. I knew I wanted to continue writing and dove into the world of freelance writing.

A few years later, my brother told me about a local man who was starting an Internet radio station in downtown Boston. He was looking for acts. I pitched him an idea on a show about dating, love, and relationships. He agreed. For the next year and a half, I produced and hosted two weekly Internet radio shows. Soon after the shows ended, I created, co-hosted, and co-produced an Internet TV show with the Pulse Network that focused on these subjects.

Given these experiences, I was becoming an expert in my own right. Not only because I had immersed myself so fully into the world of dating and relationships from a professional perspective, but also because, for many years, I was experiencing that world firsthand on a personal level: the innumerable dates, a few relationships here and there, and the emotional ups and downs inherent in the dating process.

I was always a thoughtful dater, dedicated to self-reflection and self-discovery, and an active one: resilient, persistent, and resourceful. Despite the myriad setbacks, rejections, and wrong turns, I tried hard to learn from every experience and to use that knowledge as I moved forward. I always maintained a vision that I would eventually find someone; even during some of my darker days, I still believed that

Looking back.

In retrospect, I had been an entrepreneurial dater. I never would have called myself that, but I definitely exhibited entrepreneurial tendencies in the way I approached dating.

vision was possible. In retrospect, after I had finally found the man to whom I'm now engaged, I realized that I had, in many ways, acted like an entrepreneur engaged in building a venture.

At thirty-three, I met Dave on Match.com. It was as though the clouds finally parted and sent me the most wonderful man. In truth, it had nothing to do with luck but everything to do with being an action-oriented, thoughtful dater, which took time and commitment. Several months into our relationship, I started to think more seriously about the essay I had once written: "Dating Like an Entrepreneur." I thought back to my conversation with Joel, to the various lectures and discussions and panels I had been attending since I started working at Babson. Could such a powerful force like entrepreneurship be used in other aspects of our lives aside from purely business scenarios? Could I harness the way traditional entrepreneurs think and act and apply it to one engaged in a personal venture to find love? Could entrepreneurship be democratized in this particular way? Was there *really* enough material to fill the pages of an entire book? Were there *really* enough parallels? I had to find out. I realized, like any successful entrepreneur, I had to stop thinking and act.

A dating-coaching business and a book are born

Because I was in a really good place in my personal life, the timing was right to not only start writing this book but also to launch a dating-coaching practice, an idea I had been flirting with for a while. After finding love with Dave, I wanted to do more than just freelance write about my experiences. I wanted to impart actively the lessons I had learned along my journey in order to inspire and empower other single

women looking for love. I had been through so many experiences similar to those of thousands (millions!) of women in the dating world, and I believed that I could thrive as a coach and expert because of this. My hope was that women would not see me as a know-it-all lecturer but as an equal, someone who could relate to and empathize with their struggles, someone whose stories they could see themselves in.

Skin In the Game would be my calling card and first product as a dating coach. As it turned out, a few months into the research and writing process, I began to feel so strongly about what I was writing that I decided my coaching practice and philosophy would be based on the spirit and lessons of entrepreneurship. Hence the name of my business: The Love TREP. Like most entrepreneurs, I'd need to bootstrap my business, so I continued to work at Babson to pay the bills and fund my new coaching practice, which I would run on nights, weekends, and vacation days. Given all of my experiences over the years—personally, as a former dater; professionally, as a writer and commentator about dating and relationships, an administrator at the #1 school for entrepreneurship education, and now a budding entrepreneur starting my own business— I felt uniquely qualified to be doing what I was doing. I had to ask: "Who better than me to write a book about how to think and act entrepreneurially in one's dating and love life?"

The idea for the book would be a little different than what I originally discussed with Joel. I wouldn't be interviewing entrepreneurs directly, but I would continue to pour myself into the world of entrepreneurship as much as possible and continue to flesh out the parallels between entrepreneurship and dating. I would then use the results as the framework for my book. My endeavor was made considerably easier, because I worked in the hub of the business school, had access

I am you.

I've been in your shoes. I can empathize and relate to your struggles. And now, I can help. Given my personal and professional experiences, who better than me to write this particular book?

to all sorts of events and activities, and had developed strong relationships with staff, faculty, students, and alumni.

I jumped into research, reading as much as I could get my hands on, continuing to go to as many lectures and forums and panels as I could, always keeping my book idea in the back of my head so that potential parallels could be explored. I subscribed to *Entrepreneur* magazine, devouring every issue the day it arrived in my mailbox. I purchased and borrowed notable books on entrepreneurship written by some of the masters in the field. I sat in on a class at Babson. Heidi Neck, the Jeffry A. Timmons Professor of Entrepreneurial Studies, whom I had worked with many times before in the management of the Two Year MBA program, was kind enough to let me come to her introductory entrepreneurship class (in the Evening MBA Program). I am indebted to Heidi for encouraging me to pursue my book idea, which I told her about before the course began. "You won't be lazy, when you have the right idea for you," she said to me once when I expressed my concern that laziness and self-doubt might stand in the way of my moving my entrepreneurial endeavor forward. Her words make so much sense to me now.

Bolstered by what I was learning at Babson, reading, studying, and observing, I felt more certain that this endeavor was entirely possible, that a book exploring these concepts could be written. My confidence began to grow even more when in the midst of writing chapter 1, my father, who I had consulted before starting this project, told me about the release of *The Start-up of You*, a bestselling book written by two serial entrepreneurs, Reid Hoffman, founder of LinkedIn, and Ben Casnocha, founder of Comcate, who argue that the key to career success in the twenty-first century is to manage your career as if it were a

start-up business, a "living, breathing, growing start-up of you." Why entrepreneurs and why start-ups? Because, as the book jacket states: "Startups—and the entrepreneurs who run them—are nimble. They invest in themselves. They build their professional networks. They take intelligent risks. They make uncertainty and volatility work to their advantage." Hoffman's and Casnocha's work inspired me even more to write *Skin In the Game*.

After several months of research, I was enthused to see that there were a ton of parallels that had legs; the article in the *Globe Magazine* was indeed, as I had surmised all along, just the tip of the iceberg.

Additionally, I felt my concept had a refreshing and timely angle for several reasons.

Firstly, entrepreneurship is a hot topic today, playing an important role in our economy and economies around the world. According to the "2011 U.S. Report" from the Global Entrepreneurship Monitor (GEM), a not-for-profit academic research consortium, entrepreneurial activity in the U.S. is up 60 percent and at the highest level since 2005. Furthermore, 12.3 percent of the U.S. adult population is engaged in entrepreneurial activity. Clearly, people and nations across the globe believe entrepreneurship is a potent force for change, understanding that it empowers individuals (not governments) to create personal, social, and economic growth.

Secondly, the world of entrepreneurship is a major point of interest in modern-day pop culture. Our society has become enamored, in recent times, with entrepreneurs and entrepreneurial success stories. Silicon Valley, the world of start-ups, and the entrepreneurs who toil

Why entrepreneurship?

Entrepreneurship is a mindset and a method. Not only does it have numerous transferrable lessons for dating, but it's also:

1. An important factor in changing today's economies

2. A major point of interest in pop culture

3. A way to get women excited and motivated again about dating and love.

4. A topic that today's career woman can appreciate.

away to launch and build new ideas, new technologies, have become points of fascination in today's culture. Just look at the popularity of NBC's *Shark Tank*, now in its fifth season—drawing millions of viewers each week—which stars some of the country's most respected, successful entrepreneurs. Billionaire Mark Cuban, one of the "sharks," credits the show's success to the fact that normal, everyday people see themselves in the entrepreneurs (also normal, everyday people) who come on the show to pitch their ideas and get funding so that they can take their ventures to greater heights. Bravo TV even made a reality show titled "Start-ups: Silicon Valley" around the lives of young twenty-something entrepreneurs risking it all to build their businesses.

Thirdly, too many dating books nowadays appeal solely to our hearts and emotions, replete with hard to grasp, touchy-feely, new-wave language and concepts: "Realign your vibrations and feel your inner goddess and limitlessness." While there's nothing wrong with these ideas—in certain ways, they can be helpful—I believe women also want and need more concrete, practical methods to help them move forward in their dating and love lives. On the other end of the spectrum are the dating books focused primarily on superficial action or manipulative tactics but sparingly on emotions and reflection: "Make him fall in love with you in less than 10 seconds with these proven tactics." These types of books, too, have some value, but are ultimately ignoring an important piece of the dating puzzle: self-reflection and self-awareness. Given these self-help book extremes (many of which I purchased back in my single days), I had to wonder: "What would a practical, twenty-first century dating approach that teaches and empowers one to *think* and *act* more critically and creatively while *simultaneously* encouraging greater self- and social awareness look like?" As

I was learning about entrepreneurship and the entrepreneurial way, I felt I could draw from the trial and error process of both reflective thought *and* action to create a balanced framework for singles to draw from.

Lastly, understanding that women today can often grow tired of hearing the same old, trite advice from friends, family, dating columnists, and dating coaches, presented in the same, old, tired, clichéd way, I believed that couching the process of finding love in an entrepreneurial context might prove to be a better way to inspire my fellow females to go after the type of relationship they proclaimed to want so desperately. Sadly, single women looking for relationships are often held back by their own negativity and cynicism, making it difficult for them to enjoy the dating process. Sometimes you can almost see the anger and frustration steaming off them when you spend time around them. But when you meet and read about entrepreneurs, their excitement, motivation, and drive is inspiring, contagious. And the reason entrepreneurs are so passionate and driven is because they are building something of value in their lives; they get to take the reins and carve their own paths. As I learned more about entrepreneurs, I began to ask myself: How could I transfer that excitement, energy, drive, and sense of purpose from the world of entrepreneurship to the world of dating? The answer became clear: By having women think of themselves as entrepreneurs in their dating and love lives, creating, building, and shaping their love stories, their futures.

I believe people are their best, most innovative, most creative, happiest selves when they feel they have some hand in shaping their own destinies. And I wanted to write a book that inspired and empowered women to take charge of their dating and love lives, just as they were

Prince Charming. Today's modern woman is over the Prince Charming fantasy. She should be!

Get excited! Treps are excited, passionate, and motivated; part of what fuels that excitement is the idea that they are creating and *building* something of value in their lives. Daters will feel excited about becoming entrepreneurs in their dating lives, because they, too, will start to feel that they are creating, building, and shaping their love stories, that the power to do so is in their hands.

doing in every other area of their lives—school, career, hobbies. *Skin In the Game* would resonate with the modern woman's values. The Prince Charming, white horse, sweep-you-off-your-feet trope hasn't done much for women in the last couple of decades, resigning them to a wait-and-hope mentality, clearly unhelpful in today's day and age.

I also believe that learning in the contrary can be an extremely powerful tool—consider the bestselling book *Fish! A Proven Way to Boost Morale and Improve Results* as an example. In this management parable, authors Stephen C. Lundin, Paul Harry, John Christensen, and Ken Blanchard tell the fictional account of a business manager named Mary Jane, who is tasked with turning around an uninspired, unenthusiastic operations department. Across the street from her office building is the Pike Place Fish Market, a real-life, world-famous, Seattle-based fish store known for its top-notch customer service and fun, passionate, energetic work environment. With the help of Lonnie, a fishmonger, Mary Jane is able to energize and transform her department by applying the lessons she learns from Pike Place. These lessons are, of course, drawn from an unlikely source, but they are transferrable and applicable to any division or department of any organization.

Indeed, you might have never expected to see a 400-page book applying the entrepreneurial spirit and entrepreneurial principles to one's love life, and that is precisely why I felt this approach would be memorable, galvanizing, and inspiring. Professor Heidi Neck also believes in the power of learning in the contrary, writing to me in an email after she had reviewed a couple chapters of this book: "I believe in learning in the contrary. In other words, I like to show things that one would not think relates to entrepreneurship but really does.

For example, in my earlier teaching years I would use the movie *Dead Poet's Society* to illustrate some concrete principles of entrepreneurship. Students didn't expect to see clips of this movie in class but I know they remember the principles because it was contrary."

From an entrepreneurship perspective, much of what follows in this book comes from what I learned by being a part of Babson College, from the various texts and magazine articles I've read, and the many conversations I've had with colleagues, friends, and acquaintances over the last several years. From a dating and relationship perspective, much of what follows comes from my years as a professional writer and speaker on these topics, my observations and research in the industry, my countless conversations and experiences with clients, friends, family, acquaintances, and other dating coaches, and, certainly, from my own personal dating and relationship history.

Practice what I preach. As intimidating as writing a book seemed, I had to practice what I wanted to teach singles: When faced with a daunting uncertain future, you have to start by taking action. And so I did just that.

PART I: PREPARING FOR YOUR ENTREPRENEURIAL JOURNEY

LOVE TREP® OATH

(Please recite out loud)

As a Love TREP, I solemnly swear to live by the following oath:

- ✓ I see limitless, wonderful possibilities for my dating and love life. My single status is an opportunity; it is not a burden.
- ✓ I believe in a growth mindset not a destiny mindset.
- ✓ I believe that my future is not out there to be discovered, but it is created by me and the people I enroll to help me on my journey.
- ✓ I see adversity and obstacles in my dating and love life as catalysts to action.
- ✓ I recognize that failures, disappointments, wrong turns, mistakes—past, present, and future—are assets if I take the time to learn from them.
- ✓ I understand that there is some element of risk involved in the dating world, and I courageously take on this risk.
- ✓ I know that when I feel overwhelmed by my dating and love life, all I need to do is breathe and take one small, smart step to start moving forward again.
- ✓ I believe that my entrepreneurial journey to find love begins with the knowledge I have at hand and grows from there as I experiment, create, and evolve.
- ✓ I am committed to a process of trial and error in the dating world.

✓ I take pride in who I am at my core, but I am willing to look objectively at myself to see where I can improve as a dater.

✓ I remain flexible in my ideas as to who can make a great partner for me and how I will meet this partner.

✓ I am okay with uncertainty; in fact, I embrace it because I know I can move through it.

✓ I will not approach dating and men with an attachment to the outcome. I will approach dating from a place of positivity—wanting to share love with someone—not from a place of fear—getting, controlling, or winning love.

✓ I am no longer satisfied standing on the sidelines watching my love life in the rear view mirror. I am no longer satisfied being a victim.

✓ I believe in myself and the entrepreneurial journey that I am about to create.

✓ I promise to release myself from the psychology of having to be perfect, so I can stop thinking so much and just get started.

✓ I am a Love TREP.

CHAPTER 1: ME? AN ENTREPRENEUR?

**"We are all entrepreneurs, only too few
of us get to practice it"**

– Mohammed Yunas, Micro-finance Pioneer, 2006 Nobel Peace Prize Winner

The Love TREP Oath. Before you begin your entrepreneurial journey to find love, don't forget to recite The Love TREP Oath, located on the previous page. This is important for new Love TREPs to do!

You might have picked up this book out of curiosity while at the same time saying to yourself: "I am *not* an entrepreneur, and this *can't possibly* work for my love life!"

You're wrong. On both accounts. You *are* capable of living entrepreneurially, and this book *can* help you find love. Before I start to break down how *you* can think and act like an entrepreneur in your dating and love life, I want to take a moment to convince you that:

1) Entrepreneurship is about more than starting a business; it's a method that can be applied to many different aspects of a person's life.
2) The entrepreneurial way has many applications specifically for your dating and love life.
3) Virtually anyone has the capabilities to create an entrepreneurial life; in fact, *you* are a natural-born entrepreneur.

4) Women in particular make great entrepreneurs.

5) You've already been living entrepreneurially in your life in ways you may never have identified as evocative of the entrepreneurial spirit and approach.

1) Entrepreneurship is about more than starting a business

The heart of entrepreneurship.

Entrepreneurship is a particular way of acting and thinking. We all have the spirit of entrepreneurship within us!

Uncertainty about your entrepreneurial ability prevails only if you take a narrow view of entrepreneurship: that it's a field of study limited to starting businesses. The truth is we all have the power to think and act entrepreneurially, in plenty of non-business contexts, because the heart of entrepreneurship is just that: *a particular way of thinking and acting* in unknowable environments. In fact, many of us have been thinking and acting like entrepreneurs throughout the course of our lives; we just don't identify our thought processes and actions as such. Indeed, we all have the spirit of entrepreneurship within us, and harnessing that spirit is less complicated then we might think.

Let me get really nerdy on you for a bit. Stay with me, okay?

I'm bringing dorky back.
Bear with me for a couple pages while I talk about nerdy things like research.

In November of 2010, Heidi Neck, Associate Professor of Entrepreneurship at Babson College, partnered with Christine Costello and Robert Williams of the Business Innovation Factory—a Rhode Island–based non-profit helping businesses innovate and grow—to develop a research platform called the Babson Entrepreneur Experience Lab. By means of extensive interviews, shadowing, observing, and self-documentation over a six-month period, these researchers visited and engaged with, either in-person or remotely through an online platform, more than 250 current start-up entrepreneurs from across the country. The goal of the first phase of the lab was twofold: firstly, to develop an ongoing understanding of the entrepreneurship experience through the lens of the entrepreneurs themselves; and, secondly, to start developing the idea that entrepreneurship is about much more than business creation, that its definition can be expanded to include entrepreneurs of all kinds, sizes, and work situations.

In a paper summarizing their findings, titled *Elements of the Entrepreneurship Experience*, the researchers write:

> "Many individuals and institutions are beginning to think of entrepreneurship as a vital life skill that extends far beyond the ability to launch a venture, a life skill that prepares individuals to deal with an ambiguous and uncertain future."

For good or ill, we no longer live in the days of predictable business as usual. The workplace itself is shifting; demographics are changing; global intricacies affect us all. Complex statistical models work only so well in modern times until they don't. Could any of these models so heavily relied upon nowadays have predicted or stopped the events of 9/11 or the financial crisis of 2008?

Even *USA Today* recognizes the changing nature of today's business world, proclaiming in a July 2012 article titled "Seeking the Elusive Credibility Factor (The Workplace)": "Uncertainty is the new normal … The old order has been so shaken that it has become impossible to describe exactly what the present or future holds. Yet, more and more people are asking: Where are we headed? What is the vision for the future?" This is precisely why a method like entrepreneurship

The unknown.
When the future is unpredictable, unknown, uncertain, a life skill like entrepreneurship is an extremely valuable tool, because it prevents us from becoming paralyzed.

is so necessary and timely for the business world of the twenty-first century: It allows people to take action in the face of the unknown.

This sentiment holds true not only for the world of business but also for the world of dating, where, whether we like it or not, the old, predictable ways of finding a partner have been left in the dust by a more frenzied, chaotic, ambiguous, unknowable process, often leaving the sexes resentful and at odds. Although you could make the argument that dating and love has always been unpredictable—falling in love, by its very nature, is not a foreseeable experience, contrary to what love-at-first-sight enthusiasts profess—there's no denying that, for better or worse, dating and relationships have become more complicated, less straightforward than ever before in our history; the proliferation of technology (namely, the Internet), shifting gender roles, and changing demographics all add to the confusion and frustration in one way or another. Pile on the pressures of career, the romanticization of the freewheeling single life, and the advent of what some have dubbed the "man-child," it's no wonder women are finding it more difficult to find commitment and love in the twenty-first century. This is why a life skill such as entrepreneurship can be such a valuable tool for the fairer sex, helping her to navigate these perplexing times.

Now that's empowerment.

To be entrepreneurial is to be empowered to create your own opportunities.

Costello and her co-authors hope by understanding and shining a light on various elements of the entrepreneurial experience within the environment for which entrepreneurship is traditionally known and best understood (the business start-up world), those in other environments will see that these same principles can be applied to opportunities in many different areas, that the *experience* can be the same despite differences in context.

"Entrepreneurship embodies methods for thinking, acting, identifying opportunities, and approaching problems that enables people to manage change, adjust to new conditions, and to take control of actualizing personal goals and aspirations," write Costello and her co-authors. "To be entrepreneurial is to be empowered to create opportunities for oneself."

In this light, entrepreneurship hardly sounds like a method consigned solely to the business world. By their definition, can't we also start seeing how entrepreneurship enables us to create change in our personal lives?

Babson College has been so devoted to the cause of broadening the definition of entrepreneurship and what it means to be an entrepreneur that they started a website dedicated to that end: www.define. babson.edu. People from all over the world have been invited to help shape this new definition; thousands have responded. By the summer of 2012, more than 96,000 people from 148 countries had visited the site, and almost 2,000 definitions from people in seventy-six countries were submitted. Entries came in from students, faculty, alumni, staff, friends of Babson, total strangers, and notable figures such as Thomas Menino, the long-time mayor of Boston, and Daymond John, serial entrepreneur and cohost of the TV show *Shark Tank*. To be sure, Babson has been the leader in this push, encouraging the world to see the field of entrepreneurship as more inclusive, full of limitless possibilities.

It is now my wish to lead this charge in the context of dating and relationships, to show the world how the entrepreneurial spirit and approach can help transform a person's love life.

2) The entrepreneurial way has many applications for your dating and love life

After all I have learned about entrepreneurship, I believe it can be viewed in the context of dating and love in the following ways:

- ✓ A platform for reinvention in your dating and love life.
- ✓ A template for how you can live your dating and love life—one that encourages discovery through trial and error: action, thoughtful reflection, and more action.
- ✓ A way for you to see any challenges in your dating and love life as opportunities, to see the possibilities in an uncertain future.
- ✓ A method that encourages, nay, demands self and social awareness.
- ✓ A tool that empowers you to innovate (personal and social innovation!) in any aspect of your dating and love life that is leaving you feeling stuck or unfulfilled.
- ✓ A method that enables you to use and overcome your fears in your dating life so that you can find a healthy, happy relationship.
- ✓ A method that empowers you to make changes in your dating and love life, to turn ideas into reality, to pave your own path, to create opportunities, to be an active participant rather than a silent observer or a helpless victim, to become a more positive, more curious, more evolved person.
- ✓ A way to build self-esteem and confidence in your dating and love life by encouraging you to take responsibility for your choices, and deal with the consequences head-on.

✓ A framework that teaches you to embrace failure and mistakes in your dating and love life by seeing those things as instructive, as assets that will fuel your desire and push you to see new possibilities.

✓ A method that discourages you from asking "Will I succeed?" and instead empowers you to ask "How will I succeed?"

✓ A way to find more fulfillment and purpose in the actions you take in your dating and love life.

✓ A way to stop feeling sorry for yourself and believe in your worth and value.

✓ A way to navigate uncertain situations and ambiguity in your dating and love life, and one that empowers you to know you'll be okay no matter what happens.

✓ A method that empowers you to trust in yourself.

✓ A method that positively—not negatively—reinforces you to experiment and practice and learn and grow in your dating and love life.

✓ A method that encourages you to work toward a vision.

Are you starting to see how the entrepreneurial way can help you in your venture (adventure!) to find love? Are you getting excited yet?

3) *You* are a natural-born entrepreneur!

Just as I was starting to formulate my ideas and write about transferring the powers of entrepreneurship to a person's dating and love life, so, too, was I running up against doubt from others close to me that the entrepreneurial way was a learnable skill for all people. Sure, the

skeptics could begin to see how the definition itself could be extended to other areas outside the business arena and how the concepts could be democratized, but, they argued, not everyone is cut out for the job of thinking and acting entrepreneurially; it takes a certain person.

In the words of Lady Gaga, are entrepreneurs just "born that way"? Would dating entrepreneurially only work for a certain type of person? Or do the words of Peter Drucker, prominent writer, professor, and management consultant, hold true: "Most of what you hear about entrepreneurship is all wrong. It's not magic; it's not mysterious, and it has nothing to do with genes. It's a discipline, and, like any discipline, it can be learned." Sorry, Gaga, but my bet is on Drucker.

When I was knee-deep into writing chapter 1 of this book, I threw the idea around with family members. One day, at a family gathering, I told a few relatives, my mother among them, that I was working on a dating self-help book about using the power of entrepreneurship and harnessing the behaviors and thought processes of entrepreneurs to inspire women to find love. "Oh but, Neel, very few people have the characteristics to be an entrepreneur no matter what the context," she remarked cynically. The other family members, a couple of them successful entrepreneurs, echoed her sentiment.

Is this true? Are relatively few people, statistically speaking, cut out to think and act like entrepreneurs? Because if that's the case, then it doesn't even matter if the principles of entrepreneurship can be extended to dating and love, because the majority of readers would be rendered incapable of employing them simply because they missed the DNA jackpot.

Or, is it possible that we all have the ability?

I remember a couple years into my graduate school position at Babson, there was a panel discussion on this very conundrum: whether entrepreneurs were born a certain way, with a basic set of traits—huge risk-takers, aggressive, fearless; in essence, alpha personality types—or if entrepreneurial drive and wisdom could be learned. A few students argued the former position; their opponents the latter—that to become an entrepreneur is not some predetermined, genetic fate, that most people can learn and be trained to think and act like an entrepreneur. Years later, when President Leonard A. Schlesinger, the twelfth president of Babson, took the helm, the notion that only a certain type of person could become an entrepreneur went straight out the proverbial window, replaced by the idea that we *all* have the ability to use the power of entrepreneurial thinking and action in our lives.

Who are treps?

Treps are not a specific type of person, born with a certain set of traits. We all can be treps, because entrepreneurship is a way of thinking and acting and not about personality, gender, sexual orientation, socioeconomic status, race, background, and the like.

Why is it, though, that many of us remain skeptical? Why do we have a difficult time viewing ourselves as potential entrepreneurs no matter what the context?

One thought is that when most of us think of entrepreneurs, we think of entrepreneurial titans—Richard Branson, Donald Trump, Oprah Winfrey. Also, we have a very specific personality profile in mind: risk-taker, visionary, controlling, confident, motivated, self-absorbed, all-knowing, dominant. The truth is that there are plenty of "average Joe" entrepreneurs out there. And there are any number of entrepreneurs who may embody all or some of the aforementioned characteristics, but there are plenty more who *do not* as well as plenty of non-entrepreneurs who do and do not fit these popular molds. One's

ability to think and act entrepreneurially in any context does not rest on a preconceived and often false notion of who and what an entrepreneur has to be.

Harvard Business School Professor Howard Stevenson, a pioneer in entrepreneurship education maintains that personality has little to do with who can be an entrepreneur: "The entrepreneurs I know are all different types. They're as likely to be wallflowers as to be the wild man of Borneo."

In other words, when you focus on entrepreneurship as *a way of thinking an acting* (a method) and not as an exclusive club open to only certain types of members, you open entrepreneurship to *everyone* to use in a variety of different environments to solve a variety of different problems.

Updated! The authors of *Action Trumps Everything* released an updated version titled *Just Start.*

In their book, *Action Trumps Everything*, Len Schlesinger, Charles Kiefer, and Paul Brown second this notion, writing that entrepreneurial abilities certainly do not come hardwired at birth. "Nothing could be further from the truth," they argue. "Not only can everyone employ the same approach to problem solving that entrepreneurs use, entrepreneurs' reasoning can be learned." The authors believe strongly that you can't determine who entrepreneurs are and are not based on their personality traits, but you can *discover and emulate how they think and act* and then use these techniques to solve problems in many areas of your life.

In the context of dating and love, *all of us* can use this distinct but consistently shared way of thinking and acting to better our own lives. You can have virtually any type of personality. You can be male or

female. You can be short or tall, skinny or full-figured. You can be straight, gay, bisexual, or transgendered. You can be any ethnicity. You can come from any socioeconomic level.

4) The rise of female entrepreneurs

Move over men. Women make fantastic entrepreneurs!

Entrepreneurship in the late twentieth century and the twenty-first century has allowed millions of women across the globe to take charge of their own lives, be their own bosses, pursue dreams and goals, feel empowered, realize their own agency, and develop economic and social independence like never before in human history.

Clearly, I'm not the only one singing its praises. In a 2010 article titled "The Modern-Day Woman: How Entrepreneurship Is Saving Us From Ourselves," author and entrepreneur Tammy Strobel argues that women are so busy taking care of everyone else's needs that "we forget to peek underneath those layers from time to time to remind ourselves of who we actually are." As a result, Strobel says, we pay the price, in the form of increased anxiety, angst, and restlessness, which ultimately prevents us from concentrating on "the role of you." It is in that sense that Strobel has found entrepreneurship to be so empowering and necessary. "Unlike a regular job, in which we merely put on another hat and play yet another role toward fulfilling someone else's expectations—that of employee—entrepreneurship awards us the opportunity to pursue something that's meaningful to us, and something that we're passionate about, and acts as a way that we can start fulfilling the role of us ... Never before has there been an easier

Changing women's lives.

Just look at the way women have used entrepreneurship to change their lives.

way to segue into the role of you, and not only that, but to make a living being you."

Although Strobel writes about entrepreneurship in the context of starting businesses, I believe her sentiments are transferrable to dating and love. It's time to focus on fulfilling the role of you, time to push past the media distractions, the pressures and expectations of family, career, friends, and society, and the blitz of regressive dating books out there. It's time to make your own rules and take ownership of your dating and love life. You can do that by using the spirit and principles of entrepreneurship; after all, as Strobel maintains, it is "the one way that you can take control of your life, rather than having your roles control your life."

Here are some impressive facts highlighting how women have turned to entrepreneurship, in the traditional sense, to create value in the world and transform their lives and the lives of others:

- In 1970, women-owned businesses were generally limited to small service businesses and employed less than one million people nationwide. They represented only 4 percent of all businesses. By 1991, women-owned businesses employed 12 million people, more than all the Fortune 500 companies combined.
- [In more recent times], women own 10.6 million businesses in the United States. They employ 19.1 million workers—that's one in every seven employees. Their businesses account for $2.5 trillion in sales.
- According to new data projections, job growth will be created primarily by women-owned small businesses.

Research from The Guardian Life Small Business Research Institute shows that by 2018 women entrepreneurs will be responsible for creating between 5 million and 5.5 million new jobs nationwide.

- One in every eleven adult women in the United States owns a business. Female entrepreneurship has been growing at twice the national average since 1997.
- Women-owned businesses now account for 50 percent of all privately held companies.
- Female entrepreneurs encompass approximately one-third of all entrepreneurs worldwide. A recent international study found that women from low to middle income countries (such as Russia and the Philippines) were more likely to enter early stage entrepreneurship when compared to those of higher income countries (such as Belgium and Sweden).

Transform.

If entrepreneurship can transform women's professional lives in so many incredible ways, why not use its principles and the way treps think and act to transform our personal lives?

Inspiring, isn't it? Truly, women all over the world have wholeheartedly and excitedly embraced entrepreneurship as a path to what I call the three S's: self-discovery, self-actualization, and self-satisfaction. *And if entrepreneurship can transform women's professional lives in so many incredible ways, why not use entrepreneurial principles to transform our personal lives?*

5) How have you been entrepreneurial in your life?

The entrepreneurial spirit and mindset are all around us, even (especially!) in the way people operate in their non-work lives—again, ways they may not even recognize as being evocative of the entrepreneurial spirit. An entrepreneurial life has the power to be a much simpler and

more accessible concept than the media make it out to be. That's not to say entrepreneurs who start businesses don't have to work hard to achieve their vision—of course they do! —but the field doesn't have to be as daunting, onerous, and exclusive as we envision it once we break it down into its component parts, into a method. Moreover, the spirit is right there inside *all* of us, waiting to be unleashed.

Before you move on to chapter 2, I want you to think of <u>five</u> ways you've been entrepreneurial in your life.

When you think about ways you've been entrepreneurial in your own life, consider situations where you took the reins and created something of value for yourself and/or for others, something you helped to shape and move forward over time, something you are proud of, something that made you feel empowered and full of potential, something that made you start seeing, trusting, and believing in your potential, and maybe even something that scared you a little because you weren't exactly sure it could be done.

What about you?

Most of us have been entrepreneurial in some shape or form during our lives. We just didn't connect the dots that we were indeed being entrepreneurial.

Here are some personal examples:

1. I started a freelance writing career without any contacts or knowing much about how to get published.
2. I started and hosted two radio programs with no previous radio experience to my credit.
3. I started and hosted a live Internet television show with no previous television experience to my credit, and having never been on a "set" before.
4. I started writing this book without knowledge of the process and no connections in the publishing world.

5. I started a dating coaching business without having any experience starting a business.

Although I never used to think I embodied the entrepreneurial spirit, I now realize that I have been harnessing the power of entrepreneurship to create change in my life for many years—not just with regard to the bullet points I listed previously but in so many other ways: academics, athletics, various career moves and experiments, and, certainly, my dating and love life. I just never thought at the time to identify any of my experiences as entrepreneurial.

So, what can you come up with?

—〰—

I hope you will be open to seeing the world through an entrepreneurial lens. Moreover, I hope you will be open to applying the ways traditional entrepreneurs think and act to the ways you can think and act within the dating world. Most importantly, I hope you will entertain the notion as you are reading this book that *you* are capable of being an entrepreneur in your dating and love life; you are capable of building and shaping your love story. Who knows, maybe I'll even motivate you to become a traditional entrepreneur and start that yoga studio, clothing store, restaurant, or website design company you've been secretly dreaming about.

Start-up. A business or an undertaking that has recently begun operation.

If it inspires you, consider yourself in the start-up phase of your dating life. And you are now about to embark upon an incredible entrepreneurial journey to find love.

Let's get started!

Up next:

As you begin this entrepreneurial journey in your dating and love life, it is imperative that you start off with the right attitude, and then maintain that attitude throughout. In chapter 2, I'll discuss why having desire, a problem-solving mindset, and vision are so important to any entrepreneur attempting to launch and build a venture.

Chapter 1 Action Steps Checklist:

Your love start-up.

Think of your entrepreneurial venture to find love as your love start-up. And *you* are the CEO.

✓ Create a list of <u>five ways</u> in which you believe you've been entrepreneurial in your life. These ways could be taken from your professional life, academic life, hobbies you've engaged in over the years, volunteer work, or your personal life.

CHAPTER 2: DESIRE, PROBLEM-SOLVING MINDSET, AND VISION

"Be daring, be different, be impractical, be anything that will assert integrity of purpose and imaginative vision against the play-it-safers, the creatures of the commonplace, the slaves of the ordinary."

– Sir Cecil Beaton, photographer, painter, interior designer

We have established that you—*yes you*—have the ability to think and act like an entrepreneur in your dating and love life. I hope I have put any concerns on that front to rest. In this chapter, I will highlight important qualities that entrepreneurs must possess before undertaking any new venture, and while maintaining and building that venture.

But first let me ask you three simple yes/no questions:

1. Do you have **desire** to find love?

Yes: _____   No: _____

2. Do you have the desire to work on or **problem-solve** your non-existent, stagnant, or unfulfilling dating and love life so that you can find a healthy, happy relationship?

Yes: _____   No: _____

3. Do you think you can create and maintain a **vision** of finding a healthy, happy dating life that leads to a healthy, happy relationship? Even if this initially seems difficult, can you commit to trying?

Yes: _____   No: _____

If you answered "no" to any or all of these questions you may not be ready to start this entrepreneurial venture to find love. Each quality—desire, a problem-solving mindset, and vision—is crucial to an entrepreneur's journey.

Desire

Desire.

Noun. A strong feeling of wanting to have something.

The process of starting a new business or venture is a considerable undertaking. I didn't mean to suggest otherwise in the previous chapter, only that the way entrepreneurs think and act can be extracted and broken down into a simpler framework that people can apply to many different aspects of their lives.

Entrepreneurs, of course, work extremely hard. They spend much of their days, especially during the start-up phases, dealing with challenges and uncertainty: *Will this business idea work? How do I get customers on board? What are the legal and financial hurdles I must face to get my business*

up and running? At the heart of what drives an entrepreneur to push past these challenges and to move her venture forward is *desire*.

Desire is one of the most fundamental qualities for an entrepreneur to possess. Without desire an entrepreneur can't get started, because it is what fuels action, creativity, and innovative thinking. Without real desire to do what they are doing, would-be entrepreneurs usually fail, unable to surmount the daily business dilemmas that come their way.

Open up any issue of *Entrepreneur* magazine and you will see desire practically steam off the pages, as profile after profile features various entrepreneurs who endeavor to create value and change in the world. The way these entrepreneurs harness their desire to achieve their dreams is contagious; they make you want to strive in your own life to achieve your goals and dreams.

Take Seattle-based iFly, profiled in the February 2012 issue. iFly operates high-powered vertical wind tunnels in which users can practice sky-diving techniques. Having spent years working in the U.S. Special Operations, founder Bill Adams, upon retirement, started the company (with his wife who he met at a sky-diving drop zone) because he wanted to work for himself, have fun while working, and create something of value for other sky-diving enthusiasts. However, it wasn't always smooth sailing for the business: Adams' original financing fell apart. But, as he notes, "we still had our dream intact, and we set off to get what we wanted." Get it they did; since finding other funding, weekends have been fully booked at their $10 million iFly Seattle location, and they have plans to open new locations in the coming months. Adams' *desire* to build and grow his business was

Desire and uncertainty. Entrepreneurs are driven by their desire, which helps them navigate a world full of uncertainties. It is their desire that helps them go after new solutions to old problems. The same is true in dating: Your desire will help you navigate a lot of uncertainties and spur you on to look for new solutions to old problems.

Do you have desire?

Singles need to have desire to find love, just as treps need desire to start their entrepreneurial adventures. Lack of resources or high levels of uncertainty does not discourage a Love TREP.

TREP talk. I
was talking to
a successful
entrepreneur
who lives in
my apartment
building, asking
him for advice
on my coaching
business. I
remember
saying, "I
should do x, y,
and z with the
company." He
replied: "Don't
do anything
because you
should do it; do
it because you
want to do it."
Good advice for
both business
and dating.

strong enough to surmount the challenges and doubts that come with any entrepreneurial endeavor.

Or consider the mindset of Jackie Summers, a friend and colleague in the dating and relationships advice world and also the founder of the Liquortorian, an artisanal liquor company. Profiled in the May 2012 issue of *Entrepreneur*, Summers, whose love and passion for creating homemade spirits prompted him to start his own company, talks about the importance of desire, although he calls it something slightly different: "We face a host of insurmountable tasks when starting a business. The key to our success is focusing on one insurmountable task each day and surmounting the hell out of it. It's tenacity—that's what powers the entrepreneurial spirit." Indeed, desire fuels tenacity, and when you are filled with tenacity you go after what you want and do the work to get there.

Desire is just as important to singles looking for love.

Meeting someone and finding love *has to be a priority for you*. You have to be ready to dedicate time to the search. You have to really want it in your life, to go after it, so much so that the setbacks and rejections and frustrations you will inevitably experience along the way will only serve to fuel your desire, not hamper it. You have to want it for yourself, not because others tell you it's what you should want. You have to be committed, even when you're not feeling all that confident or have doubts or are scared by the uncertainty of dating, even when you feel lazy or uninspired. That is desire. If you're wishy-washy, skeptical, half-committed, or not ready to look inside, this probably isn't the book for you.

It sounds tragically unromantic, I know: thinking of your love life as something you need to actively pursue, strategize over, and work at. But if you think about it, you pursue and work at just about everything else in your life, so why not love? The "it will happen when it happens" mentality just doesn't cut it for singles and for entrepreneurs alike, especially in a world where life moves fast, competitors are lurking around every corner, and the paradox of choice (so many options!) leads to indecision, misguidedness, and mediocrity. Entrepreneurs can't sit idly, waiting for things to happen. They'd be out of business, left in the dust by smarter, more innovative, more dedicated businesspeople who have more desire and create better choices for their customers. Both traditional entrepreneurs and Love TREPs must act. They must "do." The main thing that drives this "doing" will be your desire. Your desire to tackle the unknowns and uncertainties in your dating and love life will spur you on to take action and experiment with new approaches to long-standing "problems."

The type of desire you bring to your venture is also important. If you go into this venture for the wrong reasons—"Being single stinks, so I guess the alternative has to be better"—you won't go very far; you'll be held back by your own apathy. Ultimately, you want your entrepreneurial journey to find love to be about moving toward something wonderful— with a sense of curiosity—as opposed to moving away from something unappealing. If you are indeed looking for a healthy, happy relationship you have to declare that with pride and excitement. You have to put a stake in the ground even if doing so is scary because of the possibility of failure and vulnerability. You have to really desire this for yourself for the right reasons, not because of what others (family, friends, society, and the like) want for you or what you think you *should* want.

Desire *not* desperation. Desire is not to be confused with desperation—"I can't *live* without love and am desperate to find it"—and neediness— "please, pick me, love me!"— unattractive qualities that often stem from a place of self-rejection as opposed to a healthy place of self-love (more on these concepts later).

If a traditional business entrepreneur ever feels like her desire to start a business comes from a place of apathy or indifference or because of pressure from others, if her heart isn't authentically in it, her venture may briefly get off the ground, but its chances of long-term survival are low. She has to really believe in what she's doing and want it.

Purchasing this book means you do have a healthy, well-intentioned desire to actively and thoughtfully find love and my hope is that this desire comes from a place of moving forward toward a future of creating abundant love with someone rather than away from something undesirable as if you were trying to fill an empty hole. I hope to make that fire in your belly burn even brighter as you read this book.

Problem-solving. How are you getting in your own way of having a more fulfilling, more connected, dating and love life?

Problem-solving Mindset

Entrepreneurs need to have desire when starting a new venture and maintaining that venture. This we have established. But what exactly do they have desire to do, aside from just starting or creating something? The answer is simple: They want to solve problems.

Most businesses begin as a response to a problem in the world. Someone says, "There's got to be a better way." Or if a business already exists, someone says, "I can do this better." Grab the latest issue of *Entrepreneur* and you will see the desire to solve problems and rid the world of outdated ways of doing or seeing things in every entrepreneur profiled.

'A' for Effort. In order to recognize and seize on the opportunities that await your dating and love life, you'll need to make an effort to fully understand the problems in your dating and love life for which solutions are sought.

Take Anna Jerstrom, an entrepreneur profiled in the July 2012 issue, who quit her investment banking job in London to move to

Costa Rica and become a surfer. While pursuing her love of surfing, Jerstrom realized that swimming attire really didn't mesh well with surfing. "You'd be out in the waves, walk out of the water and literally you've lost your bottoms," she said. Fueled by a desire to fix this problem, Jerstrom got to work on sketching swimwear that would stay on even in rough surf. Her California-based company, Calavera, is well on its way to revolutionizing women's swimwear.

Or consider Olga Vidisheva, founder of Shoptiques, who was profiled in the August 2012 issue. Vidisheva, an HBS graduate and former Goldman Sachs analyst, was frustrated with the lack of online, unique women's apparel boutiques. Vidisheva, a fashionista and former model, knew other women also wanted to buy from distinctive stores that offered limited-edition, hand-crafted apparel and accessories. The problem was that most of these boutiques were so small they had no ability to sell commerce electronically; many had no online presence at all. That's when Vidisheva's Shoptiques was born, providing independently-owned boutiques the opportunity to sell to the masses, enabling the customer to "take a virtual shopping trip to India, Bali, Hong Kong or wherever you want to go."

Like Jerstrom and Vidisheva, and millions of other problem-solving entrepreneurs, you, too, see problems in your love live that you want to understand and solve. Just as important a problem to tackle as ill-fitting swimwear or a lack of unique online apparel boutiques, is a deflated or broken love life. It's a problem that can and will be solved.

Lest you be concerned: Please don't misunderstand me by thinking I use the word "problem" in a negative sense. Not at all. In this context, problems are meant to be seen as the obstacles that are holding

Read all about it! Want to read more about problem-solving TREPs and their business stories? Subscribe to *Entrepreneur* magazine.

Entrepreneurial leaders. As explained by Greenberg, McKone-Sweet, and Wilson in the Introduction of their book *The New Entrepreneurial Leader* (see Bibliography), "Entrepreneurial leaders refuse to cynically or lethargically resign themselves to the problems of the world. Rather through a combination of self-reflection, analysis, resourcefulness, and creative thinking and action, they find ways to inspire and lead others to tackle seemingly intractable problems." *Be an entrepreneurial leader in your own dating and love life!*

you back in your dating life and from finding love. In the world of entrepreneurship, obstacles represent opportunities for discovery and growth; therefore, your single status, as a Love TREP, is a tremendous opportunity for, well, discovery and growth.

Within your dating and love life, look at problem-solving in the following way:

- To create a healthy, happy dating life that leads to a healthy, happy, committed relationship, it will be important to adopt a problem-solving mindset on a continual basis when obstacles—small and large—arise. So whenever an issue sprouts in your dating life, you roll up your sleeves and take active steps to discover the cause, how to work through it, and how to change it. Problem-solving on a continual basis in this way will help you reach your overarching objective.

Problem-solving in your love life requires you to start thinking differently than the way you've been used to thinking. "When you look at problems," says Gregory Burns, author of *Iconoclast* and a neuroscientist at Emory University, "you tend to perceive them in well-worn paths in ways that you've perceived them before. That's the first roadblock in innovating, overcoming your perceptual biases. Most people work in the same place every day. We get used to thinking in certain ways in certain environments."

The good news, though, as Joe Robinson writes in his interview with Burns in the March 2013 issue of *Entrepreneur*, is that our biochemistry craves novelty. Robinson continues: "Just the anticipation of a novel

event can set off the release of dopamine, the brain's built-in motivational prod-and-reward system for learning. To break the cul-de-sac in perception, Berns suggests shaking up your routine, traveling or doing things you haven't done before. Getting away from the ties and people that bind opens up possibilities that would go unimagined when you're operating on autopilot." Purchasing this book is your first step in shaking up your routine.

As a Love TREP, instead of making excuses for your problems in dating and love, you'll feel inspired and empowered to start finding answers and solutions. This ability to turn problems into opportunities is at the core of entrepreneurial leadership.

Make a list of "problems" that you see on a daily basis popping up in your dating and love life. They could be anything from your attitude to your lack of energy, time or opportunities to self-esteem issues.

Here are five examples:

1. I feel angry at men.
2. I don't seem to have any time to dedicate to dating.
3. I don't feel very good about myself in a lot of ways.
4. Often, I don't have the energy to date; I'd rather hang out on my couch and read a good book.
5. I prefer not to force things; I'm waiting for him to find me.

Now it's your turn. List anything that comes to mind. Pay attention to your thoughts, feelings, and actions (or lack thereof) when it comes to dating, love, relationships, and men. Any problems that go on your list will be ones that you will work to solve as you begin your

This is your brain. The human brain, has a tendency to behave like a stubborn two-year-old, say David Rock and Jeffrey Schwartz, authors of a riveting article titled, "The Neuroscience of Leadership." They maintain that if someone else tells your brain what to do and think it automatically pushes back. "Partly this phenomenon is a function of homeostasis (the natural movement of any organism toward equilibrium and away from change), but it also reflects the fact that brains are pattern-making organs with an innate desire to create novel connections. When people solve a problem themselves, the brain releases a rush of neurotransmitters like adrenaline."

Vision.

Setting a vision and believing it is possible, attainable, is important. But remember to be flexible in your ideas about how you get there and about who might make a good partner for you.

entrepreneurial journey. As you identify new problems during your journey, you can add them to your list.

Vision

More often than not, entrepreneurs have a vision of what they want to create or a problem they want to solve, or, at the very least, a vision of knowing they want to create *something*. Fueled by their desire, they go out into the world and create their vision. Doubts and challenges and risks (oh my!) will be lurking around every corner. All the while, entrepreneurs need to hold tight to their vision and believe in their ability to see it through and pivot strategically from that vision when necessary (more on the concept of pivoting later).

Surely, in the uncertain and constantly changing business world we live in today, the ideas and goals that entrepreneurs start out with may change over time as they grow and learn about their industry and real-world scenarios, but they usually stay true to that core vision of wanting to solve a problem, make something better, or create something new and different. In a 2002 *Inc.* survey of *Inc.* 500 founders, when asked if a formal business plan was drafted before launching their companies, only 40 percent responded "yes," and of those, 65 percent said they had "strayed significantly" from their original business conception, adapting their plans as they went along. My guess is for most of these entrepreneurs their overarching vision remained the same, but they learned not to get stubbornly locked into a very particular idea of how that vision would come to fruition or how their concept would eventually be delivered or experienced. As Naveen Jain writes in an *Inc.* magazine piece titled, "10 Secrets of Becoming a

Successful Entrepreneur," you have to be "flexible but persistent …
and continuously learn and adapt as new information becomes available. At the same time, you have to remain persistent to the cause and
mission of your enterprise."

Let's look at a specific example. Profiled on *Inc.*'s website in January of
2012 in an article titled, "5 Tips From an Accidental Entrepreneur,"
Joe Hill, entrepreneur and father of two autistic sons, wanted to create
an affordable tool that could help autistic children learn. Eventually,
he went to market with an iPad app called Aeir Talk. Although his
grand vision was still intact, along the way he ended up having to
change his product multiple times to create something that had lasting value, not something that people downloaded, used once, and
abandoned. Article author Jeff Haden explains that if Hill hadn't
allowed for his ideas to change, his overarching vision of helping
autistic children learn through an affordable tool might have failed
entirely: "The development cycle would absolutely have been a lot
faster and a lot less expensive, but the app would have also been far
less beneficial," writes Haden.

TREP talk: "If you are clear about your vision and honest about your present realities, you don't have to figure everything out. Things start happening of their own accord. Vision is a lot more than putting a plaque on the wall. A real vision is lived, not framed. For vision to become a reality, what's important is how it's created, how it's communicated, and how it's lived." – Ken Blanchard, management expert, and Jesse Stoner, leadership consultant.

So, too, must you hold tight to your overarching vision of finding
love, while simultaneously understanding that your ideas of what you
want and need in a man and how you go about finding him might
evolve as you go courageously into the dating world and start learning
about yourself through experimentation.

As you launch your entrepreneurial venture to find love, I encourage
you to start trusting your ability to enjoy the dating process—to see
the worth and purpose of not just the good times but the challenging
times as well—and to be in a loving relationship in which you feel

Faculty-speak.
As a member of Babson's tenured and distinguished macroeconomics faculty once said to a few of us gathered for a meeting: "I've been trying to impress upon my students the notion that the future isn't predictable, but it is conceivable." Indeed, you won't be able to predict your exact path to love, and the exact type of person your partner has to be, but never waver from believing that you are capable of finding a wonderful relationship, that it *is* conceivable.

fulfilled and happy. See it. Believe it. As a Love TREP, you will need to believe in your capacity to give and receive love and have the desire and determination to *do the work* to get to that place.

During a presentation to the Babson community, Babson MBA alumna Rachel Greenberger spoke about the importance of belief in your vision. She recounted to the audience her exploits in the filmmaking world. One day, she said, she woke up with a vision: "I'm going to make a film." Given her love of movies since she was a child, her declaration wasn't that ridiculous a notion, but she had no knowledge of the film industry. So, how would she succeed in this venture?

In true entrepreneurial fashion, Greenberger started by taking action, one small, smart step at a time. She went to the library and checked out a book on screenwriting and filmmaking, read it cover to cover, and got to work on achieving her vision. A few years later, she produced an exquisitely-made, twenty-minute short that screened at various film festivals.

"The first rule of being an entrepreneur is to ignore the voice that says 'who do you think you are to do this?'" said Greenberger. "You've got to shut that voice down." In other words, you've got to believe in your vision and go after it.

You don't even have to be an entrepreneur in the traditional sense of the word to know about believing in your vision. Consider the words of Maria Sharapova, tennis superstar. Sharapova may not be an entrepreneur in the traditional start-up sense, but she certainly has adhered to the entrepreneurial spirit while managing her tennis career and brand. After winning the French Open (a win that came

after a slump of several months), she said to reporters, "I could have said, 'I don't need this. I have money; I have fame; I have victories; I have Grand Slams.' But when your love for something is bigger than all these things, you continue to get up in the morning when it's freezing outside, when it is the most difficult day, when nothing is working, when you feel like belief isn't there from the outside world, and you seem so small. You can achieve great things when you don't listen." Yes, Maria! I knew I liked that girl from the moment I saw her running around Bollitierri Tennis Academy as a twelve-year-old saying she was going to be the best tennis player in the world someday. (I was there during the winter break of my senior year of college to train.) Seeing the world through an entrepreneurial lens, Sharapova chose to see her life not as it was during her slump, but as it could be again. She silenced the negative voice, tuned out the media pundits, and held tight to her vision of making a comeback.

How many times have you let that voice run wild in your head? How many times have you lied to yourself about not needing love in your life? How many times have you said to yourself it's impossible to meet someone? How many times have you verbalized to others that you're going to die alone? How many times did you not believe finding love could happen to you and then reinforce that faulty belief again and again … and again?

Shut it down. Is there a part of you that says *I can't do this? I'm not worth it?* Shut that voice down!

Plenty, I'm sure. I was there. I understand what you are feeling. The exhaustion. The frustration. The deflation. Unfortunately, that voice has the power to become a self-fulfilling prophecy, which is why you need to silence it starting today. That's right: Starting today, you are going to put an end to the negative voice in your head that says you

can't create a fulfilling, loving relationship and then create an official vision for your dating and love life.

Yes, let's make it official.

Your stated vision from here on out is the following: *To create a healthy, happy dating life that leads to a healthy, happy relationship.*

In this book, when I write about creating a healthy, happy dating life that leads to a healthy, happy relationship, I do not mean to say that you will always experience flowers and rainbows in your dating experiences. I do, however, mean that a healthy, happy dating life should be seen as something that includes both the joyful and difficult moments (often it's in the difficult moments when we learn what we're made out of). If you are committed to learning about yourself and your needs through the dating process, if you can start looking your fears in the face and acting on them, if you can see failures and wrong turns as productive and instructive forces that will set you on a better path, you have found a healthy, happy dating life. When you start making this attitude shift, you will create the type of person that is ready for and attracts a healthy, happy relationship into your life. It may be hard to see the forest for the trees at times, but someday when you've found the love of your life, you may even look back on your single days with a sense of fondness for not just the fun times but also the struggles.

I'll be showing you how to make this official vision come to fruition throughout this book, but let's first work on starting to solidify your new vision.

Visualization Exercises

To help solidify your new vision, I've come up with a couple of visualization exercises.

As humans, much of our brainpower is set to visual stimulus. Dr. Lynell Burmark, Ph.D. Associate at the Thornburg Center for Professional Development and writer of several books and papers on visual literacy, echoes this sentiment: "...unless our words, concepts, ideas are hooked onto an image, they will go in one ear, sail through the brain, and go out the other ear." In other words, if you can create a vivid, visual objective, you have a better chance of meeting it.

Visualization exercises.

These are helpful as long as they're followed by action!

As I learned in my master's degree work, visualization exercises can indeed be enormously powerful. I received a Master's of Education in Counseling, with a minor in Sport Psychology, from Boston University. In one of the program's classes we learned about the importance of visualization techniques—many of which I had used throughout my tennis career at Amherst College. One of the reasons I was such a successful collegiate athlete (NCAA Division III national singles champion and national team champions) was my ability to be mentally tough. Visualization was one of my secret weapons. Before many of my more competitive matches, I'd sit and visualize myself hitting winners, playing the correct patterns, fist-pumping. By imagining these scenes, I was setting myself up for achieving them on the actual court.

In the introduction of professor and serial entrepreneur Michael Gordon's book *Entrepreneurship 101,* billionaire and real estate guru Donald Trump speaks to the importance of visualizing your dreams:

Without a vision, nothing of consequence will happen. In 1974, I looked at the old Commodore Hotel, next to Grand Central Station in New York City. I did not see a huge, dilapidated, nearly empty building in a seedy neighborhood. I did not see a bankrupt city or the New York real estate market, struggling to survive. I saw a magnificent, first-class convention hotel complex—grandiose, luxurious, and noteworthy. I was a young man of 27, and my vision felt right-sized.

Like Trump and his ability to visualize hotel grandeur, and like my visualization techniques on the tennis court, you need to start visualizing your success in the dating world and in finding love.

The first exercise I'd like you to practice is focused on establishing your general vision. The second exercise is focused on helping you visualize taking small, smart steps in your dating and love life.

Exercise 1— for your general vision:

- Close your eyes and visualize that a healthy, happy dating life has brought about your ideal outcome of a healthy, happy relationship. That outcome of having a healthy, happy relationship with an amazing, committed, loving man has now become your reality! Visualize yourself with your partner and take note of your environment: Where are you? What are you doing together? What colors do you see? Is there anybody else there with you? What do you smell? What do you feel? Do not visualize in detail what this man looks like, what he's wearing, or what he does for

a living. (Remember: The things you thought you knew about love and relationships and the things you thought you wanted in a man may change as you progress in your venture).

- Retain this visual and commit it to memory. Do this exercise for a few minutes every day.

This exercise can also be enormously helpful to women who are stuck in a dead-end dating situation with a particular man. Typically, I start my private coaching sessions with clients by having them visualize their end goal using visualization exercises. On several occasions, I've had clients tell me that doing this simple exercise immediately helped them step away from non-committal, wishy-washy men. When I had a former client named Angela visualize making her vision of a healthy, happy relationship a reality, she described a delightful scene: *Her future husband and her hanging out in the kitchen in their pajamas with their child, on a lazy Sunday afternoon, everyone laughing and acting silly.* Immediately after our session that day, she received a text message from a guy who appeared sporadically in her life, asking her to get together. She thought of the dream she envisioned during our session together and realized that this man was never going to be the man in her dream. And just like that, she had the power to let him go.

Sometimes, though, visualizing your ideal partner and relationship can feel difficult, weird, and forced. If that is your experience while attempting this exercise, that is perhaps a sign that what's going on internally (the way you feel about yourself, men, relationships, and the like) is not in alignment with your conscious desire to find a healthy, happy relationship. And so, even if you try to visualize these things

Small, smart steps. When your dating life seems daunting, when you wonder what you should do when you don't know what to do, all you have to do is take one small, smart step. And then another. And another.

on the surface level, it won't feel authentic. If visualizing this scene feels really difficult, chapter 3 will be important for you to read.

If you are interested in doing more of these types of visualization exercises, there are many guided, self-hypnosis and meditation videos on You Tube that can help you create similar empowering visual images.

Exercise 2 – for taking small, smart steps:

Because I recognize that visualizing the end goal of a healthy, happy relationship in exercise 1 may be too far removed for those of you beaten down by troubling experiences in the dating world or for those of you who are struggling with issues of self-worth, I have a second visualization exercise for you to try. So, after attempting exercise 1, I want you to give exercise 2 a shot.

- Close your eyes and visualize taking a small, smart step in your entrepreneurial journey to find love. Maybe that means visualizing yourself asking a friend to set you up with someone for a date; maybe that means visualizing yourself signing up for an online dating site; maybe that means approaching a man. It's your choice.
- When visualizing yourself taking a step, take note of your environment: Where are you? What colors do you see? What do you smell? What do you feel?
- Whatever first step you choose, visualize it every day for one week and then do it!
- Once you've taken action on a step, visualize taking another step, using the same process as described above and then take it.

The most important thing of all about visualizing steps is that you actually *act* on them. Vision without execution is pointless, and by practicing visualization techniques you help get yourself in the right frame of mind to execute. You will start to see that *you* have the power to make things happen and move your love life forward. The progress you make in your dating life with your small, smart steps will make it easier for you to visualize confidently your ultimate goal of a healthy, happy relationship and truly believe that it can become your reality.

In this chapter, we determined you have desire to find and create love in your life, you want to actively solve the problems in your dating and love life that are keeping you from finding and creating love, and you have an official vision of what you desire to create. It will be important to maintain desire, a problem-solving mindset, and your vision throughout your entrepreneurial journey.

You're off to a great start.

Up Next:

Now that you understand the qualities and type of mindset that you need to begin and maintain an entrepreneurial venture, you need to get to the heart of what is holding you back from finding love. Once you identify the obstacles that are impeding your ability to act, make changes, and grow more entrepreneurially in your dating and love life, you can start addressing them, one by one. In chapter 3, I will

discuss how to identify these obstacles and how to begin taking action on removing them.

Chapter 2 Action Steps Checklist:

✓ Make a list of "problems" that you see popping up in your
   dating and love life. You can continue to add things to
   your list as they come up for you during your entrepreneurial dating journey.
✓ Practice visualization exercise 1 every day for at least a few
   minutes.
✓ Identify a small, smart step you can take in your dating
   life, and then practice visualization exercise 2 in the days
   leading up to taking that small, smart step. For example,
   if you have been thinking about signing up for online
   dating, start visualizing yourself taking this action for a
   few minutes every day and then do it. The most important
   thing is to always take action on any step you visualize.

CHAPTER 3: WHAT'S HOLDING YOU BACK FROM FINDING LOVE?

**"Most of the shadows of life are caused by standing
in our own sunshine."**

– Ralph Waldo Emerson, essayist, lecturer, and poet

Let's return for a moment to Donald Trump, who writes about his
own entrepreneurial journey in the introduction of Michael Gordon's
book *Entrepreneurship 101*:

> The start-up phase of my first business was an exhilarating
> struggle, often intense, sometimes scary, always filled with
> raw passion. I felt really alive. My mental image was this: I
> was standing on one side of this terrifying chasm, a bottom-
> less start-up pit where flames of risk were waiting to engulf
> me. I was like a deer frozen in the headlights—stuck on the
> wrong side. I could envision myself on the other side, suc-
> cessfully growing my own business. But how to get there?

The world of entrepreneurship isn't so different from the world of dating. Let's take a look at this statement with just a few words changed:

The start-up phase of **[finding a loving relationship]** was an exhilarating struggle, often intense, sometimes scary, always filled with raw passion. I felt really alive. My mental image was this: I was standing on one side of this terrifying chasm, a bottomless **[dating]** pit where flames of risk were waiting to engulf me. I was like a deer frozen in the headlights—stuck on the wrong side. I could envision myself on the other side, successfully **[finding love]**. But how to get there?

How many times have you thought about your love life in the way Trump describes—the intense challenges involved, the exhilarating (and often frustrating) struggle, the anxiety of it all? How many times have you pictured yourself standing on the precipice of a chasm, desperately wanting to see yourself on the other side, the side of happy couples who have found love and have started families, with you still stuck on the singles side, unfulfilled, confused, and exhausted? Maybe, like Trump, you could envision yourself on the other side, but the inevitable risks and potential obstacles seemed too overwhelming, too daunting, to the point where it was easier to not even try to "get there."

A "Wantrepreneur."

A person who wants to be a trep.

The process of starting a new entrepreneurial venture (be it business or love) is a large undertaking. A wannabe entrepreneur may have desire and a vision for something she wants to create but feels as though there are too many obstacles in the way. As a result, she creates excuses as to why it can't be done. You can be sure that most traditional entrepreneurs sit up at night held back by obstacles. Fears and self-doubt, for example, are common impediments to an entrepreneur's journey: *What if I can't do this? What if I fail? What if I look like*

a fool? What if I'm not smart, talented, or good enough to do this? I've cried enough tears to fill a river, worrying about my capabilities as a budding entrepreneur and coach, terrified of failing. It's taken a lot of soul-searching and pointed reflection to understand what's behind these fears on a deeper level and to push past them. Whenever I have anxiety over taking a particular step in my business, I now ask myself, "OK, what's really behind this fear, and how can I work through it so that I can take that positive step forward?" This approach doesn't mean I will eradicate my fears forever, but at least I'm aware of where they come from and can learn to manage them as I grow my business and as I evolve.

Marie Forleo, best-selling author, speaker, web TV host, and trainer in personal development, entrepreneurship, and marketing, talks often about this aspect of entrepreneurship as she works tirelessly to inspire women across the world to start their own entrepreneurial ventures. She understands that every entrepreneur faces obstacles—from things like money, time, and resources to limiting internal beliefs about personal ability. But she encourages women to push past those obstacles by first getting to the root of them and then taking the steps to transforming those obstacles into unlimited possibilities for their lives and businesses.

Singles, too, deal with myriad obstacles. These obstacles show up in the form of limiting beliefs about themselves, men, intimacy, and relationships as well as more surface-level impediments (lack of time, money, energy, network, opportunities, and the like). In order to empower you to use your desire purposefully and make your vision burn brighter so that you can start building and growing your venture, it is imperative to start identifying and unpacking the obstacles that are

TREPtalk: "I started too late—because of fear of failure or a lack of belief in myself. I toiled in a job I hated for a long time, instead of starting a blog or building a business I loved. Knowing what I know now, I'd have started a decade earlier. Not starting is the worst-case scenario." – Leo Babauta, best-selling author and entrepreneur.

Excuses, excuses. Are you making excuses as to why your venture to find love can't get started? "Maybe next year" or "It can't be done" or "I'm not the person to do this." What's behind those excuses, and how can you problem-solve the barriers that are behind them?

holding you back from giving and receiving love. The end goal is that you will no longer use these obstacles as excuses.

In this chapter, I will help you develop an awareness of the barriers (both internal and external) in your life that are preventing you from greater entrepreneurial engagement in your love life and then prompt you to start problem-solving those barriers. It's imperative that budding Love TREPs go through this process. As Michael Gordon writes, "Entrepreneurship is a personal voyage, and your chance of success is greater the more clearly you understand yourself, your goals, and the obstacles you face."

Everyone has unique obstacles to unpack and work through. While there are general pieces of advice I can give to daters about their approach and mindset, I can't tell you what your particular obstacles are and how precisely to overcome them because I don't know you. The formulaic, generic dating tips and instruction available on the Internet will only get you so far. This chapter will guide you in uncovering your particular obstacles and give you suggestions as to how you can start removing them.

Affinity and Fishbone Diagrams

Use fishbone and affinity diagrams to jump-start:

1. Excitement
2. Creativity
3. Productivity

When it comes to identifying your obstacles, I believe using *affinity* and *fishbone diagrams* will be useful. Entrepreneurs can (and often do) use these diagrams to help them clear the fog in the context of entrepreneurial engagement, to help their businesses prosper; we can apply the same process to help people move their love lives forward. The questions and diagrams that follow will help you clear the fog in your

love life and determine actionable steps you can take to reach your vision. You'll need paper, a pen, and plenty of Post-it notes. Ideally you'll have a blank wall or easel pad on which you can secure your notes.

As you create these diagrams, you'll be asked to do the following:

1) To think more deeply about your *internal obstacles*—toxic, limiting core beliefs about yourself, men, relationships, and the like.

2) To think more pointedly about your *external obstacles*—any impediments existing on more of a surface-level (that may feed your internal obstacles).

You will develop solution-oriented plans for both your internal and external obstacles; these plans will help keep you on track as you begin and move through your entrepreneurial journey.

Should I do this alone or with friends?

While you can certainly do the following exercises on your own, I encourage you to invite your friends over to your place and make this a group effort. When you're alone, your thinking can often be limited and myopic; listening to other people's suggestions and ideas may be eye-opening for you. Moreover, people are often more comfortable with decisions and intentions if they feel they get to first share their ideas and thoughts with others. Ideation exercises, like the ones you are going to do, are often more illuminating, productive, and fruitful when done in groups because of the diversity of backgrounds and experiences, which usually leads to more ideas, opinions, and solutions.

Thank you note. Fishbone and affinity diagrams help organizations organize ideas and data. I'm indebted to Carl Sanders Edwards for introducing the concepts to me in the context of entrepreneurial thinking. Carl was a standout MBA student at Babson College. Not only did he achieve great things while studying at the school, but he also, simultaneously, ran a consulting business, Jumpshift, which he started before coming to Babson.

Side benefit of working with a group. Certainly, a common obstacle for women navigating the dating world is an inability to be vulnerable in front of others, which is why a side benefit of doing these exercises with friends is that you get to work on exposing your vulnerabilities, eventually empowering you to feel more comfortable doing the same with men.

And, surely, dating and the prospect of finding love seems a lot less intimidating, a bit more manageable, when you know you're not alone in your desires, frustrations, and challenges. I'll never forget the time at a friend's bachelorette party when several of us were gathered in front of a psychic for a group reading. Although I don't believe in psychics, I do believe that what I experienced that day was powerful and therapeutic. Many of the ladies present at the reading wanted answers about their love lives. As they started to talk, the tears started to flow. One by one, the women in the room began to reveal their deepest fears, vulnerabilities, and insecurities. There was barely a dry eye in the room as we listened to each other's stories—stories that illuminated our shared guilt, loneliness and struggles as lovers, spouses, singles, mothers, and careerists. The group reading truly unified us as imperfect, vulnerable women; it allowed us to feel safe with one another while sharing the frustrations, realities and challenges we face as women in life and love. It helped us feel relevant, validated, appreciated, heard, and not so alone. It helped us to begin difficult conversations with one another that might have never been broached had a stranger not prompted us to start talking.

When it comes to relationships and love, I truly believe that single women don't talk *enough* with each other about their real fears and struggles not only because they don't want to appear vulnerable but also for fear of (gasp!) actually having to admit they really want to find love. Sadly, though, we live in a world in which women wanting love just as much as, if not more than (double gasp!), a career is often looked down upon or criticized; as a result, women put up rock-hard facades designed to show others they don't care about having love in their lives. They then isolate themselves,

believing they need to gain mastery over their lives on their own. While rugged individualism is celebrated in this country, it often works against women in many aspects of their lives. What's worse is women get angry at themselves for not being able to surmount challenges on their own.

It's time we start admitting to each other that we want a partner with whom we can share love and grow. It's time to start supporting each other in this area, to deconstruct together what's stopping us from having a better shot at finding love, rather than feeling like we're on our own and have to gab and guffaw about our unsatisfying hookups at Sunday brunch. These exercises encourage women to own up to the fact that they do want a loving relationship, to say it proudly to themselves and others, and to start living like they really mean it.

Ladies night!
Make sure the women who join you in this exercise are open to the experience, positive, and supportive.

If you do make this a group effort, attendees can be single or in a relationship. The important thing is that all participants are positive, open to the idea and to others' suggestions and thoughts, and supportive of one another. Be prepared to be open and raw with one another. Tears are a good thing!

Affinity Diagrams

The purpose of affinity diagrams is to help you organize lots of ideas and make sense of overwhelming data or information.

There are four questions that will follow. As you answer each question, you'll build affinity diagrams. The fishbone diagrams will come later.

Cry it out!
Crying in front of other women can be incredibly empowering, liberating, and therapeutic.

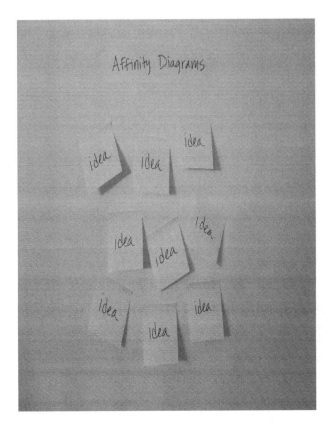

(An example of what an affinity diagram looks like)

Directions for Affinity Diagrams:

- If you are doing this exercise with a group, read all the instructions aloud.
- For each question, write down as many possible answers as you can on a Post-it note in a two to three minute period.
- When the time is up, secure these notes to a piece of paper or easel pad or wall underneath the question, which should be written at the top.
- Don't think too much about your answers. Write them down, one at a time (one idea per Post-it note), as quickly as they come to you and place them on the surface you are using underneath the question. Don't go into any detail

about your answers. Note: If you do this exercise alone, you can write your answers on a piece of paper instead of placing Post-it notes on a wall or easel.

- Don't limit your ideas. Get creative! Play! Have fun! Laugh!

Question 1: Why would you want to find love and/or what's good about love?

Go!

Sample answers: *Having someone to laugh with; stability; safety; comfort; companionship; great sex; a best friend; someone who supports you emotionally; someone who encourages your career goals; someone who takes away your tears; someone to talk to about the news, politics, world affairs; etc.*

(Example of an affinity diagram for question 1 based on my sample answers)

<u>Question 2: What relationship do you truly admire and hope to emulate someday? What makes it great? No Hollywood couples allowed!</u>

Go!

Sample answers: *My parents. Because they are still madly in love after all these years; they are affectionate with each other; they are caring with and kind toward each other; they laugh with each other; they support each other's careers and ambitions; they raised me with good morals; they have shown me what it takes to get through tough times together; they argue respectfully; etc.*

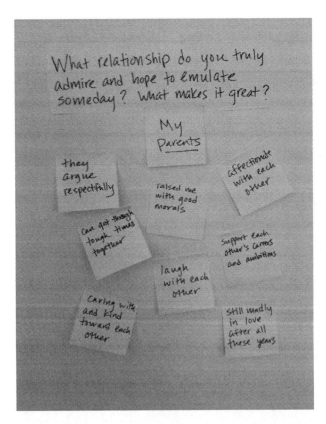

(Example of an affinity diagram for question 2 based on my sample answers)

WARNING: Don't read any further until you've completed the exercises above.

Directions continued:

- Move your answers for each question into themes or categories.

<u>For question 1, for instance, what are the general themes that emerge?</u>

In my sample answers, the themes that emerge are: *emotional, physical, professional,* and *intellectual.*

Your answers. My guess is that none of your answers to questions 1 or 2 have anything to do with money, superficial qualities, status, career industry, and the like.

(Example of moving ideas into themes for question 1)

<u>For question 2, what are the general themes that emerge?</u>

In my sample answers, the themes that emerge are: *physical, emotional, mental, professional, intellectual support,* and *consistency.*

Picture time.
If you're doing these exercises with a group. Take a photo of the answers you come up with or write them all down on a separate piece of paper and bring the lists home with you so that you can refer back to it when needed.

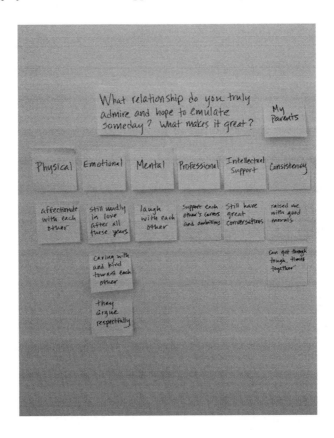

(Example of moving ideas into themes for question 2)

As you can see, when you organize all your ideas into themes, both questions come down to very similar categories: emotional, mental, intellectual, physical, and professional support/health. Some answers could certainly be placed in more than one theme. For instance, "safety" could be placed in both the "emotional" and the "physical" themes.

These are all great reasons to want to find love!

And you can be assured that many of these reasons and themes are similar to ones that emerge when aspiring entrepreneurs ask themselves similar questions about entrepreneurship. They want to become entrepreneurs for many of the same reasons people want to find love: fulfillment, intellectual stimulation, purpose, freedom to be who they are, and opportunity to create value in their lives and for others' lives.

Questions 1 and 2 are focused on fueling your desire to find a healthy, happy dating life that will lead to a healthy, happy relationship and illuminating what love can bring to your life. You may be so jaded and cynical about dating and love that you've lost sight of or forgotten what can be so wonderful about dating and finding love. It's thus important to create visual, tangible reasons that you can use to bolster your resolve when failures and rejections threaten your path. Indeed, if you've spent years thinking negatively about men ("All men are pigs") and love ("It's not good for anything"), your dating life will be negatively affected, because your thoughts create your reality. You can use the lists you create as a resource whenever you're feeling upset or cynical about dating and love to remind yourself of all the wonderful things that love, a good man, and a healthy, happy relationship can bring into your life.

Let's move on to questions 3 and 4, which will help you identify your particular internal and external obstacles.

Internal obstacles – your beliefs

Before I ask you question 3, I want to briefly explain what I mean by internal obstacles.

When you focus on your internal obstacles, I want you to think about your *core beliefs*—the beliefs you have about yourself, men, love, dating, sex, and relationships. Beliefs can limit you or empower you, hold you back or motivate you to move forward. Ultimately, you want your beliefs to work for you not against you, especially in the dating world and certainly in the business world, too. When your core beliefs are working against you, they keep you stuck and single. They may keep you safe, allowing you to hide behind walls or always blame others for your problems, but they will never allow you to grow and achieve what you want in life.

If it helps, think of your beliefs as the foundation on which your entrepreneurial venture sits. Now imagine your venture as a physical space, say, an office building. Before we can grow your venture and take it in all sorts of new and wonderful directions, we need to address the foundation. If the foundation that is holding up your building is weak or shaky, you will never be able to move beyond your current limits. You will therefore need to replace your current foundation with a stronger one that enables you to start from a place of strength and stability, a place that empowers you to take your venture to new heights.

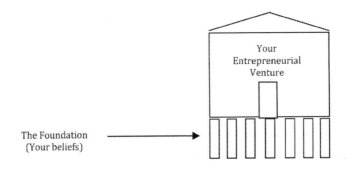

Your limiting core beliefs about yourself, love, relationships, and so on and so forth, can often be traced back to certain periods of your life, such as childhood, adolescence, or young adulthood. Some foundational beliefs come from your relationship with your parents. Some come from what you saw in your parents' relationship with each other. Others may have taken root in your past romantic relationships.

Wherever they came from, your limiting core beliefs need to be identified, worked through, consciously replaced with new, empowering beliefs, and then acted on. Otherwise, you allow these negative beliefs to continue throughout your life—they manifest themselves as patterns that you unconsciously follow again and again, at once protected and held back by them. When you don't break the cycle of your limiting beliefs, you keep reinforcing them in your life.

A former client of mine named Sally had a limiting core belief that she couldn't trust men. After discussion, we traced her belief back to her relationship with her father, who was abusive and unreliable. She spent years unconsciously seeking out unavailable, untrustworthy men, because that's what felt familiar to her based on her relationship with the first man she ever knew, a man who was supposed to love her.

In her dating life, by not trusting men or by believing that all men are inherently untrustworthy, Sally unconsciously chose men whom she couldn't trust, thereby reaffirming and reinforcing her core belief. Often, she would sabotage her own experiences by testing and pushing men away first before they had the opportunity to let her down. The more unavailable, untrustworthy men she dated, the more the belief kept getting hammered deeper and deeper into her psyche,

enabling her to always protectively declare: "See, I knew I was right not to trust men." Moreover, if Sally could push men away first, she wouldn't need to make herself vulnerable by actually having to trust someone. Because if she did allow herself to love and trust someone, he could hurt her.

But Sally wasn't getting anywhere with this approach.

So we worked together to replace her core belief with a different possibility: "Yes, *some* men are untrustworthy, but not *all* men. Just because I learned I couldn't trust my dad, doesn't mean I can't trust men. I can walk away from men who show me that they are untrustworthy. I can trust in *myself* to do that."

Once she identified and understood the old belief, and took responsibility for enabling it to continue over the years, we were able to replace it with a new, empowering belief. She could then repeat this belief over and over to herself and act on it out in the dating world. When the old belief was triggered by something a man said or did, she practiced *mindfulness*, which meant stepping into the present moment with intention but without judgment and consciously telling her mind to go with the new belief. Acting on her new belief in this way meant not only giving men a chance to show their trustworthiness, but also walking away from those men who showed their true colors and not taking their behavior personally. Instead of having a mind that was in charge of her, Sally used her mind for what it is: a tool for making smarter decisions.

Another one of Sally's core beliefs was that she was somehow unlovable or not good enough to deserve love. Again, we looked to

Mindfulness. "Paying attention in a particular way—on purpose, in the present moment, and non-judgmentally." –Jon Kabat-Zinn, Professor of Medicine Emeritus and founding director of the Stress Reduction Clinic and the Center for Mindfulness in Medicine, Health Care, and Society at the University of Massachusetts Medical School.

her childhood and relationship with her father, who hurled verbal insults at her and was incapable of providing consistent, loving support. And if a man who was supposed to love her couldn't show or give his love to her, what did that *mean* about her? That she was bad? That she wasn't good enough? That she was unlovable? Sally attached her father's behavior with *meaning* about who she was, when it reality it had nothing to do with her. Just because Sally took away from her fractured relationship with her father *a* truth ("I'm not lovable"), that didn't mean it was or had to be *the* truth. There were plenty of other reasons why her father behaved the way he did: maybe his parents were abusive with him; maybe he didn't feel good about himself; maybe he had no support system. None of those reasons had anything to do with Sally's worth; none of them meant that she was definitively unlovable.

But yet she somehow always found men who made her feel unlovable and not good enough, men who also, deep down, felt inadequate— like attracts like, as they say. This belief was also not serving her well. Sure, it kept her safe, so that no man could ever really get close enough, but it also kept her stuck and single; it was a defense mechanism that served her well as a child when she didn't know any better or know how to manage her feelings on her own, but it wasn't serving her well as an adult.

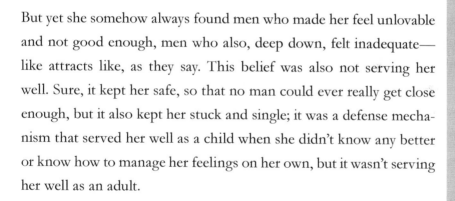

We worked together to understand the belief, to raise it to a conscious level. She then accepted responsibility for perpetuating it in her love life, and, finally, replaced the belief with a more compassionate one: "My father's treatment of me has nothing to do with who I was then and who I am today. I have so many wonderful qualities, and I can celebrate these daily. While I will always be a work in progress, I like

me, I love me. I want the person I end up with to like me and to love me for those wonderful qualities but also my flaws. I won't allow men who don't treat me well and don't ever address my needs to affect the way I see myself. Who they are and what they do has nothing to do with who I am and what I can do." As she stepped into the dating world, Sally, once again, practiced mindfulness, replacing her old belief with her new one.

This process took time, patience courage, and compassion, but when armed with her new beliefs, attitude, and approach, Sally became friendlier, warmer, more open, more sure of herself, more emotionally available, and more vulnerable with men. Her new beliefs have helped her enormously with dating confidence and attracting emotionally available men.

These are just two examples of a limiting core belief that can hold a woman back from giving and receiving love freely and joyfully. Other examples include:

> *I'm not pretty/smart/cool enough for the type of man I want to be with; I better enjoy this while it lasts, because the guy is going to leave, anyway; It won't hurt as much if I don't get too attached; My love life will never turn around; I'm cursed; There's no good men left in this city; all the good ones are taken; All men care about is sex; All men cheat; I can't trust men; they always disappoint me in the end; There are no good men out there that can give me what I want or need; I'm too old to find love; I'm just lucky if this guy is talking to me; I've got too much baggage; I should sleep with him, because that's all I'm good for; I'm always doing something to screw things*

up, I always blow it somehow; Men only want younger women; I'm not capable of settling down.

This is by no means an exhaustive list; it's simply a sampling of the many toxic beliefs that women drag around with them. During coaching, many of them are presented immediately to me and are at the conscious level, but a woman can't see how she's being unconsciously driven to seek out certain kinds of men. Others' toxic beliefs are unconscious and come out a little later in the coaching process after the client starts paying more attention to her thoughts and feelings, at which point we can consciously work through them. And still others take a while for a woman to recognize. I had a client who consciously said she believed she was worthy of love and good enough and thought highly of herself, until we really drilled down into her pattern with men and dating. Although she never had seen the connection before, it became clear that she had a history of chasing after men who didn't want her or rejected her and a history of rejecting and sometimes being repulsed by men who did want her. We traced the pattern back to one that started in high school but was truly drilled into her in college, when her first boyfriend and love broke her heart.

Fortunately, as you saw from Sally's experience, there is a way to change and overcome limiting beliefs. In summary, the model is as follows:

- **Identify** your limiting core beliefs.
- **Understand** your limiting core beliefs (where they came from, why you believe them), bringing them to a conscious level.

Stuart Smalley: Remember Al Franken as Stuart Smalley in the *Saturday Night Live* skit? "I'm good enough, I'm strong enough, and doggone it, people like me." Affirmations are great. Just be sure to follow them with action.

- **Accept** your limiting core beliefs as ones that YOU are perpetuating and reinforcing.
- **Replace** your limiting core beliefs with new, empowering beliefs.
- **Act** on your new, empowering beliefs (remember: entrepreneurs must take action).

The affinity diagram brainstorm will help you identify these limiting beliefs. You will then need to do some deep reflection on your own about where they came from and why you believe so strongly in them. Next, you will learn how to replace them with new, empowering beliefs. Finally, you will need to go out into the dating world with your new beliefs and act on them. Thought without execution is pointless. It's not enough to just think about your new beliefs and repeat them to yourself. As a Love TREP, you have to *act* on them, so that you build enough confidence to believe they are true. Ultimately, the new beliefs will become your default beliefs.

Directions continued:

- Take a few minutes to read the "Internal obstacles" section in this chapter so that your friends will understand what limiting core beliefs are and how to reframe them.
- Take several minutes to answer Question 3, following the same brainstorming process as with the first two questions, in terms of the Post-it note procedure and affinity diagrams, although you won't need to organize your answers into general themes or categories this time around.

Keep your answers general. You will eventually have an opportunity to drill deeper into specifics.

- If you are with a group, read through the sample answers to offer examples. Everyone can participate by offering their own limiting beliefs (married or coupled friends can think back to the beliefs they held during their single days). After several minutes of brainstorming on your own, place your Post-its on a shared space (a wall or an easel pad). Feel free to discuss all of the ideas together. If you do this exercise alone, you can use a piece of paper to write down your answers.

- This isn't an easy question to answer. Please be as honest and as raw as possible. You won't get anywhere by hiding things.

Question 3: What internal obstacles are holding me back from giving and receiving love?

Go!

Sample answers: *I'm unlovable; There's something about me that isn't good enough for the men I want to be with; I'm not skinny or pretty enough to attract a man; I always pick the wrong men who disappear on me; I'm too picky, but I don't want to change that; If I tell men what I need, they'll leave me; I am just cursed in dating; If I let someone in, he'll abandon me; If I get too close, it will hurt more when they leave; If I don't have sex with a man early on, he'll leave me; I can't trust men; Men just want sex; If I push him away first, I won't get hurt; I tend to be demanding of men; I need a man to love me to feel good about myself; I give men a hard time to test them; I can't get men to like me no matter what I do; etc.*

Your obstacles. Your answers to questions 1 and 2 will help fuel your excitement about finding love. Your answers to questions 3 and 4 will help you begin to uncover your roadblocks.

Ask yourself.
Look at your
answers to
Question 3. And
then look at
your answers to
Questions 1 and
2. How can you
expect to give
and receive love
with a wonderful
partner, when
you believe
everything you
write down about
yourself, men,
and dating for
Question 3?

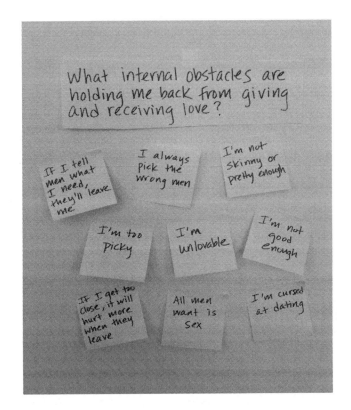

(Example of an affinity diagram for
question 3 based on my sample answers.)

When you get to the fishbone diagram section, you'll begin to flesh
out your answers to question 3.

External obstacles

Sometimes there are also external impediments to moving your love
life forward. These can be things like time, money, physical appearance, an uninviting home, old mementos and gifts from or photos of
an ex, meddling family members or friends, and the like. Oftentimes,
external obstacles create or exacerbate internal obstacles. It is important you identify these types of external obstacles and begin to figure

out ways to start removing them so that you make your path to finding love as uncluttered as possible.

Lauren, a former client, was feeling a lot of pressure from her parents to find a man and settle down. Her mother, in particular, was constantly making her feel bad about being single, to the point where Lauren felt she was getting into various relationships with incompatible men, just so she could tell her mom that she had a boyfriend. Her grandmother would also make comments every time they talked. Lauren was afraid she'd make a wrong decision because of her desire to please her family.

Eventually, she realized that she couldn't make thoughtful choices in her love life when she was living it for other people. As hard as it was, she asked her family members to back off. She told them that she didn't want to talk about her love life with them at all and explained why. Meanwhile, her parents and grandmother had no idea their behavior had affected her so deeply, and so they agreed to her request.

Lauren felt like a heavy weight had been lifted. She was now free to date as she pleased and not having her family's voice in the back of her head helped her enjoy both the dating process and family time a lot more.

Directions continued:

- Take several minutes to answer Question 4, following the same brainstorming process as with the first three questions in terms of the Post-it note procedure and affinity diagrams, although you won't need to organize your answers

into general themes or categories this time around. Keep your answers general. You will eventually have an opportunity to drill deeper into specifics.

- If you are with a group, read through the sample answers to offer examples. Then, after several minutes of brainstorming on your own about external obstacles applicable to your own life (married or coupled friends can think about the external obstacles they had during their single days), place your Post-its on a shared space (a wall or an easel pad). Feel free to discuss all of the ideas together. If you do this exercise alone, you can use a piece of paper to write down your answers.

- Note: Some of your internal and external obstacles may overlap, which is totally fine. For instance, you may put "overweight" in external, but that also could be seen as an internal problem if you have significant body issues

<u>Question 4: What external obstacles are holding me back from giving and receiving love?</u>

Go!

Sample answers: *negative family members; energy sapping friends; work issues; stuck in thankless job; inadequate online dating profile/photos; not enough free time; old gifts or mementos from or photos of an ex-boyfriend; too many commitments; overweight; lack of money; not many outside activities from work; small network; negative support system with friends; reoccurring ex-flame; lack of style know-how (clothes, hair, makeup); uninviting home/ apartment; etc.*

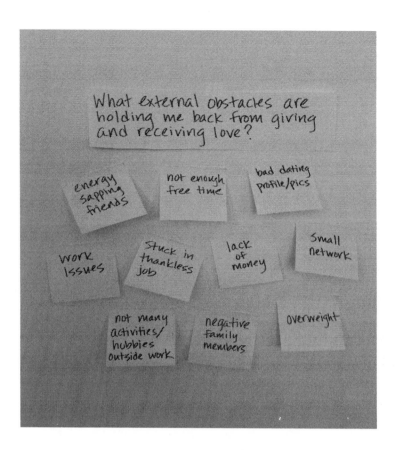

(Example of an affinity diagram for
question 4 based on my sample answers.)

Now that we've identified your internal and external obstacles in questions 3 and 4 using Affinity Diagrams, we can move on to the Fishbone Diagram process to dig deeper and to identify solutions.

Fishbone Diagrams

According to Wikipedia, a "fishbone diagram is often used when there are no clear comparisons between the problem's contributing factors or when there are too many factors to consider." A silly name for a serious diagram. In the context of dating and love, now that

you've identified some of your internal and external obstacles, you can start digging deeper and addressing them. Fishbone diagrams will aid you in this process.

Internal Obstacles Fishbone Diagram

Directions for internal obstacles fishbone diagram:

- Use the blank fishbone diagram on the following page, to fill in your answers from *question 3*. If you are doing this with a group of women, they can recreate the general shape of a fishbone on a piece of paper.
- Use six of your answers (the ones you feel are holding you back the most from giving and receiving love) to question 3. Maybe something someone else wrote resonated with you—feel free to use one or more of the beliefs that the other women added if you feel it is a belief that you hold.
- Write the answers in each of the six, top boxes. See page 68 for a completed sample diagram.
- In the lines underneath, go into a brief description of where you think the belief stems from. This may take time and pointed reflection, because some of these beliefs have been operating at an unconscious level, pulling you to certain men and dating situations, for many years. Start with 10 minutes and if people need more time you can certainly give it to them.
- If you can't come up with six, put down as many as you can.

Fill in your answers.

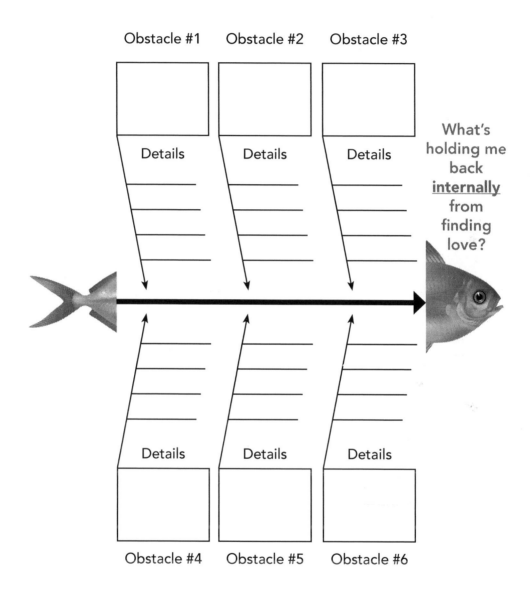

Obstacle #1   Obstacle #2   Obstacle #3

Details   Details   Details

What's holding me back **internally** from finding love?

Details   Details   Details

Obstacle #4   Obstacle #5   Obstacle #6

Here is a completed sample diagram for *internal obstacles* based on a few of my sample answers to question 3:

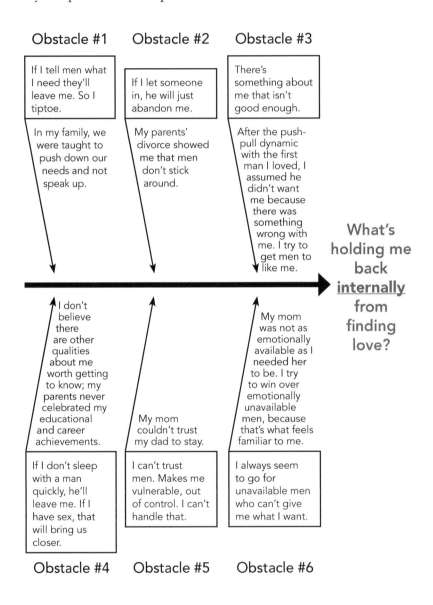

Obstacle #1   Obstacle #2   Obstacle #3

If I tell men what I need they'll leave me. So I tiptoe.

If I let someone in, he will just abandon me.

There's something about me that isn't good enough.

In my family, we were taught to push down our needs and not speak up.

My parents' divorce showed me that men don't stick around.

After the push-pull dynamic with the first man I loved, I assumed he didn't want me because there was something wrong with me. I try to get men to like me.

What's holding me back **internally** from finding love?

I don't believe there are other qualities about me worth getting to know; my parents never celebrated my educational and career achievements.

My mom was not as emotionally available as I needed her to be. I try to win over emotionally unavailable men, because that's what feels familiar to me.

My mom couldn't trust my dad to stay.

If I don't sleep with a man quickly, he'll leave me. If I have sex, that will bring us closer.

I can't trust men. Makes me vulnerable, out of control. I can't handle that.

I always seem to go for unavailable men who can't give me what I want.

Obstacle #4   Obstacle #5   Obstacle #6

If you're finding it difficult to understand where these beliefs come from, spend time chatting with your friends. Some of these beliefs

may be difficult to discuss and confront, and your friends will be there to hug and support you.

Directions continued for internal obstacles:

- Now that you've fishboned your internal obstacles, on a piece of paper, create a chart similar to the one on page 69-70.
- Fill in your old beliefs on the left side and then replace them with new, empowering beliefs on the right side (examples of how to write a new belief can be found in the "Internal beliefs" section on pages 54-60 or on pages 69-70 if you're having trouble coming up with them).
- Once you have your new beliefs, read them aloud to the group.

Sample Chart of Old Beliefs/New Beliefs:

Old Obstacles/Beliefs	New Beliefs
1. I'm afraid to tell men what I need because I fear they'll leave me. I tip-toe around them so I don't rock the boat.	1. During the getting-to-know-you stages of dating, I can articulate that I am looking for a relationship. If I've been consistently dating a man for, say, 2-3 months and want to know where his head is at regarding a possible relationship, and he hasn't already broached the subject, there is nothing wrong with speaking up in a caring, kind way and talking to him about what's going on. If he is dismissive of me and my needs, tries to manipulate me, or stops communicating with me, he is not the type of man I choose to be with, anyway. There are plenty of other men out there who are commitment-minded and will listen to my needs.

2. If I let someone in, he will just abandon me. Afraid I'll get divorced or choose wrong partner like my parents.	2. Life has no guarantees. There's a chance that I could meet someone and let him in to my heart, and it still might not work out. There's also a chance it will work out and be wonderful. If I am doing the work I need to do on myself and thinking more pointedly about my dating experiences and the men I date, that's all I can do, and my chances of finding a healthy, happy relationship are much better than if I were doing nothing.
3. There must be something wrong with me or not good enough about me.	3. Just because certain men haven't been interested in me doesn't mean there's something wrong with me or I'm not good enough. Sometimes men won't be attracted to me. That's okay. I can't control what other men want or do. I can work on myself and become the best version of myself, so that I am presenting my most open, warm, and authentic self while on dates.
4. I sleep with men too quickly because I'm afraid they'll leave me if I don't.	4. I will pay more attention to my motives for sleeping with men before we have talked about the status of our relationship. I understand that having sex does not obligate a man to be with me or make him see me as his girlfriend. I can trust in myself and listen to myself to do what feels right to me and is in line with my needs.
5. I don't like trusting men, makes me feel vulnerable, out of control. I can't handle that feeling.	5. Some men aren't trustworthy, but that doesn't mean all men aren't trustworthy. If I don't know a man, I can't assume he is either one. But I can trust in myself to make informed, smart choices. If I trust a man who abuses my trust, I can walk away from him and know his behavior has nothing to do with me and what I deserve. If a man is consistently kind and trustworthy, I will openly and lovingly give him my trust. I can only control what I do.
6. I always seem to go for unavailable men who can't give me what I want.	6. Things don't *just* always happen to me. I am not a victim. I can choose to date men with integrity and walk away from the ones who can't or won't give me what I need. I don't have to pick a man because he picks me. I am the chooser.

On a personal note: Not only did I use this type of old beliefs/new beliefs chart for my love life with regard to my limiting core beliefs, but I have also used it in other areas of my life. When I was in my early to mid-twenties, I began to suffer from panic attacks. They were few and far between, maybe a handful of times a year, but I had no idea what brought them on or when they would occur, which made me worry about them occuring at inopportune times, especially if I was in the company of other people. To make matters worse, I soon began to worry about worrying. It was a vicious cycle.

One day, I ordered some tapes and workbooks that promised to help people think about their anxiety and stress differently. One exercise within the workbook encouraged people to rationalize their fears by replacing the beliefs that caused them worry with different, more compassionate beliefs. That exercise changed my life. For example, one of my biggest fears was that I would have a panic attack in front of a lot of people and be terribly embarrassed. The workbook had me reframe my fear and replace it with a more compassionate belief. Therefore, "What if I freak out in front of people and embarrass myself?" became "Okay, so what if I have a panic attack and people look; what's the worst that could happen if that did occur?"

It took a little practice to believe in my new beliefs, but, eventually, I realized that the worst that could happen wasn't so bad, that life would go on. Once that happened, my panic attacks vanished completely. Once I realized that I was my safe person, that I had the ability to soothe myself, to calm myself down using my own thoughts, I was liberated from my old beliefs and empowered to act on new ones.

Affirmations.

Affirmations are great, but all talk and no action doesn't get you very far. You need to strengthen your affirmations by taking action, proving that you are living by your affirmations

Directions continued for internal obstacles:

- It can be helpful to do this with a group, and if you do decide to complete these exercises with other women, spend some time reviewing your answers another day when you are alone. You may need to spend more time on your own thinking about your limiting beliefs and re-working what you've written for your new beliefs.

- At least twice a week (or daily if you like), review your old beliefs/new beliefs chart. Read your old beliefs and then immediately replace them by reading your new beliefs.

- Now that you have more specifics about each internal obstacle, have begun to understand where they come from, have accepted your responsibility in perpetuating and reinforcing them, and have replaced them with new, empowering beliefs, you must follow the final step as explained in the model: act.

- Entrepreneurs must *act* to experiment with and solidify their ideas. So, over the next several weeks, as you begin acting in the dating world, either going out on dates or in your various interactions with men, I want you to really practice becoming the embodiment of your new beliefs.

- Whenever your old beliefs are triggered (for example, a man asks you out, and you immediately jump to "he's just going to flake or end up disappointing me" because of your limiting belief that men always disappoint you), you will take responsibility for these beliefs and push yourself to step away from them, but be compassionate with

yourself (these beliefs have been entrenched for years!)
when they do come up.

- Then you will push yourself to jump into your new belief.

This process takes time, effort, and practice, but it is absolutely worth
it to push yourself to be mindful about your beliefs and to create new,
empowering ones that you can live by.

External Obstacles Fishbone Diagram

Directions for external obstacles fishbone:

- Use the blank fishbone diagram on the following page,
  to fill in your answers from *question 4*. If you are doing
  this with a group of women, they can recreate the general
  shape of a fishbone on a piece of paper.
- Use six of your answers (the ones you feel are holding
  you back the most from moving forward in your dating and love life) to question 4 and write them in each
  of the six, top boxes (again, keep them fairly general).
  Maybe something someone else wrote resonated with
  you—feel free to use one or more of the obstacles that
  the other women added if you feel it is an obstacle that
  is in your way.
- Then go into detail about each one of them in the lines
  below the boxes.
- It's okay if you can't come up with six categories, but, at
  the very least, try to come up with four.

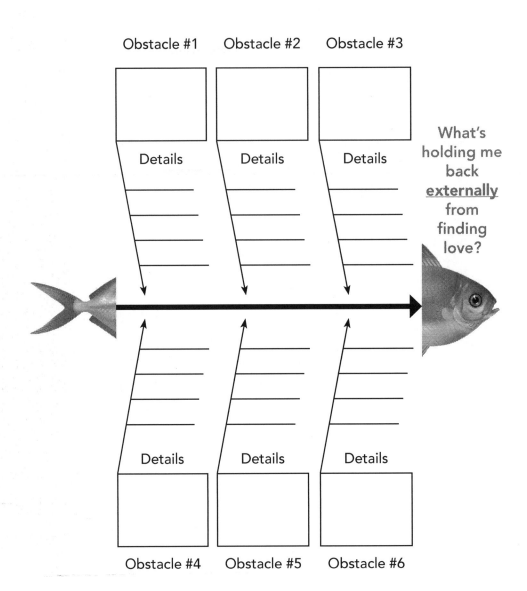

Obstacle #1   Obstacle #2   Obstacle #3

Details   Details   Details

What's holding me back **externally** from finding love?

Details   Details   Details

Obstacle #4   Obstacle #5   Obstacle #6

Here is a completed sample diagram for *external obstacles* based on my sample answers to question 4:

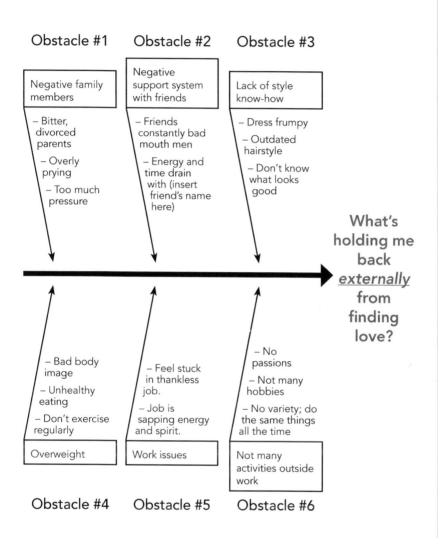

Obstacle #1   Obstacle #2   Obstacle #3

Negative family members

Negative support system with friends

Lack of style know-how

– Bitter, divorced parents

– Overly prying

– Too much pressure

– Friends constantly bad mouth men

– Energy and time drain with (insert friend's name here)

– Dress frumpy

– Outdated hairstyle

– Don't know what looks good

What's holding me back *externally* from finding love?

– Bad body image

– Unhealthy eating

– Don't exercise regularly

Overweight

– Feel stuck in thankless job.

– Job is sapping energy and spirit.

Work issues

– No passions

– Not many hobbies

– No variety; do the same things all the time

Not many activities outside work

Obstacle #4   Obstacle #5   Obstacle #6

Remember: This is a sample fishbone. If you like the Obstacles categories I've chosen and they apply to your life, feel free to use them. Or create your own categories as you see fit, providing details about each in the corresponding lines. Over the next several months, you may identify more external obstacles in your life. Feel free to add them to this list and go through the fishbone diagram process.

Directions continued for external obstacles fishbone:

- On a piece of paper, create an Obstacles/Solutions chart similar to the one on page 77.
- For each obstacle in your fishbone, I want you to select one subheading obstacle. Using my example on page 75: underneath "Negative family members," you might choose "too much pressure"; underneath "Negative support system with friends," you might choose "energy and time drain with (insert friend's name here)"; and so on and so forth.
- Then create at least one solution for each obstacle (one is enough, but you can create more than one if you like).

Sample chart for external obstacles:

OBSTACLES	SOLUTIONS
1. Negative family members → Too much pressure	1. Talk to family members and kindly ask them to not ask me, pressure me, etc. about my love life. Explain that I fear the pressure may make me choose the wrong person.
2. Negative support system → energy and time drain with (insert friend's name here)	1. Talk to friend and tell him/her how his/her negativity is affecting me. 2. Surround myself with more positivity and people who are optimistic about men and dating and who are in healthy relationships. 3. Join a local social organization to meet new, more positive-minded friends.
3. Lack of style know-how → Don't know what looks good on my body type.	1. Book appointment with stylist. 2. Ask stylish friend to help me and go shopping with me.
4. Overweight → Don't exercise regularly.	1. Find work-out buddy and commit to going to gym twice a week to start.
5. Work issues → Feel stuck in thankless job.	1. Each week dedicate two hours to looking for new job. 2. Talk to manager to ask for more responsibility and communicate my needs in a mature, professional way.
6. Not many activities outside work → No variety; stuck doing same things.	1. Brainstorm list of 10 activities or hobbies that would be fun to try. 2. Brainstorm list of five local, professional organizations that have events (more on identifying opportunities in chapter 10).

Directions continued for external obstacles:

- If you are with a group, read your obstacles/solutions list aloud.

- Within the next two weeks (yes, two weeks—entrepreneurs don't sit idly!), I want you to take action on four of

Small, smart steps. Remember to take action on the four solutions you identify in the next two weeks. Treps take action!

your solutions. As a Love TREP, you will be taking small, smart steps toward achieving your vision. This is just the beginning of your forward motion.

O   Using my sample Obstacles/Solutions chart, I have chosen the following four items. My small, smart steps are:

- talk to my parents (or email them, send them a card);
- brainstorm list of 10 activities (again, more on this in chapter 10);
- find a friend who knows about style and ask her to come with me on a shopping trip.
- find work-out buddy and commit to going to the gym twice a week to start.

Nice job.

Nobody said this would be easy. So keep it up. You're off to a great start.

Once you've taken these steps, I encourage you to take more steps, based on the other obstacles and solutions you've uncovered. If you are hesitant to act, consider visualizing taking these steps, as described in visualization exercise 2 in chapter 2, so that you can start prepping yourself for action. Of course, you actually have to then go ahead and take that action on the solutions you've identified. Remember: you're an entrepreneurial problem-solver!

—〜〜—

Many new entrepreneurs need to think about how to overcome both internal fears and external impediments. While you might not believe it, many of the answers or categories of answers listed in questions 3 and 4—low self-esteem, fears, insecurities, trust issues, negative family members, lack of monetary funds, small network, no or negative support system, and

so on—are the same issues that hold traditional entrepreneurs back from exploring and going after their business ideas and dreams.

With regard to internal obstacles, traditional entrepreneurs often undergo a similar process as explained earlier in the chapter: *identifying* the belief; *reflecting* on and *understanding* where it came from (self-doubt: "My family never supported my creativity and need to branch off in a non-mainstream way."); *accepting* their responsibility in allowing the belief to perpetuate, recognizing that their past experiences don't define who they are, who they can become, and what they can do; *replacing* old beliefs with new, empowering ones; and then *acting* on a new understanding of themselves as they move forward with their business idea, focusing on where the journey takes them as opposed to wondering if the journey is even possible.

With regard to external obstacles, traditional entrepreneurs also need to identify and confront these types of roadblocks. By creating a tangible list, they can then begin to address each obstacle by taking steps to remove it or come to terms with it (money: "To financially support myself and pursue my dream of starting this business, I'll have to get a day job, but I can work somewhere that has set hours and allows me to pursue my passion on the side; here are the jobs that might be a good fit for the time being.")

The same process with regard to internal and external obstacles is imperative for daters to go through.

I know it can be difficult to drudge up all the things that might be standing in your way, to confront yourself and certain people in your life, to tackle your demons head-on, but it's a necessary part of your entrepreneurial journey to find love. Some of you may have less daunting problems to

handle (though I suppose it's all relative), and some of you may have been dealt a really shitty hand in life. I've known some women whose terrible upbringing and traumatic childhood issues prevented them from finding men who would treat them well. But I've also known women who had happy childhoods and seemingly mild issues to confront as adults, yet they still struggled to find intimacy and love. Whatever your internal and external issues are, they are *your* issues to surmount.

So get going!

Up Next:

You've created new, empowering beliefs to tackle your internal obstacles and started taking small, smart steps to remove a few of your external obstacles, and I urge you to practice your new beliefs often and to remove as many external obstacles as you've identified as you go through this process. Now that you are on your way to making your path a little lighter, less burdensome, it is important to assemble a group of people who can consistently help guide and support you, who will believe in you as you continue this journey. In chapter 4, I will discuss creating your Board of Advisors.

Chapter 3 Action Steps Checklist:

✓ Complete the four affinity diagram exercises either alone or with friends.
✓ Use your affinity diagram answers from questions 1 and 2 to create a list that you can turn to when feeling

cynical about men and/or disappointed by your dating experiences.

✓ Use your affinity diagram answers from questions 3 and 4 to fill in your internal and external obstacles fishbone diagrams.

✓ Using your internal fishbone diagram, create your Old Beliefs/New Beliefs chart.

✓ Over the next several weeks, repeat your new beliefs daily. More importantly, practice using them with men you are meeting. You can even practice your beliefs with other people in your life. If you have trust issues, for example, you can work on giving more of your trust to other people in your life, like friends and family members.

✓ As you progress in this book, you may identify more internal obstacles and you should certainly work toward replacing them using the Old Beliefs/New Beliefs chart.

✓ Using your external fishbone diagram, create your Obstacles/Solutions chart.

✓ Using this chart come up with at least one way to remove each of the obstacles listed.

✓ Within the next two weeks, take action on four of these specific obstacles by following through on the solution steps you've identified.

✓ As you progress in this book, you may identify more external obstacles and you should certainly work toward removing them using the process documented in the Obstacles/Solutions chart.

CHAPTER 4: ASSEMBLING YOUR BOARD OF ADVISORS

"I was sustained by one piece of inestimable good fortune. I had for a friend a man of immense and patient wisdom and a gentle but unyielding fortitude. I think that if I was not destroyed at this time by the sense of hopelessness which these gigantic labors has awakened in me, it was largely because of the courage and patience of this man. I did not give in because he would not let me give in."

— Thomas Wolfe, novelist

Entrepreneurs are always in a state of forward motion. To facilitate that forward motion, it is necessary to enroll a group of advisors and confidantes to come along on your journey. This group of people, your Board of Advisors, will be there every step of the way alongside you, guiding you to make smarter, more informed choices, support-ing your efforts and dedication.

Part of what I am encouraging you do in this book is to go out into the dating world and take action, experiment, learn from your experi-ments, and then go out and experiment some more (see part II of this

book for my Date. Learn. Repeat. model of entrepreneurial dating). In a sense, you have already begun to act by identifying and removing some of your obstacles on your own—certainly, this will help facilitate your forward motion. At this point, though, it will be important to surround yourself with people who will support you and help you *consistently* reflect on your experiences, offer objective analysis, and encourage and support you in your entrepreneurial venture. Without this consistent reflection, your actions and experiments in the dating world may lose their meaning and instructive power.

People like to say dating is a numbers game. While I agree to a point (the more people you date the more you discover who's right for you and weed out incompatible men) and encourage you to date frequently and purposefully (more on this in later chapters), I also believe you could date until you're blue in the face and not feel like you're getting anywhere. If you're not ready—physically, mentally, emotionally—or at least in the process of readying yourself, through support, counsel, and feedback loops, you won't have much luck attracting a compatible partner, let alone a healthy relationship.

In other words, action in the dating world is key, yes, without a doubt. But action without *any* guidance is as futile and unproductive as guidance without action.

Surround yourself! For traditional treps, coaches, mentors, and advisors have proved to be invaluable. So, too, for singles.

Recognize your weaknesses. Seek guidance. That's what smart TREPs do!

Many traditional entrepreneurs have people advising them, even (especially!) the smartest, most successful ones. That's because smart,

successful entrepreneurs admit their weaknesses; they're not too proud to say, "I can't do this on my own." They realize their vision would be more difficult to achieve without the expertise of objective consultants who've been there before them and who possess certain strengths to fill their gaps.

Consider the team of advisors that Facebook founder and billionaire Mark Zuckerberg assembled to help grow his company. Despite being viewed as cocky, selfish, and Machiavellian by many, Zuckerberg understood that he couldn't achieve the vision and direction he had for his company without leaning on the support and advice of successful entrepreneurs: Apple's Steve Jobs, LinkedIn's Reid Hoffman, Accel Partner's Jim Breyer, and investor and PayPal founder Peter Thiel, to name a few.

In their Entrepreneur Experience Lab research (see chapter 1 for first reference), the authors found that many of the entrepreneurs they studied believed that forward motion almost always trumps reflection. However, understanding the importance of reflection in the entrepreneurial process, entrepreneurs are increasingly turning to formal mentors and personal coaches to provide that crucial mechanism of reflection. They highlight the work Steve, an Austin entrepreneur developing new LED lighting technologies and products, does with an executive coach on a weekly basis: During these meetings he's held accountable to reflect on the past week, assess progress toward identified opportunities, and plan for the upcoming week. "The coach provides Steve the opportunity to actively reflect on his experiences in a productive manner," they write.

So, too, are droves of singles turning to various advisors and guides (dating coaches, relationships columnists, spiritual gurus, therapists,

TREP talk: "My biggest mistake was trying to do it all myself. As a founder, I felt like I knew everything I needed to know about media, content, even the technology involved to reach my audience. And I did. I just didn't know anything at all about making a viable business: finance, marketing, advertising, and human resources. After a few years of rapid growth my company had stalled out, and I was spending more time fighting fires than I was doing the stuff I loved (and that made us money)."
– Leo Laporte –
Founder of the TwiT Network.

Ask yourself.

If finding love
is your most
important
venture, why
wouldn't you
seek to plug your
knowledge gaps?
You probably
do this in every
other area of
your life, correct?
So why not with
dating and love?

and the like) to inspire them, hold them accountable, help them re-flect, and develop better self-awareness. For traditional entrepreneurs and Love TREPs alike, it's crucial to understand the things you don't know and to bring others along on your journey who can support you and plug your knowledge gaps.

As a single woman navigating this often confusing world of dating, it will be important for you to admit what you don't know and ask for help. Reaching out to others doesn't mean you've "lost," as I've heard some women say when describing their antipathy toward therapists, dating coaches, or dating self-help books. You aren't failing by asking others to help you learn, grow, and move forward in your life. Why should someone seeking, arguably, the most important thing in the world—love—be alone on this journey? I'm baffled by women who have no problem asking for help in every other area of their lives but become embarrassed or proud when it comes to asking for help in matters of the heart. They go after everything else in their lives, but all of a sudden decide to leave love up to fate. It doesn't make sense.

Your Board members will be your partners, your confidantes, people who believe in you. As Schlesinger and his co-authors write in *Action Trumps Everything* with regard to discussing the need to bring others along on an entrepreneurial venture: "The committed stakeholders who join you will help change your original idea—if they're brought in early enough in the process. They end up being collaborators and taking ownership of what is created. They become, in the very real sense of the word co-creators. The initial vision becomes shared, it expands, and it becomes 'ours' instead of just yours." It will be reas-suring to you in the coming months to know that you are not entirely alone on this journey.

Your ultimate vision is to create a healthy, happy dating life that leads to a healthy, happy relationship. As you work with your Board and work on yourself, your mindset, and your approach to dating and relationships, your idea of the man you want to end up with may very well change. You may even discover that what you want is very different than what you actually need. Your Board will be there with you throughout this journey to encourage this type of self-growth and inspire you to action to achieve your vision.

The following board members are merely suggestions for an effective board. You are certainly free, though, to ask anybody who you believe will be supportive and thoughtful and can help you move your entrepreneurial venture forward to achieve your vision. I don't want to limit your thinking when it comes to choosing advisors, but I will suggest a few of my own ideas based on my personal and professional observations and experiences.

At the end of this section there are suggestions as to how you can pick and choose from my suggestions the way you see fit.

Suggested Board Members

1. The Therapist

Wait! Don't close the book yet. Hear me out.

Far too many people balk at the idea of therapy, even though therapists are really just unbiased people who endeavor to help you make sense of your world. Sounds harmless, right? But for many, by seeing a

Objectivity.

If part of the goal of your Board is to offer you objective guidance, who better than a therapist?

Your past.

Learn from your past—the lessons are there for the taking, if you take the time to understand them.

How our past affects our present.

Not everything you discuss in therapy has to go back to your childhood, but oftentimes it is true that we suffer in the present, in part, because of the past. Once we come to terms with, accept, grieve over, understand our past and how it may have affected our current realities, and then take responsibility for it moving forward, our present lives can be easier to navigate.

therapist, it's as if they've admitted defeat. To that I say: defeat in what, and by whom are you being defeated? The word itself is defined as "a victory over (someone) in a battle or other contest." Are you in a contest or battle with yourself? It's ludicrous. Self-help books can be great aids (otherwise I wouldn't be writing one), but all the self-help books in the world can't cater uniquely to you. Where do you think many of the authors of dating and relationship self-help books get their material, specifically the ones written by licensed therapists, psychologists, and psychiatrists? Most of the insights come from their work with normal, everyday women, just like you and me, who want to better understand themselves and strengthen their dating and love lives.

Some of you may have a pattern of choosing noncommittal men. Maybe you have trouble with trust, intimacy, or real connection. Maybe you've been entering into the wrong relationships and engaging in self-sabotage as a way of passively avoiding your hidden fears. Maybe you have years of built-up low self-esteem. Whatever your specific issues or beliefs, you owe it to yourself to identify them and think more deeply about them on a consistent basis. Isn't it possible that there's something deeper to your decisions in love, and that maybe someone can partner with you to help uncover what's beneath your choices and beliefs? I've seen countless women date their faces off only to get the same results again and again. I've also seen many women consistently turn a blind eye to the lessons they could have learned from past experiences, ignoring the possibility that maybe there were deeper issues that needed unearthing before any sort of progress in their love lives could be made. These women refuse to get help and often resign themselves to endless bad dating habits and patterns, which often stem from unconscious places they haven't been able to access or fully understand.

Sure, a woman may say that she *has* learned from her dating experiences and made certain surface-level adjustments, but if she doesn't have help connecting the more superficial dots ("I don't like when a man shows too much interest in me, for example") with some of the more entrenched ones ("I felt abandoned by my parents as a child"), poor choices may continue, and any sort of a-ha moments that spur on self-awareness, self-understanding, and self-acceptance may lose their instructive power.

In chapter 3, I asked you to start wrestling with and moving past some of your toxic beliefs and that's a good start, but the truth is this journey isn't an overnight process. It will be important for you to have someone by your side to consistently aid you in your self-awareness and self-growth. Because a lot of what drives you comes from an unconscious level, it will be helpful to have a professional by your side to help bring some of those unconscious, hidden fears to the surface, so that you can move forward in your dating and love life from a place of awareness.

Indeed, the unconscious is a powerful force. Years ago, I enrolled in a fear of flying program run by Dr. Albert Forgione, a Boston-based psychologist, who had been holding group therapy sessions since the 1990s for those with flying phobias. During one session about how our unconscious fears often get projected onto objects, experiences, or people (a fear of losing or not having control gets projected onto a plane or pilot), Dr. Forgione relayed a story about driving home one night during his youth. He awoke in the driver's seat of his car in his driveway after driving home from a late night out. But he had absolutely no recollection of how he got home, even though he clearly had driven himself home. The story was meant to relay how powerful

Invest in yourself.
Seeing a therapist was the best thing that I ever did for myself. It wasn't always easy, but it helped me grow in ways I don't think would have been possible had I not gone. You can't have a healthy, happy dating life, unless you have a healthy, happy relationship with yourself.

Remember your internal obstacles?

The ones you identified in chapter 2? A therapist is a great person to talk to more in depth on a consistent basis about those limiting core beliefs.

the unconscious can be. His unconscious had, in fact, taken over that night and led him to a familiar place, because he was too tired at the conscious level to pay attention. Relationships and dating often have the same magnetic pull. We are attracted to certain men and types of relationships because we are being unconsciously pulled. The goal is to bring our unconscious motives to the conscious level, so we can break the cycle of being pulled unconsciously toward unhealthy men or situations that don't truly satisfy us. A therapist can be very useful in this regard (as can hypnotherapy, self-hypnosis, and guided meditation).

I wholeheartedly endorse the experience of therapy, probably because I feel it has been instrumental to my journey. At twenty-five I found myself in a roller-coaster relationship. It was demoralizing, unhealthy, and exhausting. I didn't understand the force that kept pulling me back to this man—because that's what it felt like, an unassailable force, a drug, an addiction, like a car steering me home. The truth is, for years I had been drawn to unavailable men or men who didn't want me, convinced they'd come around someday, that I could change them, that they'd eventually see how wonderful I was for them. I had only been in one serious relationship that lasted about nine months, but it was rife with arguments and tumult.

I entered therapy around that time, determined to understand my unhealthy dating patterns. My therapist partnered with me to work through childhood, parental, intimacy, and commitment issues, and modern-day dating challenges, and she helped me understand my unconscious fears and to dig deeper into my conscious fears. She helped me understand why I consistently exhibited certain behaviors with specific types of men. She helped me to become a more whole,

grounded woman, who was more accepting of and compassionate with herself. She helped me to *fall in love with myself.* Ladies: If you don't understand and love yourself first, how can you allow another person to understand and love you?

Eventually, through both the reflection I was doing in therapy and the action I was taking in the dating world, I was aware and confident enough to self-correct, make smarter choices in men, and better able to give and receive love and thus experience true intimacy. Though it took me a handful of years of therapy and experimenting in the dating world, I eventually found someone amazing (to whom I'm now married). I credit Dr. Cohen, who I continued to see long after I met Dave, with helping me to become more self-aware and with providing different perspectives than my friends or family ever could. Moreover, she has been there to just *listen* to me. Ah, to be heard. In a world in which fewer and fewer people have the time to just sit and listen, a therapist is a great asset.

I'm asking you to try this. If you haven't tried therapy, how do you know it won't be helpful? I want you to keep an open mind going into your sessions. One hour a week—that's all I'm asking. If you go into this experience with a negative mindset, it won't be of any help—that I can promise. Look at it like an entrepreneur would, as an opportunity to further your venture. You don't even have to look at it as "therapy"; rather, it's simply time to breathe, reflect, and talk about subjects that matter only to you.

Therapy bonus.
A person who is dedicated solely to helping you. No one-uppers or competitive friends who have their own issues to discuss or project onto you.

When searching for a therapist, you can certainly look for practitioners specializing in women's or relationship issues in your healthcare plan network, but I'd start by asking for referrals from family and friends

(that's how I found mine). Seek out someone with whom you have a good rapport. If you don't feel comfortable with or like the manner or demeanor of your first therapist, try someone different—but give it at least four sessions (one month's worth) before changing. This selection process is kind of like dating—you'll learn what personality type (and therapeutic modality) works best for you and you can make pivots based on what you learn. Don't be defeated by incompatible matches.

Once you find someone with whom you feel relatively comfortable, stick it out with that person for at least six months. Ideally, you'd have this person as part of your Board until you've achieved your vision, although it's often helpful to have someone to talk to even after you've found the type of personal success you desire. Life and relationships will always be filled with challenges, and who doesn't need an unbiased confidant along the way with whom you can unload and unburden yourself?

Know this: Therapy isn't all flowers and rainbows. Many of my sessions over the years were filled with tears, anger, and feelings of guilt. But many were filled with laughter and the joyous a-ha moments that have helped me move my love life forward. Also, don't enter therapy expecting to find a husband as an outcome of treatment; it doesn't work that way. Your time with a therapist can help prepare you for meeting and connecting with men, but it cannot guarantee that a man will magically pop into your life within a certain timeframe. Therapy, like the entrepreneurial journey, takes time. As Professor Bob Caspe opined in an article titled "Advice to the Class of 2012," in the spring 2012 *Babson* magazine, "Entrepreneurship is a life choice where one chooses to focus on the pleasure of the journey as opposed to the destination." Give therapy time. Focus on what you're discovering about yourself and the world around you, not the endgame. Besides, getting married

Fiction.

Only the crazies go to therapy. Nonsense!

isn't necessarily a sign of growth or health—I know plenty of married ladies that could benefit a whole lot from talking to a professional.

But … therapy is not enough

I acknowledge the criticisms of therapy: All that thinking and analysis can sometimes create a cycle of inaction and a tendency to overanalyze. In the words of Sigmund Freud, the founding father of psychoanalysis: "Sometimes even a cigar is just a cigar." This is why it will be important to temper therapy with action-oriented work. In Part II of this book, I will be asking you to go out into the dating world to learn and grow from your experiences while simultaneously asking you to draw from what you're learning in therapy.

As a dating coach, I endorse using both coaching and therapeutic practices; in fact, I believe both modalities should be used together, holistically, to propel a person forward. Here is a chart examining the differences between coaching and therapy:

THERAPY	COACHING
Assumes the client needs healing	Assumes the client is whole
Roots in medicine, psychiatry	Roots in sports, business, personal growth venues
Works with people to achieve self-understanding and emotional healing	Works to move people to a higher level of functioning
Focuses on feelings and past events	Focuses on actions and the future
Explores the root of problems	Focuses on solving problems
Works to bring the unconscious into consciousness	Works with the conscious mind
Works for internal resolution of pain and to let go of old patterns	Works for external solutions to overcome barriers, learn new skills and implement effective choices

(Adapted from Hayden and Whitworth, 1995)

As a dating coach whose philosophy is grounded in the spirit and principles of entrepreneurship—facilitated by action, reflection, and more action—I wholeheartedly support everything listed on the right side of that chart. But, as someone who has a master's degree in counseling and has personally gained from seeing a therapist, I also believe in the power of therapy to promote growth, self-love, and change in the individual. Ideally, one would combine therapy with an action-oriented, problem-solving, conscious-minded approach.

For instance, a woman could uncover that her fear of abandonment, which began in childhood, has affected her ability to form lasting bonds with men, but if she wasn't consciously pushing herself to take action and make changes in the dating world, she may continue her pattern repeatedly or sit on the sidelines to avoid hurt for years upon years. Conversely, a woman may be action-oriented in the dating world by dating a lot of men, but if she's not getting to the heart of why she keeps choosing men who always seem to end up hurting and disrespecting her, she may be destined to repeat the same bad patterns for years upon years. This is why many of the concepts within the ET&A model that I referenced in the preface—a balance between using thought and action and knowing when to choose one over the other or how to use them in tandem when making decisions—are so well suited for singles.

Action is key.

Remember: Entrepreneurship is about balancing thought with action. It's not enough to just think about your problems; you must act on them.

Kudos if you already have a therapist with whom you've been working. Clearly, you've already taken that first step to finding a healthy, happy dating life that leads to a healthy, happy relationship.

2. The Mentor

For our purposes here, I will be using the pronouns "she" and "her" to refer to your mentor (as well as the other board members I suggest). However, your mentor can either be male or female.

Because you'll be going out into the dating world to date and interact with men frequently, you'll need someone to support you and offer feedback as you learn and grow from your experiences and therapy sessions. Having a mentor is of paramount importance for many entrepreneurs. There are hundreds of competitions—MassChallenge and TechStars being two of them—and college-sponsored programs or contests throughout the country designed to provide budding entrepreneurs with the mentorship and support they need, from honing their business model to securing funding.

I asked you in chapter 3 to identify someone whose relationship you admire, the point of which was to remind you and help you appreciate all the wonderful things that a healthy, loving relationship can bring to your life. I want you now to bring that person into your journey by asking her to be a part of your Board of Advisors. Ask her if she'd consider mentoring and supporting you as you embark upon this entrepreneurial venture to find love. Tell her about your vision and about your desire to find what she has found. If she declines or is worried she might not be able to give you enough of her time, there's bound to be other women in your life whom you can ask who are in positive, healthy, happy relationships.

Your Mentor.

- doesn't need to be your BFF but can be;

- shouldn't be a family member;

- ideally is married, engaged, or in a long-term committed relationship.

If you selected your parents as your role-model couple in the chapter 3 Affinity Diagram brainstorm exercise, my advice is to find someone else to serve as your mentor—family members, even more so than close friends, can be tricky when serving in an advisory role of this sort, given their emotional and physical attachment and bond to you. It's best to consider someone who is not a family member.

Most people will be flattered that you've singled out their relationship as one you admire and respect. My bet is whoever you ask will be honored to be a part of your Board, even if she has a busy life. Keep in mind, though, a person is much more willing to come along on your journey if your venture is something that excites or interests her. Many women (probably more so than men), especially those in fulfilling relationships, are happy to help others find love, because, in general, women enjoy talking about men, dating, and relationships. However, your mentor can either be the woman or man in the relationship you've identified (whomever you feel more comfortable with).

Your mentor doesn't have to be a best friend although she certainly can be, but someone you know well enough that asking her to serve in this capacity wouldn't be an awkward or unreasonable request. Close friends can sometimes be competitive with regard to dating and relationships and therefore not the best advisors, *but* because this friend is happily involved (and therefore has more of an ability to focus on someone else's relationship happiness and is not competing with you for the affection and romantic interest of others), she could certainly work well in this role. Lastly, it can be difficult for close friends, like family members, to be objective because of the bond you share, so you should articulate that you are ready for their honest feedback throughout the process.

Your mentor doesn't have to be married (though it's great if she is). However, it helps if she feels certain an engagement is in the near future because an engagement means more stability in her life, thus allowing her to better focus on helping you. If you're getting counseling, you can tell your mentor so she knows she's not alone on this Board and not solely responsible for providing support, encouragement, and feedback.

Again, an ideal mentor is someone who, from what you know, has a healthy, happy relationship that you admire and would like to emulate in some way. That doesn't mean she and her partner never argue, have unhappy moments, or get annoyed with each other—all couples do!—but it does mean she and her partner exhibit genuine happiness for each other and the relationship they've forged.

The Mentor's role

Now that you've got someone in mind to ask, you'll need to explain what her responsibilities will be.

Your mentor would benefit by reading this book. Doing so will give her some background into the entrepreneurial way and help her to help you keep the spirit of entrepreneurship alive and well in the dating process. By no means, though, is reading the book a requirement for your mentor; she should, however, look over these responsibilities.

The Mentor's responsibilities:

- Your mentor will be there for twice a month check-ins.
  - ➤ Arrange this bi-monthly meeting on a day and time that is convenient for both of you but especially your

mentor. An hour should be enough. You can talk via phone or in person. She agrees to keep these meetings focused on you.

➤ During these meetings, you can discuss the dates you went on or any interactions you had with men since the last time you spoke. You can talk about who you liked, who you didn't like, who you aren't sure about, and why. You can talk about any surface-level confidence issues you are having (first date nervousness) or surface-level dating dilemmas (texting vs. phone calls, sexual contact quandaries, deciphering a date's behavior, etc.). If you haven't had any dates, feel free to talk about dating and relationships in general or anything on your mind.

➤ For the most part, leave the heavier, deeper conversations for your therapy appointments if you are seeing a therapist. Ideally, your mentor should not be playing the role of a professional therapist.

➤ She will offer as much objective feedback as possible based on what you are telling her about your experiences each week. But understand that she only knows about these experiences through you, so be as open and honest as possible with her.

➤ During these meetings she will provide you with support, encouragement, and positive reinforcement.

• Your mentor will consistently encourage you to reach your vision: a healthy, happy dating life that leads to a healthy, happy relationship.

➤ If your vision wavers at any point, she will do her best to make sure it remains intact.

- Your mentor will be patient with you, understanding that finding love takes time, and includes a lot of wrong turns, failures, and rejections.
  - ➤ She understands that a healthy and happy dating life doesn't mean you will never experience disappointment, but that it's more about enjoying the present moment and the journey and learning from your experiences. She will therefore encourage you to see dating as purposeful, meaningful, and an adventure in self-growth and self-discovery.
- Your mentor will understand that your wants and needs may change over time and will thus encourage healthy pivots throughout the dating process. Your mentor needs to know what you're looking for in a man. Give her a list of the top-ten fundamental attributes or qualities you think you want and need at this time in a partner. (In chapter 5, I will talk more about creating this list and how you may deviate from it as you start dating.)
- Your mentor will remain committed to recognizing non-committal or incompatible men you are meeting, and to discouraging you from continuing to see, date, or stay in touch with these types of men.
  - ➤ Happily partnered people have a good antenna for bullshit and will be quick to identify men who aren't showing you the respect and attention you deserve.
  - ➤ She will give your dates the benefit of the doubt at first, but will encourage you to walk away from men who become repeat offenders of bad behavior. She will not, under any circumstances, enable you to give these types of men third and fourth chances.

- Your mentor will encourage you to date lots of men until a man you are really interested in offers you commitment (as in, asks you to be his girlfriend).
  - ➢ Because she will be consistently engaging you through-out this process, she will be able to see what men lift you up and what men bring you down. She will also be able to bring you back down to reality when your mind wants to take flights of fancy with unworthy or non-committal men.
- Your mentor will encourage you to push past your limit-ing core beliefs about yourself, men, dating, and love, and challenge you to practice your new beliefs.
  - ➢ Give her a copy of the Old Beliefs/New Beliefs chart you created in chapter 3.
- Your mentor will be supportive but will also be honest with you about your dating strengths and weaknesses, and will strike a balance between being empathic and forth-right. (I will talk more about creating your list of dating strengths and weaknesses and asking others to contribute to it in chapters 5 and 7. Once you have created your list, you should give it to your mentor.)
  - ➢ She will not sugarcoat her feelings but will be open and candid.
- Your mentor will help brainstorm with you opportunities to meet other singles.
- Your mentor will also pledge to actively play matchmaker for you by setting you up with men she meets and deems compatible for you. (In chapters 9 and 10, I will discuss how to use networking and opportunity identification for

the purpose of meeting new people and being set up on dates.)

Your mentor is NOT someone who:

- Has all the answers.
  - ➢ She will work with you to the best of her ability, but you must understand that a mentor can't predict anything for you or give you magic answers that will solve all of your dating dilemmas. She can, however, help you reflect, guide you to come to your own answers, and encourage you to take small, smart steps toward achieving your vision.
  - ➢ Like your therapist, she cannot change your life. Only you can change your life.
- You can overwhelm with phone calls and emails every day.
  - ➢ You should not be inundating her with every thought, question, and anxiety that pops into your head on a daily basis, or unloading onto her your deeper-felt psychological and childhood issues. Remember: If you're working with a therapist this will be his or her area of expertise.
  - ➢ For the most part, try to wait for your check-in meetings, unless she agrees to talk more often. You can keep a list of things you want to bring up when you meet rather than shooting off an email every time something pops into your head.
- Tells you what you want to hear.
- Will be there for you all the time.

> ➤ She may need to cancel or reschedule every now and
>   then. After all, she does have her own life to lead and
>   is doing something very generous for you, so be sure
>   to cut her some slack.

As the mentee you promise to:

- Give your mentor the benefit of the doubt.
  - ➤ She found a healthy, happy relationship, which means
    she understands the general qualities that are crucial
    for long-term success.
- Respect and be open to what your mentor has to say.
- Express gratitude and appreciation throughout the process
  for your mentor's commitment to your Board.

You can certainly talk with other people about your dating and love
life, but I'd advise you to keep your stories and updates short. You
don't want their influence to affect your decisions too much. Years
ago, I had a friend who was in a very bad place; her negativity about
men had the power to influence my attitude about men, so I stopped
talking to her about my and her dating experiences, not only for
her sake, because she wasn't actually dating all that much, but also
because I didn't want her attitude and outlook toward dating and
relationships to affect mine. Think about your friends who are currently involved in dysfunctional, unhealthy relationships. Why would
they ever be people you'd want advice or feedback from with regard to your own dating life? Temper your urge to blab; you'll be
a lot better off by leaning on your Board and your own intuitions,
which you'll be learning to trust as you gain more self-awareness and
self-confidence.

3. The Stylist

Sometimes all an entrepreneur needs to get more customer attention is a packaging tweak.

First impressions.

First impressions are important. The way you present yourself to the world can be the key to getting your foot in the door. It's not *everything*, but it's still important.

Take Bryce Organics, an online organic skincare brand, profiled in the March 2012 issue of *Entrepreneur.* Founder Adrian Bryce Diorio was disappointed in sales, but realized after talking to customers that packaging was to blame—photos on the site did not do the products justice. "People couldn't tell what was inside the $28 bottle," said Diorio "Even though *I* liked the look, it wasn't speaking loudly enough to customers online. How would anyone know that our product wasn't the typical boring white lotion when you couldn't see it?" The solution? Switching the containers, using more vivid photographs and improving his retail merchandising tactics. The results? Sales skyrocketed, up 150 percent six months after the changes.

Sometimes all you need to get a little more attention in the dating world is a style tweak.

Men appreciate when a woman looks vibrant and put together. This doesn't mean you have to weigh ninety-eight pounds; in fact, men like women with a little meat on their bones—just look at the various men's magazine surveys on this topic. It also doesn't mean you have to shop at Barney's or Neiman's to buy the latest brands that will inevitably break the bank. It doesn't mean you need to cake on the makeup like a beauty pageant queen. It doesn't mean you have to get $500 haircuts.

It does, however, mean that it's important to feel confident in your body, find clothes that look great on your body, use makeup to

accentuate your best features, and have a haircut that looks great on you. These things will help attract more men and get you excited about going out into the dating world. You want to exude confidence on the dates you'll be going on, and when you look good and feel good, confidence will happen naturally. Ever notice how sexy and in charge you feel in a great pair of heels, or how pretty and feminine you feel after purchasing a hot, new lipstick, or how unstoppable you feel in a certain pair of jeans that frame your body perfectly, or how on top of the world you feel when your hair looks great?

Your exterior.
Your style and the way you present yourself physically is indeed part of the package. It is *not* a substitute for the work you're doing internally.

Updating your look (clothes, makeup, hairstyle, and the like) is never a substitute for the work you'll be doing with the other members of your Board, but these things are a piece of the puzzle. The human being who exists underneath the makeup, clothing, and hair is paramount to the superficial stuff—with more comfort and stability in who you are as a person, the more confidence you'll exude—*but* your physical appearance is something important to consider in the world of dating, not just for attracting men but also for a little ego boost.

Judith Sills, a clinical psychologist and the author of *Getting Naked Again,* couldn't agree more. Interviewed in *More* magazine, Sills believes that the superficial can go a long way. "Cosmetics have always been an attitude enhancer," she opines. "We don't paint our faces just to attract the opposite sex. If you're feeling schlumpy and depressed, a manicure, a haircut and a little lipstick can work like medicine. It's easy to dismiss all that as superficial, but it has a deep impact on our sense of self and our willingness to connect with other people. It says, 'OK, I'm going back out into the world now. I'm not in retreat.'"

My guess is you have a friend who has style and knows what looks good on different body types. Someone who has sartorial skills also probably knows how to wear makeup and can recommend great products and colors that will work for you. He or she will also probably have great recommendations for your hair, or at the very least, can refer you to a reasonably priced salon stylist who will know what shape and color will work best for you.

If you don't have much money to spend, tell your stylist to start with the *resources you have at hand* (something you'll be hearing a lot more about in chapter 5). Ask your stylist to go through your current wardrobe and cache of accessories to see if she can maximize what you already have. If you do have money to spend, let your stylist know your budget so that she can figure out what stores to take you to. You don't have to spend thousands of dollars on designer duds; in fact, what a man finds sexy and fashionable is often different than what a woman appreciates. A man doesn't care if you're wearing Chanel or Target, as long as it looks good and flatters your shape. A man couldn't care less about the on-trend parachute pants that all the celebrities are wearing, but he does care to see your curves and the way you fill out a pair of sexy jeans.

For both entrepreneurs and daters, tweaking your packaging is an excellent strategy. According to *Branding for Dummies* co-author Barbara Findlay Schenck, in an interview in the November 2012 issue of *Entrepreneur,* "it's a proven means of regaining market relevance and rekindling consumer interest."

4. The Entrepreneur

I've written a book about emulating the spirit of traditional entrepreneurs and the way they think and act to help single women find love.

$$$$$$$. You don't have to have gobs of money to look good. There are plenty of inexpensive clothing, makeup, and hair options out there. Your stylist can help show you where to go.

Flattery will get you everywhere. Remember: Most people are usually flattered and happy to help when you reach out to them for guidance. That's because you are essentially saying you admire and respect them.

You can hardly be surprised then that I'm encouraging you to ask a traditional entrepreneur to be on your Board.

Again, for our purposes here, I am using "she" as the pronoun, but feel free to approach either a male or female entrepreneur.

Having access to a hard-working, dedicated traditional entrepreneur who is dealing with many of the scenarios you are experiencing throughout your entrepreneurial venture to find love—frustrations, self-doubt, fear, rejections, setbacks—as well as someone who exhibits the qualities I've told you are important throughout the dating process—desire, a problem-solving mindset, vision, adaptability, an action-oriented approach—will be a constant source of inspiration for you and a reminder that as a Love TREP you are not alone. Moreover, a traditional entrepreneur's determination and enthusiasm are contagious—he or she will motivate you to keep moving forward toward your vision.

You will also bear witness to the truism that nothing worth having in life comes easy. Entrepreneurs are reminded of this on a daily basis as they work hard to build their businesses. Why should this be any different for your love life? Who ever said finding love would or should be easy? I remember emailing with a 30-year-old entrepreneur friend of mine who was doing well with her business but when it came to her love life she admitted to making repeated unhealthy decisions. She said to me about her dating life: "It's never easy, Neely." I had to laugh a bit, because my friend was so adept at moving her business forward, making adjustments and looking for solutions when problems arose, but when it came to her love life she kept repeating insecure behavior thinking she'd get different results. Apply that logic to her business

and she'd be *out* of business; apply the adaptability and openness to new ideas and possibilities that she exhibits in her business to her search for love and she'd most likely have different results. It's never easy, but it can get *easier.*

Your entrepreneur Board member can be at any stage of her business. Her venture could also be any type of business—from a consulting firm to a catering company to a home-based jewelry line. The important thing is that she is dedicated to seeing her venture thrive.

TREP talk.
Talking to treps will inspire you to move forward in your own life. After years of working among traditional treps, I can tell you firsthand that their enthusiasm and passion for life is contagious.

Ideally, you'll meet with this person once every other month to talk. From her answers and insight, you'll be able to discern plenty of parallels to *your* entrepreneurial venture. You can then apply these parallels to your dating and love life and let them serve as inspirational reminders along your journey.

You'll want to learn the following during your first meeting:

➢ How did she arrive at the idea for the business? What was her vision?

➢ What was she willing to risk when she started her venture?

➢ What may have, initially, stopped her from becoming an entrepreneur and how did she rid herself of those impediments?

➢ Has the idea changed or morphed along the way as she has learned from her experiences?

➢ What obstacles did she have to overcome to get the business going? Did she ever have any doubts or fears about what she was doing when she started the business? Does

she still have doubts and fears and how does she deal with those?

➤ Were there any major setbacks or failures along the way as she built or has begun building her business and how did she cope?

➤ What are her plans for the future? Does she plan to expand and grow the business? What does that entail?

Now that you have her background, during subsequent meetings you can discuss ongoing issues she deals with as she continues to grow her business.

It may help if this person is a friend, because she is more likely to share with you the challenges she's encountered (without worrying about your stealing her ideas or competing with her product or service). If you don't know anyone who has started a business or is in the process of starting one, undoubtedly your friends know people who have, and you can always ask your friends to make an introduction. Maybe even think about tapping into your college and/or high school alumni networks.

People love talking about themselves and what they've learned in their lives, and my guess is most would be happy to chat with you every couple of months about their business and the subject of entrepreneurship. You don't need to tell them about the book (though you certainly can, and I encourage you to do so if you're comfortable sharing—this will especially rule out their suspicion that you are somehow competing with them), but you can simply say you're interested in the process of starting a business and in entrepreneurship in general, and that you would love to pick their brain every now and then about what they're up to.

If the formality of this arrangement is off-putting, consider just chatting up any and all entrepreneurs you meet along your path. You can always use these questions as conversation starters.

As an alternative you can think about subscribing to *Entrepreneur* magazine. The stories and profiles inside will inspire you to action in your dating and love life as they did for me in regard to starting this book. Maybe even become a fan of the magazine on Facebook and check out the articles and updates they post.

Lastly, consider joining entrepreneurial-minded groups on LinkedIn or Facebook and listen to what the men and women are talking about when it comes to building and maintaining their ventures. My favorites are Marie Forleo's Facebook page and Melanie Duncan's Entrepreneuress Academy Facebook page.

What about an actual dating coach for your Board?

You may be surprised to see that I did not immediately suggest myself or a dating coach for your Board. I want you to believe that you can assemble an effective support system around you, without having to spend lots of money (even a therapist is covered by most insurance plans) by accessing your networks. Understanding that some of you don't have gobs of money to throw at people for this entrepreneurial venture, I wanted to initially suggest other, non-paid members for your Board. However, if you don't feel comfortable asking a friend to serve as your mentor/coach, or you simply cannot find anyone, I am available for personal coaching: www. thelovetrep.com. There are benefits to having your mentor be a paid coach—a coach, even more so than a friend, is able to give

unbiased feedback and, perhaps, a firmer kick in the pants every now and then.

Certainly, given my personal and professional experiences, I understand the entrepreneurial process of finding love better than anyone. I can definitely support and encourage you as your coach/mentor if you wish. We can check in twice monthly via phone or we can meet in person if you live in the Boston area.

The makeup of your Board is ultimately up to you

I encourage you to have all four of the members I've suggested on your Board, but I recognize you might have misgivings. Maybe you're saying to yourself: "Geez, this all seems like *way* too much work. And I'm uncomfortable with the people you are suggesting."

If you have concerns, consider these options:

- If you feel your style or physical appearance is fine as is, no need for the stylist.
- If you are totally averse to having the therapist, be sure you have the mentor on your Board.
- If you don't feel comfortable asking someone to serve as the mentor, be sure you have the therapist on your Board.
- If you prefer having a coach instead of the therapist or the mentor, I am available to serve in this capacity. Check out my Web site for coaching packages. You can also consider the services of other coaches, either in your area or available via phone and/or Skype. There are a ton of

dating coaches out there, and I encourage you to choose someone who will help you explore your internal beliefs and unconscious motives, as well as more surface-level dating concerns, as opposed to people who focus exclusively on superficial manipulation tactics and techniques. On its own, that type of superficial advice is not powerful enough for you to have the kind of long-lasting results you are looking for. Most coaches have Web sites that will explain in detail their philosophy and how they work with people.

- If you don't want to officially enlist the entrepreneur to sit on your Board, consider the other options I mentioned within that section. This board member is mostly for inspiration purposes and to keep you believing in the power and spirit of entrepreneurship to create value and change in your dating and love life.

- *At the very least, use this book (and the workbook if you choose to purchase it) as a guide and employ the services of one other Board member,* who must be either the mentor or the therapist (or a coach as mentioned in the above bullet point).

You will have the best results if you utilize the skill sets of all four members, but I think you can still accomplish your vision with a smaller board.

And while having a full board of four may seem overwhelming and time-consuming, just think of it this way:

The Therapist – one hour a week;

The Mentor – one hour (or so) every two weeks;

Comfort zone. Life is too short to never practice stepping outside your comfort zone. Remember: This is one of the most important aspects of your life. It deserves a little time and attention, as much as your career, your physical health, hobbies, time with family and friends, and the like.

The Stylist – a few shopping trips or consultations about clothes, hair, and makeup;

The Entrepreneur – one hour every couple of months.

That's really not all that much time in the grand scheme of things. Think about how many hours per week you spend at work, watching TV, surfing the Internet, focusing on your hobbies, or working out. Isn't it worth dedicating a little time to focus on your dating and love life? A healthy, happy relationship has the power to be one of the most important, fulfilling aspects of your life and it thus deserves your time and attention. Most successful entrepreneurs and business-people will admit as much: when interviewed and asked what they are most proud and appreciative of, indubitably, they will say either their family or spousal relationship.

Up Next:

By assembling your Board of Advisors, you've ensured that you will have guidance and a solid support network throughout your entrepreneurial journey. In chapter 5, the first chapter of Part II of this book, I will encourage you to start taking action in the dating world and how to start thinking about your action differently. Also, I will show you how to create various inventories and affirmations so that you will have personal knowledge and inspiration to draw from while out there dating, thereby helping you to make smarter decisions as you move forward in your entrepreneurial venture to find love.

Chapter 4 Action Steps Checklist:

- ✓ Figure out who you want to be on your Board. You can follow my suggestions or create your own Board.
- ✓ Once you've figured out whom you want to help guide and support you, take action. Start reaching out to these people and asking them to be a part of your venture.
- ✓ Schedule times for meeting with or talking to your Board members. Getting dates and times on the calendar is good motivation for sticking with the process. Don't cancel these meetings!

PART II: EXECUTING YOUR ENTREPRENEURIAL JOURNEY

TREP TUTORIAL

In Part I of this book, I focused on preparing you for your entrepreneurial journey.

Let's review:

- In chapter 1, I discussed why the entrepreneurial spirit, mindset, and approach is such a potent force to emulate in one's dating and love life. Moreover, I hope I convinced you that you—*yes you*—are a natural-born entrepreneur, that you have the capacity to think and act like an entrepreneur in your dating and love life, to date entrepreneurially and innovate in your love life.

- In chapter 2, I explained why certain attributes—desire, an interest in creating solutions to problems, and vision—are necessary to possess as you begin building your entrepreneurial venture to find love. Also, I showed you why it's important to remain flexible in your ideas and build off what you discover along your journey.

- In chapter 3, I asked you to take some time to reflect on what might be stopping you or holding you back from greater entrepreneurial engagement in your search for love and encouraged you to start removing those obstacles, so you can move forward, freer and less burdened. I asked you to continue to unpack and remove any obstacles you identify throughout this process so that your desire and vision can burn bright, which is especially important when you encounter failure and disappointment.

- In chapter 4, I asked you to consider that one important key to success in entrepreneurial endeavors is bringing others along on your journey. By surrounding yourself with competent, caring confidants and mentors who can inspire you and help you make sense out of and learn from your experiences, you make your chances of achieving your vision much stronger.

CHAPTER 5: DATE
(DATE. LEARN. REPEAT.)

"Act or accept"

– Anonymous

Now that I've laid the foundational groundwork for your entrepreneurial venture, in the next few chapters I will discuss how to start taking *action* in your venture, more specifically by *acting your way into thinking*. One very important way that entrepreneurs learn is through doing—the doing is often what provokes the thinking. When an entrepreneur is faced with an unknowable situation, she must act to create opportunities.

Acting Your Way Into Thinking

With regard to your budding venture, I want you to undergo a mind-shift when it comes to thinking vs. action. There are times when you, as a dating entrepreneur, can use premeditated analysis and your knowledge of the past to predict future occurrences and common recurring dating patterns, and there are times when you must choose

"CreAction." The authors of *Action Trumps Everything* came up with the term "CreAction": an approach to building entrepreneurial ventures that combines acting and thinking, or rather, acting your way into thinking. So, when faced with the unknowable, treps act, but more specifically, they act their way into a new way of thinking. You can imagine my delight when, toward the end of their book, I read about their idea to use "CreAction" in the dating world! I couldn't help but chuckle over the fact that three successful business

to use experimentation and action to identify new ways of thinking. In this section of chapter 5, I want to talk about the latter approach.

In *Action Trumps Everything*, the authors put an interesting spin on taking action in entrepreneurial ventures: "Instead of *thinking* your way into a new way of acting, which is at the heart of using prediction, you need *to act your way into a new way of thinking*. That's what entrepreneurs do when faced with the unknowable—and it is an approach that will work for you as well." They believe this approach can be used in all areas of life.

In the margin:

professionals and a dating coach had the same notion about using the principles of entrepreneurship to help your love life, although my guess is they have no plans of their own to bring their idea to fruition. They title their facetious book, *Action Trumps Everything: Navigating the dating scene in an uncertain world.*

In your entrepreneurial dating life, it will be important to start *acting your way into thinking by taking small, smart steps.* Instead of hemming and hawing about actually doing something ("should I sign up for online dating or should I spend more time researching sites?" or "What if I go to this date/event/party/, and it's not what I wanted it to be?") or trying to predict what your results will be if you take a certain action ("If I do this, will it get me the exact results I want?"), you just take action, which, inevitably, offers you access to new knowledge, ideas, and possibilities. You can then use what you learn to take your next step. A small, smart step can be the littlest decision, such as purchasing this book, or a bigger decision, like saying yes to a date with someone you might not normally go out with. Whatever that next step is in your journey, take it, learn from it, and then take another one!

In a sense, you have already started acting your way into thinking about your love life by completing the various exercises in chapter 3, by taking small, smart steps to remove obstacles, and by assembling your Board of Advisors. Good work! Each of these steps required you to take a form of action, and each of them will facilitate new

information and new ways of thinking about your dating and love life.

You will now continue this theme of acting your way into thinking in Part II of this book.

You can provoke change in your thoughts, beliefs, attitude, and mindset about dating, love, and yourself through your experiences in the dating world. To do that, sometimes you have to push yourself to have those experiences. (I'll show you how to create your own experiences and opportunities in chapters 9 and 10). In their article "The Neuroscience of Leadership," David Rock and Jeffrey Schwartz write, "Large-scale behavior change requires a large-scale change in mental maps. This in turn requires some kind of event or experience that allows people to provoke themselves, in effect, to change their attitudes and expectations more quickly and dramatically than they normally would." The authors cite a 2006 Northwestern University brain study to bolster their argument. The study finds that "at a moment of insight, a complex set of new connections is being created. These connections have the potential to enhance our mental resources and overcome the brain's resistance to change. But to achieve this result…we need to make a deliberate effort to hardwire an insight by paying it repeated attention. That is why employees need to 'own' any kind of change initiative to be successful." The same goes for making changes in your dating and love life. You need to own your change, to provoke yourself, to generate your own insights through *action*. The primary way you'll take action in the dating world is by doing things to move your love life forward, and by increasing your dating experiences and interactions with men.

Cyclical approach. Dating, like entrepreneurship is a cyclical approach. Date. Learn. Repeat. As simple as that.

Small, smart steps. When you ask yourself, "what do I do when I don't know what to do?", the answer is to just take action using small, smart steps. I encourage you to continue to take small, smart steps in your entrepreneurial journey to find love.

Dating Uncertainty. "Uncertainty refers to a situation in which no historical data exists to help the decision maker. Uncertainty cannot be modeled or predicted. It is a future that is not only known but also unknowable." – Stuart Read and co-authors. *How can you turn uncertainties in your dating life into opportunities, like Jessica did?*

A client of mine named Jessica was hesitant about going to a networking event, which I had emailed to her, mentioning it would be a great place to meet men. She also was nervous about going alone, so I told her I would attend the event with her. An hour or so into mingling, during which Jessica had already met several men who asked for her card, she exposed the real reason she was hesitant—she felt embarrassed by the fact that she was attending these types of events actively looking for men; her belief was that she shouldn't have to put herself out there in that way (it was an ego thing for her). Also, her sister chastised her earlier that evening for going to the event for the sole purpose of meeting men, saying that it was ridiculous to search for dates that way. Instead of hemming and hawing about going to the event and spending time letting her internal voice (and the voices around her) convince her to stay home, Jessica pushed herself to go to the event. From that action, she learned that NOBODY cares why you're at a networking event, the only person who can make you feel embarrassed is yourself, and that there were plenty of eligible men who were quite happy she attended that night whatever her reason.

Jessica gained these insights by *taking action*. There's no way she could have learned any of these things by trying to predict the outcome of a situation for which she had no historical data (she'd never attempted to meet men at a networking party before and therefore had no way of knowing if it was a good way to meet men).

From every date and experience you have in the dating world, it will be important for you to reflect on what you learned (acting your way into thinking), as Jessica did. Push yourself to take away some sort of lesson or knowledge that can be applied to your

dating and love life moving forward. In chapter 6, I'll show you how to engage in various reflection exercises as you date, so that you'll be actively thinking and learning about new ideas and possibilities for your dating life, and developing better self- and social awareness. You'll then take that knowledge and date some more, *iteratively* and *incrementally* building on the knowledge you're gaining through this action-based approach (more on these concepts in chapter 7).

That trial and error approach is the crux of this book and the entrepreneurial way: action and thought working together, as a repetitive process to facilitate forward motion while simultaneously building a better understanding of self and the world around you. This is the approach I encourage my clients to take in their dating lives and it's the approach that successful, entrepreneurial-minded leaders use as well.

Take Suzanne Sengelmann and Mary Jo Cooke, vice presidents of new business for Clorox's laundry home care division, who helped bring the "Green Works" product line to market.

In 2005, Sengelmann and Cooke were tasked with introducing a new Clorox brand to consumers. A "green" line for Clorox, a company that specialized in chemical-laden products, would have been deemed far-fetched if conventional business analytical approaches had been used—presumably, market research would have concluded that the risk would not be worth the reward for Clorox. But according to Danna Greenberg, Kate McKone-Sweet, and H. James Wilson, authors of *The New Entrepreneurial Leader*, in which they tell the story of the successful Green Works

Applied discipline. Like entrepreneurship, dating is an applied discipline; it can't solely be taught using formulaic, scientific techniques—do *this* and get *that*—because relationships are about human interaction. Humans are not robots responding to computer codes. You need to get out there and experience your way into insights and new ideas and possibilities.

product line, the entrepreneurial leaders at Clorox had a different worldview of business. "They used an alternative decision-making approach in which they started by taking action, rather than just analysis, to build the new brand." After overcoming various challenges and forming a strategic partnership with the Sierra Club, a well-known environmental activist organization, Green Works was brought to market in 2007 and met with resounding success—it captured 42 percent of the market share within 6 months of launching. The women involved in the success of the product "acted their way into an innovative solution" for Clorox. Rather than start with traditional analysis, Sengelmann and Cooke relied on an action-oriented decision-making approach and in so doing helped change the industry and the way Clorox does business.

Throughout much of your entrepreneurial journey to find love, I'm going to encourage this approach: *acting your way into thinking*. This doesn't mean that taking action is *always* preferable to using prediction—understanding and analyzing your past to make better decisions moving forward—in your dating and love life, but it does mean figuring out when an action-oriented approach versus an analytical one will serve you better. "You can still use the past and your instincts," write Stuart Read and his co-authors in their book *Effectual Entrepreneurship*, "but you will also need to test the waters as you go, learn patterns, and find ways to adapt to the new patterns wherever possible…"

Date. Learn. Repeat. These are simple concepts.

Control-freak. How do you control a future you can't predict? The dating world is full of uncertainty, and you won't be able to predict much of it. So what do you do? The answer is you just have to get started by taking action via a small, smart step. Pause. And then ask yourself: What did I learn and how can I use that knowledge to take my next step?

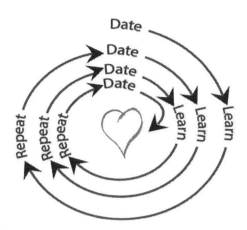

(My Date. Learn. Repeat. model of entrepreneurial dating.)

Yet, as we grow older, dating has a tendency to become an overly complicated, scary, and daunting process, often prohibiting people from taking action. Why is this the case?

Think back to when you were a child. The world seemed full of possibilities. We could work in any profession or industry, go anywhere we wanted (certainly in our minds, at least), and be whoever we wanted. As we grew up, we faced some of life's harsher realities. We started to make mistakes, began to fail at things, and learned that mistakes and failure (things that, incidentally, are crucial for success in dating and entrepreneurship) were bad. We started to realize how difficult it is to be vulnerable. We began to erect walls to keep out pain. We became jaded, cynical, especially regarding matters of the heart.

Kids' corner. When you were a kid, the world was full of possibilities. It still is!

In adulthood we frequently become paralyzed by fear and self-doubt, the kind that didn't exist when we were children. As adults, we over-think, overanalyze to avoid failure. We learn to think about our lives and the world around us through elaborate and often unnecessary prediction models. Far too often, we end up silencing our inner voice,

"Marshmallow Challenge." In this challenge, kids usually perform better than adults!

Kids' corner. How would a kid view the challenges of dating?

the one that's screaming "Just go for it!" And the truth is that the lessons and cautionary tales we had drilled into us as we grew into adulthood—that we should be careful about taking action lest we fail or make a mistake or be vulnerable—can oftentimes be counterproductive, incompatible with, and injurious to the process of dating. By the time we get to be adults, many of us have lost the capacity to take a chance.

That's a notion that I think Tom Wujec of Autodesk, the world's leader in 2D and 3D technology, would agree with. In a segment on National Public Radio, Wujec discussed his experiences facilitating "The Marshmallow Challenge," a design exercise that "encourages teams to *experience* simple but profound lessons in collaboration, innovation and creativity." As I listened to Wujec describe the challenge—teams have eighteen minutes to build the tallest free-standing structure out of twenty sticks of spaghetti, one yard of tape, one yard of string, and one marshmallow, which needs to be placed on top—I couldn't help but laugh when he said that kindergarten students routinely perform better than MBA students, erecting taller structures. How is that possible? As Wujec explains, business students focus on mapping out complicated plans before taking action, which ultimately hampers creativity, locking them into a particular way of doing things based on their plan; they become too wedded to a very narrow goal. The kindergarten students, on the other hand, just start building and prototyping from the moment the clock strikes, learning quickly from their iterations in terms of what works and what doesn't, and then incorporating that knowledge as they try new ideas; they don't get bogged down by a plan, an exact blueprint.

No doubt, that curious, imaginative, innovative, optimistic, open-hearted, action-oriented little girl, unafraid of making mistakes, is still there within you, hidden, pushed deep down inside, waiting to exhale, to see the light of day. Let's view dating through the eyes of that bold, adventurous, unspoiled child. What would that wide-eyed little girl tell you to do when it comes to your love life?

I decided to ask a few of them. At a family gathering, several months into writing this book, I asked a few children, ages nine through eleven, the following question: "What would you do if you were a woman trying to find a partner to settle down with?" Their answers, all offered with little thought, analysis, or debate, were as follows: "Search all over the world"; "Get on the computer"; "Just go out there and show your true self." Simple, straightforward suggestions, proffered with little evaluation and based purely on unfiltered thoughts. The underlying premise of their advice was to *just start acting and stop thinking so much.*

Kids' talk. Here's what the kids I asked had to say about dating:
- "Search all over the world."
- "Get on the computer."
- "Just go out there and show your true self."

Ask adults the same question and they might start to overanalyze the situation and debate the best possible courses of action. They might develop a system of rules you should follow to get your desired result; if you do A, B, and C, you will get X, Y, and Z results (as suggested in the infamous dating book *The Rules*). But when you live in an uncertain, constantly changing, fast-paced dating world, employing any sort of prediction models or strict, prescribed plans to achieve your vision is often futile. In today's worlds of dating and entrepreneurship, it often doesn't work that way. Entrepreneurship, like seduction, like flirting, like dating, is not an exact science but often more of an art form, where one creates her own painting from scratch rather than following a prescribed paint-by-numbers process.

Now, I'm certainly not saying that finding love is as simple as following through on the innocent advice of a ten-year-old who hasn't been hit with the complexities of life, but I am saying that sometimes the dating world (like the entrepreneurship world) doesn't have to be as complicated, scary, and daunting as we make it out to be or have been taught. And that sometimes we just need to "go for it" and start acting, one step at a time, in order to achieve a vision. When you view dating through this lens, when you break it down into a simple, uncomplicated framework, it can seem a lot less overwhelming, and, dare I say, fun!

It's a sentiment Sam Hogg, an entrepreneur and adjunct entrepreneurship professor at the University of Michigan's business school, would agree with. In an article he wrote in the October 2013 issue of *Entrepreneur*, he opines, "Over time, I've noticed that many of my answers [to questions from my students] seem to come straight out of a kindergartner's mind." When Hogg is asked "How do I get started on my business?", his typical reply is "Act before you think." Explaining this advice, he writes:

> Too many people spend far too long thinking and planning when they should be doing. I say, just start. I don't care how. Get moving: Build something, sell something, see where it goes. If you spend too long analyzing how difficult it's going to be to launch your business, you will likely learn that, yep, it's too hard to even start.

Using Action *and* Prediction in Your Dating and Love Life

Traditional entrepreneurs favor action and experimentation over prediction and analysis to grow their ventures. They like to discover

new ways of thinking, new ideas, and new possibilities through the actions they take (acting their way into thinking). This is the approach I'm encouraging you to take much of the time in your entrepreneurial journey. However, there is certainly an important place for prediction in the entrepreneurial method. The best entrepreneurs are skilled at cycling between action and prediction to innovate and manage change in their venture—they know when to lean on one approach over the other—and they understand that often the two are intertwined.

Prediction is, as Greenberg and her co-authors argue in the Introduction of *The New Entrepreneurial Leader*, an extension of the scientific method—thought, evaluation, and then action toward a predefined goal or objective. "The premise underlying prediction logic," the authors write, "is that one can protect against or control the future through detailed analysis…data mining, market research, and traditional statistical tools to develop opportunities." They continue: "A prediction approach assumes that an uncertain future can be predicted and that decisions can be made based on those predictions." Certainly, entrepreneurs rely on predictive methods to move their ventures forward.

On the flip side, however, entrepreneurs take action to create and discover the future (as opposed to predicting it). Action and experimentation work well when a situation is new or complex enough that it inhibits any sort of predictive capabilities. In these types of situations, it's difficult to predict cause and effect (*if I do this, I will get that*). Historical data or analysis is of little help. "In unknowable situations," Greenberg and her co-authors write, "action is needed to generate data and insight, to further assess the problems and opportunities, and to select the next course of action." Surprises and

challenges will inevitably arise when action in unknowable situations is taken, but the best entrepreneurs learn how to adapt or overcome them, and future actions are guided thoughtfully by the new data and ideas that are uncovered from the previous action.

When you translate these concepts to your love life, I hope you can see where I'm going. Read those last three paragraphs again, keeping your dating and love life in mind. As a Love TREP, there will be many times when action (acting your way into thinking) is the best route to take, there will be some situations when you can lean on prediction to make better decisions for yourself, and there will be times when you use prediction and action in cooperation with each other to move your love venture forward.

Doing the limiting beliefs work in chapter 3 and completing the forthcoming self-knowledge inventories in this chapter (as well as the exercises on risk in chapter 8) will aid you in your prediction abilities: They give you an enormous amount of information that you can draw from to start making better decisions moving forward in your entrepreneurial venture to find love. And as you begin to understand and push past your beliefs, as you start to identify, embrace, and build on who you are and what you know, and as you start to recognize your patterns, you are empowering yourself to date smarter (or differently) and to experiment and take action in new ways than you've acted before. Maybe that means giving different types of men a chance; or meeting men in different ways than you've been used to; or new ways of honoring your feelings, your voice, and your needs; or working on news ways of communicating and connecting with men. The possibilities are limitless!

Alternatively, taking action can lead to solutions in your love life that could never be predicted through analysis or lengthy discussions with, say, friends, a coach, or a therapist. As you take action in your dating and love life, you will also start discovering new things about yourself, gaining confidence, and trusting in yourself. The most effective kind of action is rooted in an understanding of who you are and an understanding of who you are in a particular context.

Let's discuss a few examples to illustrate how singles can use action (acting your way into thinking), prediction, and a combination of both.

Example 1:

A woman who continually meets and falls for unavailable men can mine her past experiences, identify the reasons behind her choices, and then, based on her analysis, make a choice moving forward to not pursue men who demonstrate non-committal, emotionally-unavailable tendencies. She can predict the consequences of going down this road again and the types of men who fit this category based on her past history. She can certainly experiment in the beginning to see what type of man he is, while she continues to date other men, but if he begins to demonstrate shady behavior, she can steer herself in a different direction. She can then choose to experiment with getting to know different types of men than she's dated in the past or, certainly, different ways to meet men than she may be used to.

Example 2:

A woman who is hesitant about trying online dating can try to predict if it will work for her: she can spend months researching different

sites; she can ruminate over the statistics of how many people meet significant others online; she can use articles that say online dating sites are in the business of tricking people to make money as evidence as to why she should stay away; she can relay the horrible experiences of friends to back up her fears. Or she can say to herself: "I've never personally tried this before. I may have certain fears, but the only way I can know more about the experience is to push past my insecurities and the statistics and the anecdotal stories and try it for myself." Once she takes action and signs up for a site, she collects data about her experience, and then experiments with new ideas based on what she learns—maybe that means hiring someone to write a more engaging profile and experimenting with different photos if she's not getting much interest, or signing up for more than one site, or putting more time and energy into searching for matches, winking at and emailing people.

Example 3:

At a discussion on "dating and relationships in the 30s," a woman is in a room of about 40 women and 10 eligible men. During the Q and A period, she raises her hand and bemoans how difficult it is to talk to men at bars when they are hanging out in a "posse." She wants to know from the men in the audience where men go or what good places are to meet men. This is a great (and real-life) example of a woman who is so busy trying to predict where the men go that she's not even seeing who's in front of her (the cute, eligible men in the room!). It's also a great example of a woman who goes to the same, tired places and is waiting for others to tell her how to experiment. In other words, talking to men is a great way to research where men go, but not at the expense of neglecting to see the opportunities in

front of you that you are currently experimenting with, and not at the expense of brainstorming and experimenting with your own ideas.

Example 4 (a personal example):

About 2 months into dating, Dave came back to my place after a night out. One steamy makeout session later, he suddenly bolted for the door. His exit was so abrupt that we barely had time to say a proper goodbye. I had no idea why he was so rushed and felt odd about the whole thing the next morning when I woke. I wanted to call him, but I was so anxious about being perceived as *that* girl—you know, the overly nosey one who calls to check in on someone who isn't even her boyfriend. But Sunday evening rolled around and I still hadn't heard from him, and I felt icky about that. In retrospect, calling to check in was a perfectly reasonable idea. The truth was, underneath the anxiety of making a phone call was my fear of rejection, of having to make myself vulnerable to a rejection by Dave. So I struggled for a while about what I should do, weighing the options carefully. Should I call or should I pull my usual routine of shutting down and putting the wall up? Maybe I should just wait for him to get in touch. Maybe I should send him an email or a text. Eventually, I realized that all the analysis in the world wasn't going to be able to predict what was going on inside his head or the outcome of a phone conversation. And I thought, the most loving act toward myself that I could take in that moment was to step into my fear and act, which meant picking up the phone and calling to express my concern and see if he was okay.

While every minute of that phone conversation was uncomfortable for me, I felt proud of myself, empowered. If a man was going to disappear on me just because I cared enough to call, then he wasn't

the man for me. Turns out, Dave's stomach wasn't feeling well and he panicked. Several months later when we became an official couple, I found out that his stomach was about to explode (if you know what I mean). He was mortified—dealing with gastro-intestinal problems while you're with a girl who you recently started dating and you really like in a foreign apartment is a nightmare scenario for any guy. By taking action that night, I got information about what happened, I learned that the uncomfortable moments aren't the worst thing in the world, that I can push past my limiting beliefs, and that I can be loving to myself by confronting my fears (acting my way into thinking). There's *no way* I could have predicted any of that.

—m—

The more adept you become at entrepreneurial dating, at being a Love TREP, the more confident you will become as far as knowing when to use prediction and analysis of the past and who you are to make decisions in the present *versus* when action and experimentation will create your future *versus* when both approaches can be used in cooperation together.

Use the resources or means you have at hand to start taking action

The means at hand. A good place to start in the dating world is with the knowledge you already have by answering:

- Who am I?

- What do I know?

Okay, okay, you get it: I want you to start dating and increasing your experiences with men, because action is key to any entrepreneur's journey. As I mentioned, I have already asked you to act by taking steps to remove any obstacles that have the power to make the dating world a negative, draining place for you and by assembling people

around you who will help support and guide you through this process. But you don't have to spend several months or years making these types of preparations before you can begin dating. In fact, I *encourage* you to date *while* you are making those preparations and while you are reading this book. Because as long as you have started thinking about various aspects of your life that may be hindrances to the process and you have enlisted people who are simultaneously offering help and encouragement, you are ready to get out there, meet new people, go on lots of dates, learn from your experiments and experiences, and "show your true self."

Waiting for the perfect moment in your dating life to get started is the wrong approach. You may think to yourself: "Well, once I lose these 20 pounds then I'll start dating"; or "Once my ex moves away then I'll start dating"; or "Once I get out of this boring job then I'll start dating." But rarely will you find that the stars have aligned in such a perfect way to create the perfect opportunity for you to start your dating journey. So while it does sometimes make sense to step out of the dating world to reset, make sure that you're not waiting for some magical, pie-in-the-sky moment to get started. Sometimes you just have to dive in and get going.

In order to make the most of your actions in the dating world, I want you to think a little bit more about yourself by answering a few personal questions. These self-inventories will be resources for you throughout your time dating and interacting with men.

In *Action Trumps Everything*, the authors encourage would-be entrepreneurs who don't know where or how to start building their venture to ask themselves three very simple questions that will aid them as they

**Who am I?,
What do I
know?**
Fittingly, these
questions are
also ones that
most dating
coaches
and pundits
encourage
singles to ask
themselves.

act. There are no elaborate, hundred-page business plans; just three simple questions to bring together to get the ball rolling and make an entrepreneurial opportunity happen.

I will address the first two questions in this chapter:

- Who am I?
- What do I know?
- Who do I know? I will address their third question a bit later, as part of chapter 9, which focuses on networking.

That's it! Using the answers to these questions will help you as you plunge into taking action, creating your dating and love story as you grow.

New ventures, both personal and professional, often begin with the means you have at hand rather than all the things you need to get started. The means you have at hand with regard to your dating life is *the knowledge that already exists within you.* In the business context, take the Clorox example. Sengelmann and Cooke, beyond their professional interest in green cleaning products, had personal passion—both were mothers of young children and were worried about the impact of harsh chemicals on children's development, and both were interested in environmental causes. "The first unique element of being entrepreneurial leaders is that these women's actions were rooted in an understanding of themselves and the communities in which they lived," the authors write. "Sengelmann and Cooke's action began out of their own value systems, founded in their personal histories."

When I do coaching work, I always prompt my clients to spend time getting at the heart of who they are and what they know about themselves. These simple questions can be difficult for people to answer. How many times have you actually sat down and thought deeply about who you are and what you know in the context of your dating and relationships experiences and environment? Inevitably, I encounter women who balk at this kind of exploration, arguing that they know all there is to know about who they are and where they've been, that there is nothing more to unearth. But the truth is we only stop learning about ourselves when we decide to stop learning. We never have to stop discovering who we are (and who we can become), and we never have to stop adding to what we know. If women did these simple clarity exercises more often, they might stop and think twice about investing their time and energy into men who they know, deep down, are completely incompatible, and situations that they know aren't healthy. ·

If you're relatively new to dating or have taken a long hiatus, you might have a fairly clean slate in terms of knowing who you are and consequently with whom you're compatible. Oftentimes, it is through romantic relationships that we discover ourselves, because we're forced, more so than with platonic friendships, to hold up a mirror to our thoughts, behaviors, and actions. That's okay—that's exactly why stepping into the dating world, interacting with men, and dating a lot will help you figure these things out so that you begin to act smarter in your love life as you learn and grow.

Old vs. new. This works for people who are new to dating and especially for people who have been dating for a while.

If you've been dating for a while, you have an incredible bank of knowledge at your disposal already and a distinct advantage over new daters. In a *Washington Post* article titled "The Case for Old Entrepreneurs,"

article author and technology entrepreneur Vivek Wadwha attempts to debunk the argument that people over thirty-five aren't capable of innovating or making change happen because they are stuck in their old ideas: "The young may have good ideas," Wadwha says, "but there is no substitute for experience." He continues: "The experience entrepreneurs have gained, the contacts they have made, networks they have formed, their ability to recruit good management teams and their education give them the greatest advantage." To be an innovator in your dating and love life, you don't have to be twenty-one; in fact, the older you get, the more experiences, knowledge, and bigger networks you have to draw from. Every experience you've had up until now is knowledge you can use to your advantage, which is why it is crucial for you to start reflecting more pointedly on your past experiences to help you move forward in different directions, and narrow in on who and what type of relationship is right for you.

It is entirely possible, though, that if you've been dating for a while and feel like you're getting nowhere, you're simply not making enough use of your bank of knowledge by engaging in deep reflection. People think they know themselves until they really start mapping out their journey. That's what these questions encourage you to do.

You will be learning about yourself if you choose to work with a therapist or mentor (or coach) as part of your Board of Advisors, but even before you enroll advisors, you can get your entrepreneurial venture off the ground by answering these two simple questions (thus starting with the resources you have at hand).

Successful treps agree: The most important thing is to "know thyself." Don't ignore the inner voice that tells you who you are.

So, whether you're relatively new to dating or have had many experiences, let's get started with the first question.

<u>Who am I?</u>

"You ultimately have to find out who you are inside and develop a set of values that are truly yourself, and then express them. If it's inauthentic, if you say one set of things but don't feel and believe those things, it won't work."

- Mark Leslie, founding chairman and CEO of Veritas Software

At the core of your entrepreneurial journey is a deep understanding of your own identity. By asking yourself Who am I?, you are trying to find out the following: What kind of a person are you; what really matters to you; what do you really value in life. Answering this question gives you a better sense of self, which helps you to better understand men who may and may not fit with you. Once you know who you really are (and like who you are), you can find someone who matches that, someone who knows who he is (and likes who he is).

When I was in my twenties, I spent a lot of time tamping down who I was for fear of scaring guys off. I dumbed myself down in certain ways, clamped off the parts of me that were uniquely me, all to attract the type of man that I thought I wanted or saw myself with. Denying parts of me always felt wrong. When I met Dave, I finally recognized how wonderful it is to be able to "show your true self" and be loved, admired, and appreciated for who you are. Dave is an excellent fit for me because he loves and accepts me for my playfulness, my passionate, opinionated side, and some of my more quirky qualities. If those parts of me couldn't come out around him, I'd end up becoming resentful. *But* allowing those parts to come out in the first place meant identifying, understanding, accepting, and, finally, embracing them, and then finding a man who would love me for them.

The best analogy that I've heard on the topic of self-acceptance and finding a compatible partner was from a man taking part in a dating panel:

> *Men are like plants. There's a wide variety of us, no right or wrong. Some plants require, shade, some have flowers, some don't, some take a long time to grow, and so on. As a woman, you have to decide what kind of farmer you want to be and be honest with what type of farmer you are. If, for example, you are a very strong woman/personality, find someone who will work well with you, and once you find out what you can and can't tolerate, and who you are and aren't, find someone who fits with you. Don't try to make an apple tree into an orange tree. You'll waste years of your life trying to change something that's not supposed to be. And you have to understand what and who you are and then go find your match. It's not a matter of who is perfect; it's a matter of in what environment does he thrive and what environment do I do well. If you give a plant exactly what it needs, it will do really well and it will take care of you, but you have to understand how that plant works. And if you are in front of a plant and say this isn't doing what I want, then go find another plant, and don't wait years of your life sticking around and waiting for it to change into something else.*

Here is an example of a happily married woman named Mallory who completed this Who am I? inventory before meeting her now-husband, so as to give you an idea of how self-knowledge helped her find a healthy, happy relationship with a great man.

Mallory -- Who am I? Inventory:

Mallory bulleted out her list, but you can create your inventory however you wish.

What makes you tick? Like everyone else, you've got strengths and weaknesses. There are no right or wrong answers.

Mallory:

- Assertive; bold; likes to be in charge
- Social
- Intuitive; socially aware
- Enterprising
- Intellectually curious
- Likes to be silly, laugh, and make others laugh; child-like
- Enjoys attention; likes the spotlight; life of the party
- A good listener
- And, in turn, has a strong need to be heard, listened to
- Conscientious
- Curious
- Neurotic; anxious
- A procrastinator
- Messy
- Stubborn
- Impatient
- Impulsive
- Bad with paying bills on time
- Self-critical
- Competitive
- Reliable
- Sensitive
- Resilient
- Likes to be in control more often than not
- Independent; appreciates alone time
- Outspoken at times; feisty
- Night person (not a morning person)
- Takes pride in physical appearance
- Athletic; in shape; but not all that "outdoorsy"

- Attractive; not a natural beauty
- Fit; healthy; slim
- Hypochondriac
- Constant muscle tension
- Well-educated; bachelor's degree; MBA
- Loves to write; curious about the world and others' stories
- Passionate about helping others, offering support and feedback
- Loves creating things
- Wants to be a thought leader; make a mark on the world
- Fairly strong work ethic but appreciates work/life balance
- Entrepreneurial; big idea thinker; forward-thinking.

By creating this list and owning who she is, Mallory might conclude that a match would be someone who is an equal partner but also easygoing, laid back, a grounding presence, sensitive to her feelings and needs, allows her to bask in the spotlight, and is secure enough with himself to support her career ambitions. This doesn't mean Mallory didn't need or want to do any self-improvement work in certain areas (stubborn, impatient, etc.), especially ones that affected her experiences in the dating world and her ability to attract men, but, at the end of the day, she realized she had to own up to who she is at her core in order to recognize compatible matches.

Looking at Mallory's list, she could probably rule out, or, at the very least, spend less time and energy chasing after dominant, in-control men, who prefer the spotlight.

Obviously, this isn't an exact science; rather, your list can provide a little more guidance for you as you are dating and meeting different kinds of men, especially when you start questioning your judgment and instincts. You can also think about the men you've liked in the past. Did these men allow you to be you? If not, why did you pursue them? If you are a playful, silly person, for example, and a man squashed this side of you, how could someone like that not make you resentful in the long-term?

You can also look through the adjectives you've put on your list and ask yourself if they interfere at all in your dating life. Do you use any of your attributes in defensive ways when you're out there in the dating world? If so, how can you keep these defenses in check so that they don't hinder you from making better connections? For example, Mallory recognized that she needed to curb her impatient behavior with men. She realized that her impatience stemmed from a deeper fear of being rejected, which prompted her to sometimes push men on their feelings or rush the pace of a budding relationship. When she became more aware of how her impatient nature was affecting her dating decisions, she was able to keep better tabs on it during her experiences with men.

Mallory also sometimes used her sense of humor to hide her fears about men and dating. Instead of openly recognizing and maturely dealing with dating situations that made her anxious, she laughed off her feelings or made fun of herself in self-deprecating ways ("I'm such a drama queen; I'm so overly sensitive; I'm a total pain in the ass"). The point of identifying this behavior was not to rid herself of her humorous, playful side (no!), but it was important that she confront how she sometimes used self-deprecation as a mask. Moving

forward, she could start dealing with her feelings in healthy, productive ways instead of shrugging them off or hiding from them behind a thick veil of humor.

Now it's your turn to create your Who am I? inventory.

Here are some questions to help you:

- What makes you tick?
- What are the things that matter to you in life?
- What are you passionate about?
- What makes you *you*?
- What is most meaningful to you in life?
- What are your strengths and weaknesses?
- What kinds of roles and responsibilities do you enjoy and feel you are good at? What sucks you dry or zaps your energy?
- What would your friends say about you if asked (both the good and bad)?
- What kind of personality do you have?
- Have you taken a personality test? What have you learned from it?
- Which traits of yours stand out to others?
- What are your best talents and natural abilities?
- What are your interests in life?

Again, you can create your list like Mallory's, bulleted out, or feel free to write long-form like you might in a diary. Save your list and refer back to it frequently throughout your dating experiences. If you have a love mentor, show him or her what you've written.

Need help creating your inventory? Ask friends

Sometimes it's difficult to describe yourself or to think about your strengths and weaknesses. If you're having trouble creating this list, ask your friends to contribute. Other people can often see things about you that you have a hard time seeing or understanding. For instance, my friend Julie never really saw herself as a life-of-the-party type who likes to take charge, but in reality, she is that person. After a roller-coaster, two-year relationship in which she dated a man who also basked in the glow of attention, I pointed out that she might be better suited with someone who lets her shine, someone who doesn't compete with her star power. She later married a man who allowed her to be that best version of herself (more on this in chapter 6), someone who was more reserved and soft-spoken.

Thank you for being a friend. Friends often see what you can't see or don't want to see about yourself.

Regarding your strengths, think of what happens at a wedding. During the rehearsal dinner and post-ceremony reception, guests toast the bride and groom and list off all of the unique qualities that make the newlyweds special. It's a real love fest. For instance, at a recent wedding of a close friend, various guests told the bride how sensitive, caring, hilarious, and loyal she was. If it was your wedding day, what would your friends say about you? *Ask them!*

It might be more difficult to get friends to fess up to what some of your negative personal traits or flaws are. Oftentimes, it can be challenging to own up to these sides of your personality. The superego is a powerful thing. The trick with receiving this kind of information is to not become overly defensive and to understand that they love you despite your quirks and flaws. Ask your friends for their honest insights, and I guarantee they will deliver them in a caring,

compassionate way. You don't need to accept everything others are telling you as the absolute truth, but be aware that this is at least how those closest to you experience you, and that information in itself may be useful to you as you head out into the dating world.

Let's now look at the next question.

<u>What do I know?</u>

Chapter 3. You've already started to investigate what you know by doing the work in chapter 3. Keep it up!

> "The past shapes the present even as the present changes our understanding of the past."
> — Salmon Rushdie

By asking yourself *What do I know?* you are mining your past for all the experiences that have helped shape and mold your world in the context of dating, sex, love, relationships, and the like. Sometimes you aren't even aware of how past events, dating experiences, and relationships are pertinent and relevant to your current-day thoughts, behaviors, and actions. As Schlesinger and his co-authors write: "You never know where the insight that leads to an opportunity will come from. That is why mentally cataloguing what you know is so important. It is not always clear beforehand which pieces of information are worth paying attention to and which are not. Everything is potentially important, at least initially. It is only later (or after the fact) that the things that are superfluous become clear."

Revisit. We will revisit What do I know? in chapter 11, in which I encourage you to look at this question from a different angle: social awareness. That is to say, what do you know about the dating world (the environment you are operating in) and about men (the people with whom you are trying to connect)?

Let's use the inventory that Mallory created in the months before she met Ben, her now-husband. As you create yours, I want you to consider the following questions:

- What do you know from your past relationships and experiences in the dating world?
  - o What have you learned?
  - o What felt good and right to you? What felt bad and wrong?
  - o What patterns did you exhibit?
- What events from your past might have affected the way you see men, love, and intimacy?

Mallory's inventory is based on various periods in her life and some of the men she was with during those periods (whether casually or seriously). She couldn't recall every man she dated casually, so she based her list on the men and experiences that stood out most in her memory. When you create your list, focus on what you know from some of your more vivid experiences, rather than trying to remember every date. Force yourself to understand the lessons. I guarantee you know more than you think you do.

It's important to be honest with yourself when creating this inventory, which may require you to sit and reflect for a substantial amount of time. Nobody is judging or criticizing you, so I encourage you to be as open, raw, and thorough as possible. Remember: Your inventory will be important information you can use in the dating world.

Bank of knowledge. You know more than you think you do. Mine your past for the lessons it has to offer.

Mallory – What do I know? Inventory:

High School:

- Hook-up culture began in my junior year. It was all new and exciting to me but often tinged with disappointment when the boys didn't call me or want deeper relationships.

- I did not like being the other woman when I was hooking up with my high school crush. He had a girlfriend but would meet me on the side. It felt exciting in the moment but devastating in so many other ways when I realized he wasn't going to break up with her for me.

College:

- I spent much of these years entrenched in hook-up culture. Reading through my voluminous college diaries, I sense rather acutely both the excitement and agony of this time in my life. I was highly boy-crazy, but also proclaimed desperately to want to settle down with a boyfriend. However, 99 percent of the time when the commitment-oriented boys expressed interest in me, I wasn't interested.
- I spent years chasing after boys who never wanted to commit, liked other women more than me, or were emotionally distant with me. I tried so hard to "win" them over.
- The one exception was my first boyfriend during my sophomore year. We dated on and off for about nine months. I lost my virginity to him at nineteen. I'm glad I lost it to a boyfriend, and it was nice to have someone finally want to commit to being with me. We had great moments together, but the majority of our relationship was filled with strife. I was very immature and perhaps craved drama, but I am grateful for the experience of having my first boyfriend.
- All of my hook-ups in college were fueled by alcohol. Alcohol gave me the courage to get physically intimate with boys at my college and the nearby university.

However, my hook-ups never went past "third base." I took the act of intercourse seriously.

- I felt momentarily empowered and excited by hook-ups and wrote about these experiences extensively in my diaries. While I felt an initial sense of power, later entries were almost always filled with disappointment and hurt when these same men avoided me or weren't interested in anything more than fleeting sexual encounters. I seemed to both hate and love feeling emotionally off-kilter.

- My self-esteem was momentarily bolstered and my loneliness briefly alleviated by hook-ups. But I was usually negatively affected in the aftermath.

Post-college:

Ages twenty-one to twenty-seven:

- Hook-up culture continued post-college. The bar scene was my primary way to meet men. For the most part, I was not interested in hooking up for the sake of sexual pleasure alone. I was looking for a boyfriend, but in retrospect, I don't think I believed I was worthy of someone loving me for more than just a quick hook-up.

- I casually dated Brian but wanted it to be more. I didn't want to sleep with him but felt if I didn't he would leave me. I gave in, but he ended up disappearing on me, anyway. I was very hurt and heartbroken by this experience. I couldn't understand what was wrong with me and why he didn't want to be with me.

- After Brian, I spent the next few years casually dating and hooking up with random guys I met at bars or elsewhere (but mostly bars).

- While I had a lot of fun during these years, I was usually disappointed by my experiences and envious of roommates and friends who had boyfriends.

- I remember having a special fondness and attraction to men who lived far away from Boston. Hmmm…

- At twenty-five, I met John. I fell hard and wanted a commitment from him, but he was never able to give that to me. He disrespected me and treated me terribly. I was in a constant state of anxiousness around him. I enabled his behavior. I thought I could get him to change. I slept with him thinking that would bring us closer or get him to want to be with me. It didn't. For more than a year, I felt addicted to the roller-coaster pseudo-relationship we had. During our "relationship," I forced myself to go see a therapist.

- After John, I had two brief relationships (three months or so) with men who were fully committed to me, but neither guy was the right fit. In retrospect, their personality types were better suited to mine than the alpha male, emotionally unavailable, bad-boy types I seemed to be attracted to.

- During this period I think I exhibited a pattern of trying to get men to want to be with me, to win them over. With men I was able to win over, I was no longer interested. The act of winning them over was addictive for me. Real intimacy was a very foreign concept for me.

- I did not like having casual sex (as in intercourse). In fact, I did not like having sex with someone until it was

established that we were in a committed relationship. I did not, however, hold true to my values. Although I never had one-night stands, I did have sex with men I was dating before ever actually having a conversation about our status (thinking that it would solidify our relationship). When these men disappeared on me or a budding "relationship" failed, I was always devastated, usually ruing my choice to sleep with them.

- I had a strong desire to sleep around like Samantha Jones from *Sex and the City*, but truthfully I was not good at or comfortable with having casual sex. It did not feel right to me, even though I would continue to do it with men I was dating, even though the culture was goading me on telling me that casual sex was no big deal. I felt like I *should* have loved having casual sex, but I never truly did.

Ages twenty-eight to thirty-two:

- At twenty-eight, I tried online dating. I liked it. It allowed me to meet people who appeared to be serious about meeting people. I met Jack and he became my boyfriend for the next two and a half years. Through my relationship with Jack, I learned what intimacy and commitment were all about. He was a wonderful guy, but I felt something was off between us. He was a bit too dull for me or maybe I just wasn't ready to settle down for life. In retrospect, his reserved, laid-back nature was exactly the right fit for my neurotic, attention-seeking self. When he moved to Philadelphia for a job, we dated long distance for about a year but eventually broke up.

- After Jack, I went in the opposite direction and briefly dated a total extrovert with a ton of passion and zest for life. While exciting, it was exhausting for me, as I reverted back to my old, chasing ways. Our "relationship" foundered after a few months.

- After that, I met Jim at a friend's party. I was drawn to his alpha-male-like qualities and bedazzled by his athletic abilities. He was, in general, a nice guy but stubborn, stuck in his ways, and not attentive to my emotional needs. He did not have the intellectual curiosity that I realized I needed in someone. We both wanted to be in control, and we ended up butting heads far too often. After a year-plus, I ended it.

Over the years, Mallory drew from her experiences and developed new perspectives on herself, dating, men, and relationships. She also learned to accept and embrace the parts of herself that would probably never change and figure out the parts of herself that she wanted to work on. And you can be sure that she was putting this accumulated self- and social awareness to good use when, at age thirty-two, she went back online determined to find a healthy, happy relationship. No longer would Mallory settle for less than she deserved, no longer would she chase men, no longer did she want to be with emotionally unavailable, dominant men, no longer did she crave flash over substance. In short, she was ready to find her partner. Mallory was able to make a wonderful choice in Ben, but only after working on herself and unearthing her unhealthy patterns, limiting beliefs, and consistently inadequate choices in men. Eventually, she understood that her inner difficulties and past conflicts were driving her selection process.

Success! Mallory's knowledge, coupled with the action she took in the dating world, led her to a wonderful man.

It's amazing what will come out when you do a deep dive into your past experiences, getting them out of your head and onto paper. Many clients have discovered patterns they never would have had they not written about their stories in detail. One client was surprised to see how much she grasped for love over the years, trying desperately but unconsciously to get men to want her. Another identified a pattern of intimacy avoidance, which was surprising to her, because, consciously, she had been trying to find a partner for years on end.

Now it's your turn again!

What do you know from your past relationships and experiences in the dating world? Put some time into creating your inventory. Afterwards, here are some important questions to ponder:

Don't forget. This is also the type of work you will be doing if you choose to speak with a therapist.

- Do you see any patterns or limiting core beliefs (see chapter 3) at work? What are they?
- What do you think you might have been getting unconsciously from some of these relationships? Power? Control? Playing a victim? Were you working through past wounds or hurt with certain types of men or relationships?
- What type of men were you attracting or attracted to? What did they have in common?
  o How do you act in those types of relationships? Are you the dominant one? Are you the submissive one? Do you try too hard? Do you get nervous about confrontation? Do you develop insecurities? What are they?
  o How do those men make you feel? Do they make you feel terrible about yourself? Angry? Anxious? On

edge? Insecure? How are those feelings different than when you are with a man who you are not romantically interested in or a man with whom you feel you have more leverage? What's the difference?

- Can you think of times when you felt confident and relaxed when you first started dating someone and then suddenly those feelings drained out of you and gave way to anxiety and insecurity? What triggered this experience for you?

- In any of your relationships or dating experiences, did you start out feeling fairly indifferent about someone or that you weren't all that compatible, but, all of a sudden, they did or said something that had you anxiously wanting them? What changed in you?

- Can you make connections between what you've written and your past, such as your childhood or your relationships with parents/caregivers, so that you might understand how your present has been affected by that past?

- In your past relationships and dating experiences, did you set boundaries for yourself based on your values and needs and then not hold the line on them? Why?

- Can you start thinking about what you might do to change your present situation?
  - o What can you change about *your* thoughts and beliefs and behaviors that would change your situation? How can you start taking action differently?
  - o Do you need to change the way you respond to certain situations in your dating and love life?

As you go out into the dating world, you will be able to use all of this knowledge to your advantage. You can be sure that as Mallory was getting to know Ben, she made a concerted effort to work on addressing much of what she uncovered in her inventory.

For instance:

- With regard to sex, Mallory decided to wait a few months. She wanted to wait and see if Ben was interested in something longer term. It turned out to be a great decision—they spent three months getting to know each other without having intercourse. The fact that he was willing to wait meant he was interested in getting to know her, not just her vagina.
- Mallory promised herself that she would only give emotionally available men a chance. She kept a lookout for red flags, behaviors she had seen in emotionally unavailable men from her past. After spending a few months dating Ben, he showed her that he was willing to be emotionally connected and was looking for a commitment.
- Mallory made a concerted effort to hold back a little when talking about herself. Instead of trying to impress Ben with all of her accomplishments right away, she focused on revealing herself slowly, allowing him to discover who she was over time. She constantly told herself: "being me without my accomplishments is good enough."
- Mallory made a concerted effort to sit back, relax, and enjoy receiving. She did not chase or push Ben on his feelings or try to control the situation. She let things unfold naturally; after three months, Ben asked her to be his girlfriend.

- Mallory embraced the fact that Ben had some beta traits—he was laid back, sensitive, and caring. She knew from her previous relationships that she was not compatible with alpha males.

- Mallory started paying more attention to who she became with the men she dated. If she felt herself becoming someone she wasn't, she took that as an important sign. With Ben, she felt her true self flourishing and expanding and liked that feeling.

So what can *you* work on based on the inventory you've constructed?

Word Cloud Your Story

A fun thing to do after creating and reflecting on your What do I know? inventory is to cut and paste all of your text into Wordle.net, a very cool website that creates "word clouds" from text you provide—giving greater prominence to words that appear more frequently in the source text.

It's an interesting way to create a visual story about the ways you think and talk about your dating and love life, and the concepts and words you focus on. As I like to say to my clients, "Tell me what your dating results are in your life, and I'll tell you what you believe." When you look at your word cloud story, are there themes that emerge? What story about your past could someone else tell by looking at some of the more prominent words that appear in your cloud?

Here's Mallory's cloud based on the aforementioned inventory she created:

Source: Wordle.net

Now that she's met Ben, she can add to her inventory, confidently believing she knows the following:

- At thirty-two, I met Ben on OKCupid.com. When I first met him, I thought to myself: I like this guy, he's easy to talk to, a real gentleman. We went out a second and third time and my attraction grew as I realized we had great chemistry and a great physical attraction to one another. We complemented each other very well, in terms of personalities, and shared similar values. He treated me well on a consistent basis, we laughed our asses off together, and he was always kind, thoughtful, and respectful. I feel at peace with Ben, safe, cared for. He made me want to be the best girlfriend I could be: more patient, more sensitive, selfless. Our relationship blossomed over the months and we developed the kind of intimacy and trust I had always hoped I'd find in a relationship. Even when we disagree, we forgive and forget easily. What I've found in Ben has opened my eyes to how much bullshit I put up with from

various men over the years and how little I valued myself. I discovered what qualities are truly important to me in a man and partner.

Now, let's look at the word cloud story that resulted when she pasted the above text into Wordle.net. As you will see, there is quite a change in the language, creating a very different visual tableau.

Source: Wordle.net

Your inventories together

By creating these inventories—Who am I? What do I know?—you'll be better prepared to make smarter decisions as you date, just like Mallory.

For example:

- You'll have better radar for incompatible and compatible men.

- You'll stop wasting time and energy on the men that don't match up with who you are and what you already know about yourself in the context of relationships and love.
- You'll be able to draw from many of your past "mistakes," "failures," and "wrong turns" to help point you in better directions (more on failure in chapter 8).
- You'll stop being attracted to and attracting emotionally unavailable men.
- You'll have less tolerance for men who aren't consistently treating you in ways that match up with values that are important to you.

Self-awareness. Become aware of yourself and how you experience the world around you when it comes to dating and relationships if you want to grow personally and professionally.

This is not to say you can't experiment and take chances (please do!), and that's not to say you won't make plenty more wrong turns, but the items on these lists will help guide you a little better and steer you back on track when you do go in the wrong direction. And as you date and interact with men, you'll be discovering more things about yourself, and you'll be adding to *who you are* and *what you know* so that you can continue to help yourself make smarter decisions. Self-awareness and your development as a dater don't just happen. They require that you pay attention to your experiences, to the way you respond to your experiences in the dating world. Your self-awareness thus evolves over time as you take action in the dating world and learn what kind of person you are. During this process of self-discovery, you may identify certain limitations. For example, a woman may wish she could have sex like "Samantha Jones" from *Sex In the City*, but she learns from her actions and experiences that she is isn't capable of living that way, because it's not who she is.

Leader or follower? Are you an entrepreneurial leader who is ready and willing to go in new directions in your dating and love life, or are you a follower who is content doing what you've been doing?

Ownership. Use your self-awareness to take ownership of your dating opportunities.

On a personal note: I, too, spent time creating these types of inventories, reflecting on them deeply and often. Putting my thoughts down on paper, whether through journaling or creating lists, and documenting my experiences was helpful for me to confront my feelings rather than ignore them by burying them deep inside. Through this work, I was able to start embracing my identity; I was able to identify patterns and limiting beliefs, which, ultimately, helped me move past them.

The power of self-awareness – it's scary but so important

Creating these lists may not be easy; it may even be painful for you to get clarity on who you are and to drudge up experiences from your past. But in entrepreneurship and in love, self-awareness truly is the foundation of success.

In a *Harvard Business Review* piece titled "How Leaders Become Self-Aware," author Anthony K. Tjan, CEO, Managing Partner and Founder of the venture capital firm Cue Ball, argues that "there is one quality that trumps all, evident in virtually every great entrepreneur, manager, and leader. That quality is self-awareness. The best thing leaders can do to improve their effectiveness is to become more aware of what motivates them and their decision-making."

But you have to commit to the process of becoming self-aware and socially aware, as much as it may scare you. Unfortunately, as Tjan writes, people don't always want self-awareness, because they can't always commit to facing the truth about themselves. He maintains: "Self-reflection and its reward of self-awareness cannot be thought

of as passive exercises, new era meditation, or soft science. They're absolutely essential. There is a reason why in rehabilitation programs the starting point is being aware enough to admit you have a problem. So, too, is the case in business leadership and personal development."

When you become properly acquainted with yourself, you begin to develop a better understanding of who and what type of relationship might be a good fit for you and thus a better appreciation for everything that makes you who you are. Ultimately, action in the dating world should be driven by who you are. All entrepreneurial leaders (in business and love) need to start from a place of self- and social awareness and this awareness will guide your decisions and behavior.

Some of today's academics and business leaders argue that the old approaches to management education aren't nearly as effective in today's day and age, because they don't help people understand themselves, which is why people at places like Babson have started to teach subjects like entrepreneurship differently, encouraging students to have a holistic mindset, developing self-aware, socially-conscious leaders who can go confidently into unknowable situations and lead. Likewise, the old approaches to dating and love don't work so well anymore either. Courtship has been replaced with an unsettling hook-up culture, technology has given us endless options, gender norms have shifted, and demographics have changed. It is in this kind of environment that a single woman must develop a keen sense of self- and social awareness so that she can go confidently into a confusing, unknowable dating world, developing her own opportunities, and creating her future instead of waiting for one to come her way.

Make the connection. Developing true self-awareness must be connected to action. You can draw from your past experiences to gain personal insight, but it will be necessary to experiment with your insights and thus create new approaches to your dating and love life. To use an earlier example: If you understand from your past experiences that you don't like having casual sex, you must experiment with new approaches (outside of sex) to connecting with men.

Your Affinity List

Building on the inventories you created with regard to who you are and what you know, I want you to now create a list of things you're looking for in a partner (i.e. your affinities).

The "Wheel of Fortune" principle

The first three items on your Affinity List are *my non-negotiables* for *you*. It is rare for me as a coach to give a mandate—I prefer to guide people to come to their own answers rather than tell them what they should think—but in this instance, I have decided to break from the norm.

Fun fact. Over 90 million Americans have never known a world without *Wheel of Fortune.*

Let's use the popular TV game show *Wheel of Fortune* as a reference. In the final round, the contestant has to solve a word puzzle after choosing various letters of the alphabet. The letters R, S, T, L, N, and E are automatically provided for the contestant—he or she has no say in the matter. Next, the contestant gets to provide four more letters—three consonants and one vowel. It is then the job of the contestant to solve the word puzzle using the letters that are showing.

Let's apply the same logic to your list.

The following three qualities are fundamentally important in a partner for long-term love. They all have to do with a man's character. Obviously, you won't be able to tell up front if someone embodies these qualities, which is why, if you click with someone, you will need to give them some time to prove themselves in these areas.

I submit to you that along with common interests and values (which we will explore in chapter 6), it is important to look for someone who has a good character. Oftentimes, when I meet with new clients and ask them what they're looking for in a man, they immediately spout off all sorts of things like "someone who's hot, tall, ambitious, charming, a good dancer, a good dresser, has good hair." Those *characteristics* are all well and good, but it's troubling that nowhere in their lists do they say anything about *character.* Who is the person behind that veneer of flash?

Understanding that women sometimes forget to think about a man's character, the following traits are ones that must be on your list:

- Kindness
  - o Because why would you ever want someone who treats you with anything other than kindness? Is he kind to you in the way he listens and remembers things about you or that are important to you? Is he kind in his gestures toward you? Is he kind in the way he supports or encourages you in your passions and goals in life? As you start getting to know a man, you will know if he is kind to you in the way you need him to be. If a man is not kind to you, he is either not in the stage of his life where he has the capacity to be kind, he isn't interested in you for a longer commitment, or he's simply a person incapable of kindness toward another human being—all reasons to look elsewhere.
- Trustworthiness
  - o Because why would you ever want to be with someone you can't trust? Is this a person you feel you can

trust with your feelings, secrets, and whatever else you choose to share? Do you trust he is who he says he is or who he portrays himself to be? If you become an item, do you trust that he will remain faithful?

- Reliability/Dependability
  - o Because why would you ever want to be with someone you can't rely or depend on? Is he constantly breaking plans? Do his actions speak louder than his words? Can you depend on him when times get tough? There's no need to waste your time and energy on someone who will never be reliable or dependable or just isn't ready to be that person yet. When you're in a committed, long-term relationship you have to be able to rely and depend on your partner for any number of things.

Dating dissonance. The difference in what we say we want in a partner and relationship and what we actually want or choose.

Some of you may even *say* you want these types of qualities in a man, but you have spent years *choosing* men who don't demonstrate them on a *consistent basis.* That sort of dating dissonance—the difference between what you say you want and what you actually want or choose—can end, but only if you make an effort to make better choices and understand why you've made the opposite choices in your past. There might be rare instances in which a man might disappoint you every now and then in the beginning with regard to these qualities. A couple months into dating Dave (who is now my husband), he was late twice for dates by an hour. I was, naturally, upset. Rather than lash out at him (something I might have done in previous budding relationships), I spoke to him calmly and from the heart. I found out he was going through some personal stuff and we moved past it quickly. He was never late for a date again.

In general, a man should display these three character traits effortlessly and the majority of the time. And women should be paying close attention to these qualities during the early stages of dating. They provide a good jumping-off point from which to build a healthy, loving, happy relationship. If your partner is consistently lacking in any of these qualities, I encourage you to think more carefully about why this is someone into whom you want to put your time and energy.

The next seven selections

The next seven selections are yours to make. The reason I cap your selections at seven is to force you to think about qualities that are really important to you. Your list will be a guide for you as you are taking action in the dating world; it cannot be an exact blueprint. Consider the infamous seventy-three-point checklist of Julia Allison, dating columnist and star of Bravo TV show *Miss Advised*. How could any man live up to that kind of elaborate checklist? Would you want to be required to live up to a man's checklist if it was that long?

The danger in creating too long a list is that you create a perfect mold of a man that doesn't exist, except maybe in Hollywood romantic comedies or storybook fairy tales or Julia's Allison's fantasy world. I want you to start reconciling your childhood fantasies with a more mature reality: that a man is going to have all sorts of foibles and imperfections and can't possibly match up to everything you think you want in someone. Guess what: neither can you. So cut the men out there some slack, ladies, and think about what is really important to you in a man.

Just say NO!

Toss the overly long checklists. Let the short list you create here serve as your guide.

Vague vs. specific. Find a happy medium with your list. You want to give yourself some direction but you don't want to box yourself into a very particular type of person.

Successful entrepreneurs don't go into new ventures with an exact blueprint of what their businesses have to look like. And neither should you when thinking about who you want to be with romantically. If you have a very specific physical "type," throw it out the window. Too many women enter the dating world searching for very specific types of men (height, hair color, skin coloring, etc.); by getting so specific, they overlook men who might make great partners, simply because they're married (no pun intended) to a very specific type or to certain superficial qualities. Yes, physical attraction is important and it's fine to put down on your list, but don't specify how tall he has to be, what color his hair has to be, how much hair he has to have, or other more superficial qualities like fashion sense and body type, *unless* you legitimately feel these qualities will be important for your mate to have until the day you die—news flash: looks fade, his hair will be gone eventually, and you can always retool his wardrobe. The same thing goes for a man's job. Don't specify what industry you want him to be in or how much money he has to make, but do feel free to specify that you want someone with career goals and dreams. A man who wants to be, say, an incredible high school math teacher may never make a ton of money, but he has ambitions to be a great teacher. He probably won't be able to shower you with riches, but he could very well be a loving, supportive partner.

On the flip side: Try to not to be too vague with your list. For instance, many women will say, "I want a man who challenges me." To which I always respond: "What exactly does that even mean? Challenge you how? In what ways?" Do you mean, simply, that you admire a man who has his own passions and hobbies and can introduce you to something new? If so, put that on your list, instead of some elusive quality that gives you little guidance. Don't be so general

in your affinities that you have little to guide you, but, of course, don't be so specific that you get locked into a very narrow vision of who is compatible.

If you have absolute "non-negotiables"—requirements or qualities with which you absolutely won't be flexible—get them down as well. For instance, if you want children and aren't willing to negotiate on that, add it to your list.

My list would be the following (in no particular order):

- Kind
- Trustworthy
- Reliable/dependable
- Similar sense of humor; loves to laugh; capacity to be silly
- A sense of intellectual curiosity about the world around him
- Physical attraction (can grow over time)
- Has passions, goals, hobbies of his own, and supports my passions, goals, and hobbies
- Laid back, easygoing
- Financially stable/responsible
- Wants children

Note that I did not write down specifics for each bullet point, such as, he *has to* love a certain type of comedy or share the same favorite authors as me or look exactly a certain way or have a certain hobby or make a certain income or want exactly two kids. In this way, I've allowed different kinds of men room to work their way into my heart and given myself room to move and evolve.

A fun exercise I like to do with clients after they've created their affinity lists is to ask them if who they've just described sounds familiar. Often, the person they're describing is the person they are or want to become. Ultimately, they realize they don't have to go outside of themselves to find those qualities or fill themselves up. They are qualities that are either right there inside of them already or ones that they can commit themselves to working on. In this light, finding love becomes about *being the person* you want to meet instead of searching for someone who possesses qualities to validate you or make you whole. You can still find someone who complements you but also someone who makes it easier for you to personally evolve. With regard to my seven selections, I am absolutely all of them, with, admittedly, an exception in certain ways to "laid back, easygoing." However, recognizing that this was something I wanted to improve upon, I spent a lot of time working on that part of myself. Eventually, I went into the dating world able to offer most of the things I was looking for in a man, understanding that my easygoing side would be a work in progress but that this type of man would be a great fit for me. Indeed, Dave is so patient and laid back that it makes me want to continually strive to be a better woman in this way.

Your affinity list will be a great guide for you, as you are acting in the dating world, but it is important not to set it in stone. As you evolve, so, too, may your list in various ways as you discover what's really important to you in a man. For example, initially, you might have selected "Ambitious in his career" for your list, but after dating and learning about yourself and what's really important to you, that item may change to "Has a job that he enjoys and believes in" or maybe you decide to eliminate a career-oriented choice for your list entirely and replace it with something that speaks more to how a man makes you feel ("Sensitive to my feelings"). To offer another example: Maybe you put down "Athletic" but discover that trait is not a crucial item for your list, freeing up space to add something you've discovered is truly important to you, such as, say, "Positive/joyful." Like any entrepreneur knows, while a vision of what is to be created should always remain intact, the ideas that get you there may shift along the way.

Once again, I will use a personal example to illustrate my points.

I met Dave on Match.com. He sent me an email to say hello. I thought he was cute, and his profile made me smile. But I was thirty-three at the time and committed to getting serious about my love life. Dave was twenty-eight. I replied but did not respond to his next email, because I figured he was too young, anyway. A month went by when I noticed he had checked out my profile again. I thought to myself, "Oh yeah, that guy; well, maybe just one date. What do I have to lose?" I finally returned his email and he was very sweet about it. He could have been angry or resentful, qualities I had seen in some men with whom I had emailed, but he was totally flexible and thoughtful. I liked that about him. We met for a drink at a local bar. He had gotten their thirty minutes early to make sure we could get seats. If it turned out we had to wait, I wouldn't have minded at all, but I appreciated that he went above and beyond. He was cute, although not necessarily the typical guy to whom I was attracted, but I liked so many other things about him that I let go of all the superficial ideals and requirements I had dreamed up over the years. Two years later, we got engaged.

One other nugget to add on this topic: I remember on our first date, I noticed that his fingernails were on the longish side (longer than

what I preferred—sorry, honey!). In the past, I'd let something like that dissuade me from going out on a second date. But I liked Dave. We had a good conversation, he listened well, and our humor meshed well. So I said yes to date number two, during which I learned that he had been trying to get over a bad habit of biting his fingernails and had inadvertently let them get a bit too long. Now he keeps his nails trim. But do you see what I'm trying to point out?

Firstly, if I hadn't pushed myself to act and kept an open mind about a slightly younger man than I thought I wanted, I would not have spent a couple hours of my life to meet Dave. Secondly, if I had ruled him out immediately because of something superficial that I had no background information about (his fingernails) or because he wasn't precisely my physical type in x, y, and z ways, I might have never met the love of my life.

Do not be so tied to your ideas that you overlook someone who may have potential otherwise.

Elevator Pitch.
A short summary used to quickly and simply define a person, profession, product, service, organization, or event and its value proposition.

Creating Your Personal Elevator Pitch and Personal Brand

At this point, you've thought about who you are and what you know, and you've created a short list about the qualities in a man you're looking for (keeping in mind that this list may shift as you date and learn). Good work.

Personal elevator pitch

Next, I want you to construct something called an elevator pitch, a business phrase and metaphor meaning a short, pithy argument that

an entrepreneur makes to potential investors. The name implies that one should be able to deliver the pitch in the span of an elevator ride, the purpose of which is to interest the investors enough that they would consider financing the entrepreneur's company or idea.

At Babson, every year, many of the students take part in a competition called Rocket Pitch, in which early-stage businesses have the opportunity to present their ideas in front of hundreds of people, including fellow students, staff, faculty, and outside investors. Each student has three minutes to prove why his or her start-up has *value proposition*, and is therefore worthy of investment. Attendees then grade the students' presentations so that they can get feedback on the effectiveness of their pitches as well as the feasibility of their ideas. Many students walk away with great insight, some with a bunch of contacts, and a lucky few with future investment offers.

In the context of this book and your entrepreneurial venture, there's a twist on the traditional pitch. Instead of pitching others, you are *pitching yourself to you*! You'll then refer to your pitch on a regular basis throughout your entrepreneurial journey to *remind yourself* of why:

- ✓ You are amazing, deserving of love, and worth someone investing in YOU.
- ✓ You are deserving of someone compatible, caring, and appreciative of what you bring to the table.
- ✓ You are deserving of someone who is willing to consistently give you their love and kindness.

Remember: First and foremost, it's important to fall in love with yourself and see your own value before you can freely give and receive

Fall for yourself. Fall in love with yourself first and a man will easily fall in love with you, too.

Validation! Rather than wait for someone else to decide you are worthy of love, start telling yourself daily that you are worthy and you'll come to believe it, and then you'll attract guys who believe it, too!

love, before you can *share* love with someone. In my coaching practice, I work with many wonderful women who for a variety of reasons cannot see their worth or value. Many of them believe they have to go outside of themselves to find a man to fill them up and validate their worth, and so I spend time asking them to acknowledge and celebrate who they are, who they are working on becoming, and why they are worth investing in themselves by doing this type of work. Eventually, they start to see their value, not only the value they have just by being human, but the value in who they are as an individual and who they are working to become. They begin to acknowledge that they are worthy of love and connection. Creating an elevator pitch to yourself that clearly states your value, the value you have to offer another human being, and the fact that you deserve love and respect from your future partner, and then reciting and reflecting on these words on a frequent basis can be an incredibly powerful tool.

Elevator pitch do's.
- Be clear.
- Be concise.
- Be positive.
- Refer to your pitch regularly.
- Believe in it.
- Be the person you write about.

Directions:

✓ Keep your pitch to under 300 words. Be descriptive, let loose.

✓ Make your pitch clear, concise, positive, and inspiring.

✓ If you discover new things about yourself during this process or want to change or make edits to your pitch, please feel free to re-write it until you feel confident that it is an accurate portrayal of who you are, who you are working to become, and why you're worth investing in yourself.

Even if you are still working on some of the qualities you mention in your pitch, such as, say, letting go of control or becoming more vulnerable, it's important to believe that you can and will become the

person you write about. I want you to see your potential. At the end of the day, if you don't believe in yourself and your pitch, nobody else will.

Here are some questions to help get you started:

- Why are you worth investing in yourself?
- What is special and unique about you? What is your value proposition?
- Why are you worthy of love and connection?

Begin your pitch by stating your name and that you are "worthy of love and connection."

Here's my personal elevator pitch:

Hi, my name is Neely Steinberg. I am worthy of love and connection. I have spent many years dating and learning about men, relationships, and myself. I have learned that I am kind, giving, loyal, and affectionate. I am also feisty and opinionated but have a soft, silly side. I love to laugh and try to find humor in the world around me on a daily basis. I enjoy making others around me feel comfortable and at ease. I have a lot of love to give to the right man who is willing to return it. Because I have spent a significant amount of time dating and working on myself, I believe wholeheartedly that I will make a good partner for the right man, and look forward to joyfully receiving his kindness and love. I hope to be compassionate and loving and willing to compromise with my partner and expect the same in return. I hope to love you for who you are and do not have any desire to change a man, and I am excited to find the man with whom I can be the best version of myself. I will let go as best I can

Pitch yourself!

Go ahead, pitch yourself. Start talking to yourself in kind, loving ways. Begin to see and celebrate all of the wonderful things you have to offer, even if you are still working on becoming the woman you want to be. You are worth investing yourself!

and not seek to control you. I hope to give you the same sense of comfort, peace, and intimacy I am looking for. I look forward to working through disagreements calmly, experiencing life's ups and downs, and growing with you if you show me that you are willing to do the same.

Your pitch is an effective way to affirm your worth and value, and to start understanding that you deserve a man who will give you the love and attention that you are willing to give him.

Repeat your pitch on a daily basis—maybe have it on a piece of paper next to your bedside table and take a few seconds to recite it every morning when you wake. If you've started dating someone new more seriously, read it often to reaffirm your faith in yourself and the power of a healthy, happy relationship. Also be sure to act on this affirmation by letting go of men who don't value and respect you.

Personal brand statement

Your final task in this chapter is to create a personal brand.

Personal brand.

A description that gets to the heart of who you are. Repeat your brand often to yourself. Be the embodiment of your brand on a daily basis. Let it inspire you in the dating world.

Successful entrepreneurs understand that building a company includes building a unique and compelling brand. Some of the most trusted companies in the world—Coca-Cola, Apple, Amazon—go to great lengths to ensure that people fall in love and stay in love with their brand, developing emotional, visceral bonds with customers. In turn, customers come to see these brands as valuable, even necessary to their lives.

Singles can benefit, too, by thinking of themselves as a brand. What does your brand say to dates, to potential suitors, to the outside world?

From your elevator pitch and Who Am I? inventory?, you can create a pithy, upbeat personal brand statement that's easy to memorize and one you can return to quickly in your mind:

- before or on a first date
- during the early stages of dating someone
- when feeling insecure or whenever you need a confidence boost

You can also use your brand as a litmus test for men you are dating:

- Does a man allow you to be your brand or does he squash who you are?
- Do you feel like you have to become someone different or become a different brand in order for a man to like you?
- Does a man take advantage of who you are, or does he appreciate and cherish these qualities in you AND reciprocate by consistently showing you his own wonderful qualities (his brand)?

Directions for creating your brand:

- When creating your personal brand statement, keep it very short—one sentence that includes three, four, or five (at most) amazing attributes about you.
- You can draw from the strengths you've identified earlier in the chapter or those highlighted in your elevator pitch. Choose a few that you feel are your strengths in the context of dating and relationships. In other words, your brand should speak to what you love about yourself, and, in a few words, what you have to offer someone else.

- Avoid using things like your job or how much money you make in your brand statement.
- Repeat your personal brand to yourself often and back it up on a daily basis *through your actions*, so that you truly become the embodiment of your brand. As soon as you start talking to and interacting with others, you are showcasing your brand. Own your brand; wow those around you!
- Find a picture of you that represents your brand and put it up in your home where you can see it. Add the words of your brand onto the picture (see my example).

My personal brand: *Playful, free-spirited woman, who loves to laugh and make others smile.*

(Me and my personal brand)

So ... what's your brand?

Up Next:

At this point, you might be saying to yourself: "I'm ready to be action-oriented. I'm ready to get out there and start dating and acting my way into thinking (and using prediction when necessary), but there's one small problem: How do I actually go about getting the dates?!" Don't worry: I will address how to network and identify opportunities in chapters 9 and 10. These chapters should give you a lot of ideas on how to increase your chances of meeting people, getting set up, and on how to create opportunities for yourself.

But hold your horses—you'll get there soon enough!

In the next chapter, I'll be showing you how to *learn* from your actions by reflecting upon the current experiences you are having or will eventually be having in the dating world.

Chapter 5 Action Steps Checklist:

- ✓ Create a personal inventory answering the question: Who am I?
- ✓ Create a personal inventory answering the question: What do I know?
- ✓ Allow yourself time to digest both inventories. Reflect on them.
- ✓ From your Who am I? inventory, might you be able to identify men who probably would and wouldn't be a good fit with you? Can you think of men from your past who you might have spent less time and energy pursuing

because they weren't compatible? Can you think of men from your past who you might have given more of a chance? Can you then apply this knowledge moving forward so that you don't spend more time and energy on men who, despite any initial chemistry, are probably going to be incompatible? Can you apply this knowledge moving forward so that you give more time and energy to see what develops with men who may be better suited for you?

✓ List how you might use some of your attributes as defenses in the dating world. And start paying better attention when these defenses surface in your dating life so that you can start making decisions from a place of awareness.

✓ From your "What do I know" inventory, what are specific patterns you can work on breaking as you start dating? How can you challenge yourself to go in new directions?

✓ Commit to acting your way into thinking in your dating life moving forward, but do think about ways and when you can use prediction to make smarter choices in your dating life. We will talk more about this in chapters 7 and 8.

✓ Construct your Affinity List. Kindness, trustworthiness, and reliability/dependability are the first three items on your list by Neely mandate! The next seven selections are yours to make. Spend a fair amount of time reflecting on what you want to put on this list. But keep in mind: It may shift and evolve over time as you begin dating.

✓ Construct your Personal Elevator Pitch. This will be a positive affirmation of your worth and value, who you are working to become, and why you are worth someone investing their time and heart into. You can turn to this pitch when you are feeling sad, frustrated, or confused to

remind yourself of the wonderful things you are and all of the wonderful qualities you have to offer someone, and why you deserve someone equally as wonderful. Or feel free to read your pitch whenever the mood strikes as a way to instill confidence in yourself and keep your vision burning bright.

✓ From your elevator pitch, construct your one-sentence Personal Brand statement. Repeat this brand mantra daily to yourself and/or before dates. Embody this brand daily through your actions. Find a picture that embodies your brand, write your brand on the picture, and put it up in your home to remind yourself of your brand (you can take it down when dates come over!).

✓ Revisit chapter 3. Are there any other internal obstacles (i.e. limiting core beliefs) to finding love that you've identified in your Affinity and Fishbone Diagrams that you can begin to unpack and replace with new, empowering beliefs? Are there any other external obstacles to finding love that you've identified in your Affinity and Fishbone Diagrams that you can begin to overcome by taking small, smart steps?

CHAPTER 6: LEARN.
(DATE. LEARN. REPEAT.)

**"Let us not look back in anger, nor forward in fear,
but around in awareness"**

– James Thurber, author and cartoonist

In this chapter, I'm going to discuss the importance of reflection in your *current* dating and relationship experiences. As Neck and Greene write in their article "Entrepreneurship Education: Known Worlds and New Frontiers" with regard to the entrepreneurial way: "Reflection is an important process by which knowledge is developed from experience." Just as traditional entrepreneurs must engage in deep reflection about themselves, the world around them, and the experiences they are having with their business ventures, it is crucial that, along with an action-oriented approach to dating, you are engaging in constant, reflective thought, so that you are not just *having* experiences but *actively learning from them* (acting your way into thinking) and adding to what you already know about your love life and to what you know about who you are. (See inventories in chapter 5.)

Purposeful experiences. Don't just have experiences. Make them purposeful. Actively learn from them. That's what treps do.

Welcome to the digital age. A world filled with manifold distractions, designed to keep us from sitting idly, reflecting. While I, of course, have great respect for these inventions and the entrepreneurs who dream them up, I also recognize the tremendous importance of turning the gadgets off and plugging into yourself.

Deresiewicz's speech. To access his entire speech, go to: http://the american scholar. org/solitude- and-leadership/

Unfortunately, our fast-paced twenty-first-century society often seems to be at war with the notion of deep reflection, if only because we have invented all sorts of ways to distract us from our thoughts, to keep us constantly busy. From smart phones, portable tablets, mobile music, games, and videos to the Internet and television, no matter where we are or go, we can distract ourselves endlessly to alleviate the pain of solitude.

We are guilty, though, of being willing participants, gladly allowing ourselves to be distracted so as to not have to engage in deep self-reflection. We want the quick fix, easy answers, a pill to solve our problems, instant gratification, anything that can keep us from having to spend time doing the hard stuff. We have become grateful to our gadgets and busy, non-stop lives for keeping us from ourselves. But it is also true that lack of solitude and reflection time can be detrimental to self-awareness and growth.

In a now-famous speech titled "Solitude and Leadership" delivered in 2009 at West Point, essayist William Deresiewicz talked about why solitude is an important pre-requisite for leadership in the business world and beyond. I would argue the same could be said about dating and love.

"Thinking means concentrating on one thing long enough to develop an idea about it," said Deresiewicz. "Not learning other people's ideas, or memorizing a body of information, however much those may sometimes be useful. Developing your own ideas. In short, thinking for yourself. You simply cannot do that in bursts of 20 seconds at a time, constantly interrupted by Facebook messages or Twitter tweets, or fiddling with your iPod, or watching something on YouTube." Deresiewicz discouraged the West Pointers from seeking the easy,

generic, formulaic answers often found in places like the Internet, TV, magazines, and newspapers. He urged the students to confront doubts and questions head-on. Deresiewicz continued:

> …*it's perfectly natural to have doubts, or questions, or even just difficulties. The question is, what do you do with them? Do you suppress them, do you distract yourself from them, do you pretend they don't exist? Or do you confront them directly, honestly, courageously? If you decide to do so, you will find that the answers to these dilemmas are not to be found on Twitter or Comedy Central or even in* The New York Times. *They can only be found within—without distractions, without peer pressure, in solitude."*

Solitude. How often do you sit and reflect in solitude?

David Meyer, a cognitive scientist at the University of Michigan, agrees with this general sentiment, urging entrepreneurs to halt their multitasking every now and then. Interviewed by Joe Robinson, a work-life trainer, in the December 2012 issue of *Entrepreneur*, Meyer opines, "If you want to be a creative entrepreneur, you ought to be setting aside large chunks of time where you just think."

Don't run from yourself. Tricks and manipulation tactics in the dating world do nothing to help you look inward, but that's where the answers lie.

Or consider the words of Lisa Bodell, founder and CEO of Futurethink and author of *Kill the Company: End the Status Quo, Start an Innovation Revolution*, who was interviewed in the October 2012 issue about improving innovation in early-stage start-ups: "We're so focused on productivity that thinking has become a daring act," she says. "In a world focused on efficiency, creating the space and ability to think should be on top of the to-do list." When it comes to dating, are you so focused on getting and having dates that you've stopped setting aside time to think more pointedly about the experiences you're actually having?

The answers will come. The answers to our dating questions and dilemmas often emerge over time, that is, if we take the time to really reflect.

Re-think Your Thinking

I'd be a terrible dating coach and cheerleader if I sent you into the dating world to have all these experiences without also encouraging you to think about and learn from them. In chapter 5, I asked you to think about who you are and what you know about yourself and the world around you in the context of dating, love, and relationships, as an accompaniment to acting, so that the knowledge you have already gained, that is right there within you already, can be harnessed and put to good use while acting in the dating world. In this chapter, I will be asking you to think about your *current* experiences with perhaps more purpose than you have ever done before. When you spend time thinking about your experiences, you help yourself arrive at the answers that work best for you.

While it's true that romantic chemistry is often an intangible quality, and not something you can think your way into, you *can* think about the people you are allowing and not allowing into your life and why. Chemistry is only part of the equation; it's not enough on its own. By engaging in consistent, pointed reflection about the men you are dating, your experiences, and attitude, you have a much better chance of resolving challenges and setting yourself on a path to finding a relationship that is healthy, happy, and right for you. Moreover, you'll end up investing a lot less time and energy on those men who make you feel less than worthy of love and commitment.

As a Love TREP, I want you to start re-thinking the process of thinking so that you are able to consistently see new opportunities and ideas, connect more deeply with men you meet, transform self-insight

into knowledge you can use and act on, and create and execute new and different solutions for your dating and love life.

What follows are suggestions on how you can reflect more purposefully and less superficially about the dates and experiences you're having. Carve some time out of your busy schedule to reflect in solitude. My favorite ways to reflect include journaling, exceedingly long showers, quiet time lying in bed, walks in nature, and driving in the car with the radio off.

The Three Reasonablies

Not only do I encourage you to spend time alone to reflect on your *past* experiences, but I also encourage you to reflect pointedly on your *current* experiences.

First thing's first, though: Be open to accepting dates from a variety of different men so that you have experiences to reflect on. That doesn't mean accepting a date from a weird, creepy-looking man thirty years your senior, who sends you a Match.com email asking for a date, but it does mean saying "yes" to every reasonable invitation from a man you might be reasonably attracted to in one way or another, even if he doesn't match up to what you're typically attracted to.

After every first date, I want you to set aside time to ask yourself the following post-date questions. I call them The Three Reasonablies:

- *Did I have a reasonably good time?*
- *Was I reasonably attracted to him?*
- *Did we have a reasonable amount of common interests?*

Are you an extremist dater? Avoid dating in the extremes. You shouldn't have to talk yourself into liking someone, nor should you dismiss someone immediately simply because you didn't feel a lightning-bolt connection from the get-go.

Nothing profound. Just three simple questions. Let's unpack them one at a time.

Did I have a reasonably good time?

When you go into a first date situation thinking in extremes you run the risk of either ruling someone out who may improve upon a second or third date or putting someone up on a pedestal and erecting blinders to their bad behavior. I've worked with women who rule out men at the slightest hint of uncertainty, using the pettiest excuses to reject a second date. I've been that woman. If you're searching for perfection, you're not going to find it. I'm not even sure why you'd want to find it. I've also worked with women who fell immediately for men after the first date despite glaring red flags. I also used to be that woman.

But let's say you go out with someone whose company you reasonably enjoyed. It wasn't, say, the best or most adventurous date of your life, but you had good conversation, you laughed, he was respectful, you left wanting to know more about this person, and you thought to yourself: "That guy was *nice*, I liked him." These are the guys I want you to give a second, even third chance. Of course, it's fantastic if you have an amazing first date; naturally, you'll be accepting a second date. The point is I don't want you discarding a man just because your first date wasn't the most sensational experience ever. Just because you didn't get immediate butterflies doesn't mean he couldn't be a wonderful match for you as you get to know each other.

This approach also helps you shrug off superficial dislikes so that those dislikes don't have the power to ruin a potential future with

a great man (remember my fingernail example in chapter 5?). One woman I coached didn't like the way her date cut his steak. Instead of cutting the meat and then switching hands to eat it, he cut the steak and ate it without the utensil switching hands—European style. This same man also got a doggie bag, despite there not being much food left over. From a dating-coach perspective, these hardly seemed like deal breakers, yet if I hadn't asked her if she had a reasonably good time apart from these minor oddities—to which she responded yes—she might not have given him a second chance. I forced her to think differently about trivial things such as how a man cuts his steak and his doggie-bag habits and to think about where these knee-jerk reactions come from in the first place. Maybe he grew up in France and adopted the European style of eating steak. Maybe he grew up poor and hates to see leftover food go to waste. Maybe he actually has a dog. She'd never get to find out these details if she dismissed him because of these petty dislikes.

Laugh at yourself. What's the silliest thing you've ever dismissed a guy over? I give you full permission to giggle at yourself.

On the flip side, I would never encourage you to go out again with someone if you had a terrible time on your first date. That's pointless. But be careful not to judge a date experience by standards that you wouldn't want your date judging you by. Do you want someone to feel you should have been a perfect date who said and did all the "right" things?

After each date, take a moment to list three things that went well on your date. Instead of focusing on the negatives, you are prompting yourself to look at the positives. If you can't think of at least one, you probably didn't have a reasonably good time and therefore no need for a second date.

Positivity. Focus on the positives of your date. Stop looking for reasons not to be attracted or interested.

Example:

1. I appreciated that he got to the bar early and got two seats for us—that was very gentlemanly and got us off on a good start.
2. We had good conversation and enjoyed a tasty beverage.
3. He seemed genuinely interested in learning about me.

Was I reasonably attracted to him?

How many times have you heard women say that the first time they met or went out with their now-husbands/boyfriends/fiancés they didn't necessarily feel an intense attraction? Plenty, I'm sure. That's because attraction doesn't always have to be an immediate experience that you feel in your loins. Attraction can grow over time.

Lest you be concerned: I am in no way encouraging you to go out a second time with someone whom you feel zero attraction toward, but as long as there is some level of physical attraction (maybe you like his eyes or his smile or his strong hands), I encourage you to give a man a second or third shot. Also, don't forget about other types of connections, like spiritual or intellectual attraction, which surely can translate to physical attraction as time goes by.

On a personal note: Every single time I felt a lightning-bolt, deep-in-my-knees physical attraction to someone from the get-go, the "relationship" was short-lived or ended in shambles.

Certainly that doesn't mean my experiences will be yours. I am simply encouraging you to not search exclusively for that elusive lightning-bolt attraction or feeling. You might also want to consider if your attraction to a particular man feels like a force, as though you are drawn to him for some unknown reason. This type of attraction could be, as we discussed in chapter 3, your unconscious at work, which is why it's so important to uncover these hidden, latent motives by bringing them to consciousness, either by doing the work in chapter 3, or working with a therapist and/or coach.

I'm not saying you shouldn't go out with men to whom you are intensely attracted from the first moment—please do!—but be on high alert that your intense attraction, wherever it comes from, can often prevent you from seeing red flags. That's because you put blinders on as a result of your knee-jerk attraction; bad behavior is then often shoved under the proverbial carpet because you're being driven by feelings of lust and perhaps other unconscious desires. It is best to be aware of this type of attraction, so that you can determine if it's coming from a healthy place or an insecure place.

After each date, take a moment to list three ways in which you felt attracted to your date. These ways could be related to physical, mental, emotional, intellectual, or spiritual attraction, or any other kind of attraction you can think of. If you can't think of at least one, you weren't reasonably attracted to him and therefore no need for a second date.

Example:

1. He was a really great listener.
2. He had a sexy smile.
3. His passion for music was a turn-on.

Did we have a reasonable amount of common interests?

It's hard to know from a first outing how much you have in common, but I think you will get a pretty decent idea.

It helps in a relationship to have common interests, but that doesn't mean you have to have everything in common. Plenty of happy couples pursue different interests and enjoy different hobbies. But they usually have some things they like doing together as well. A first date will uncover some of your common and different interests, but do not discard someone just because several of his interests do not match up with your own.

If you met through a common interest (a running club, political cause, etc.), you're off to a good start. Now is your opportunity to see if you share other things in common, and if your personalities mesh well. Or you may have met someone online who says they share one or several of your interests, and a first date is the opportunity to explore those interests and each other more in depth.

After each date, take a moment to list two or three interests you have in common. If you can't think of at least one that you talked about during your date, you probably don't have all that much in common and therefore no need for a second date.

Example:

1. We both like going to museums.
2. We have a shared love of tennis.

The second date

If the answers to these three questions are "yes," and you were able to create your lists fairly easily, go out on a second date and see what develops. After your second date, ask yourself the following questions.

- *Did I continue to enjoy my time with him?*
- *Did my initial (reasonable) attraction grow at all?*
- *Am I interested in exploring with him some of our common interests?*

After your second date, if the answers are "no" to any of these questions, it's probably not worth a third date (unless you have good reason to think otherwise and want to give your suitor more time). If you answered "yes" to the first question but "no" to the second, it may be worth giving a man one more shot to see if the attraction can grow.

If all three answers are "yes," at this point, it's pretty obvious you have a keen interest in this person and your budding attraction and admiration has the potential to grow even deeper. You also have things in common and you're excited about the possibility of exploring those interests together. Go out on a third date and see what develops.

Second time is a charm? Give a man a second chance to see what develops. You never know what switch inside you might flip.

The third date and future dates

After your third date and any future dates, I want you to start reflecting more deeply on the following questions:

- *Do I feel good about myself when I'm around him?*
- *Do I feel good about the bond and connection we're forming?*
- *Do we value similar things in life?*
- *How is our relationship growing?*

Let's break down these three questions one at a time.

Do I feel good about myself when I'm around him?

In the summer of 2012, I was at a close friend's wedding. During one of the toasts, my friend's sister said the following: "We know Mike is right for you, because ever since you've been with him, you are the best version of yourself." Read that sentence again.

Best version. Does he allow you to be the best version of yourself? Or does he squash who you are?

I can't stress enough how important it is to be with someone who appreciates and allows you to be who you are and feel good about that, someone who brings out your best attributes. When a man allows you to be the best version of yourself (remember your personal elevator pitch and personal brand?), you will feel a sense of peace and gratitude, a sense that all is right in the world. Someone who consistently makes you feel on edge, anxious, emotionally off-kilter, confused, restrained, and that being you isn't good enough, is not the person you want to be sitting next to in the rocking chair when you're old and gray. How could you not end up resenting someone like that?

I want you to start considering that the way you *feel* about yourself when you're with a man is an important ingredient in determining if a relationship has long-term potential. Of course, it starts with *your* feeling good about who you are and loving yourself, but when a man appreciates who you are and allows you the space and freedom to be that person with him, it's the greatest feeling in the world.

So, you obviously won't know all of this just by a few dates. But, trust me, you will start to get a read fairly early on if you pay attention and reflect on how you feel about yourself when you're around him.

Do you feel fairly at ease? And I'm not talking about the early-stage dating butterflies that erupt simply because you're excited to be around this person; rather, do you feel like you can be yourself in his company? For instance, if you're an animated person, does he allow you to express yourself in such a way that you feel comfortable doing so, or does he constantly try to censor you or get embarrassed by you? If you're more reserved and introverted, does he appreciate this side of you, or does he constantly make you feel like you need to be more social? If you're talkative and opinionated, does he like to listen, or does he constantly interrupt and talk over you?

A feeling of safety is important in a relationship, a feeling that it is safe to be the best version of yourself. If you find yourself drawn to men who leave you feeling emotionally unsafe or off-kilter or not good enough in some way, you'll want to explore why you seem to be attracted to those types. Or maybe you find that you consistently turn away men who treat you well and make you feel safe. That's surely something to investigate. Remember that you're looking for the patterns in your love life that leave you unfulfilled. Pay close attention

Warning! If you're constantly anxious when you're not around him, worrying or stressing out about when you'll hear from him, there's usually a reason for it. Reflect on why that may be. When you ask women in healthy, happy relationships about the early stages of dating with their now boyfriends, they'll exclaim how easy it was, how they didn't worry so much in between spending time together.

to the feelings you'll be experiencing with the men you start to date more seriously; more than likely, your feelings will give you guidance as to who and what will make you happy long-term.

By paying attention to and honoring your feelings, and then acting accordingly in response to those feelings, you allow yourself to hold the power in the dating world. You don't pursue or enable men whom you feel emotionally unsafe around or who make you feel bad about who you are, and you do pursue and appreciate men who you feel safe around and who make you feel good about who you are—that being you is good enough. A therapist (or your mentor or coach) is useful in this regard, because he or she can help you sort through the feelings you're experiencing in a budding relationship.

One quick caveat: Being who you are doesn't give you license to be obnoxious, selfish, or rude, if that's who you are. The chances of finding a man who wants to put up with a lifetime of narcissism and anger are pretty darn low. Remember: Being who you are means being the best version of yourself. If you exhibit these qualities on a regular basis, you should consider getting out of the dating pool temporarily and working on yourself either via therapy or coaching so that when you do start to meet men, you don't ruin potentially great prospects by smothering them with your insecurities and anger.

Do I feel good about the bond and connection we're forming?

Here are two scenarios to highlight the distinction between one woman who feels anxious about a new suitor and one who feels confident and relaxed.

In the first scenario, Mary, a smart, attractive, successful woman, has four dates with Joe. She has great physical chemistry with him but also feels as though she has to try really hard to be the woman she thinks he would like. In between these dates she feels very anxious and on edge. She obsesses about when he's going to call, text, or email, mostly because he's sporadic in his communication. She likes Joe a lot but feels unsure about his feelings toward her. She considers using sex to strengthen his feelings for her. She's so invested in a potential relationship with Joe (even though she doesn't really know him all that well) that she doesn't want to go out with other guys she meets, for fear of ruining what she might have with Joe. She thinks often about how to win or get him and how to become more impressive, more attractive so that he'll just see how great she is. Although she feels she has the power to be sexy with Joe, other parts of her feel constrained.

In the second scenario, Jane, a smart, attractive, successful woman, goes out on four dates with Brad. She feels it's easy to be herself around Brad, and she likes that feeling. In between these dates she feels relaxed, assured, and confident that he'll call, text, or email. She likes Brad a lot and sees that he returns these feelings because he communicates consistently with her twice a week, whether via email, phone, or text. She likes Brad but not to the point where she's already envisioning their wedding. Her feelings don't feel rushed; their relationship is progressing naturally and organically. She holds off on getting physically intimate (as in, intercourse) until she has more information about her feelings, who Brad is, and what he's looking for. Brad respects this boundary. She continues to have a full life, while she figures out what might happen with Brad and as she allows their bond to slowly deepen.

Butterflies vs. termites. Butterflies or anticipatory nerves in the beginning of a new romance are normal; all-encompassing nerves that eat away at your stomach and heart are a sign to re-examine your connection, your feelings, his interest level, and if your needs are getting met.

Let's consider the differences between Mary and Jane.

- Mary feels super anxious about herself and the bond she's forming with a man; Jane feels confident about herself and the great bond she appears to be forming with her new suitor.

- Mary's feelings rush over her in an instant, and she thinks about ways she can change herself or manipulate Joe, as if this guy *has* to be The One; Jane allows her feelings for Brad to progress at a slower pace as she gets to know him and as she continues to open up more of herself to him.

- Mary doesn't feel entirely comfortable being herself with Joe, but she assumes their physical chemistry must mean they are right for each other; Jane feels relaxed on her dates with Joe, as if it's just easy and natural to be herself around him, which makes their physical chemistry grow organically.

- Mary spends her time apart from Joe feeling anxious and uptight, as if the whole world will come to an end if their relationship doesn't work out. Inconsistent communication from Joe makes her feel even more uneasy; Jane looks forward to another date, but she feels relaxed and confident that Brad will call again. She doesn't stop living her life simply because she's met one guy with whom she clicks.

- Mary considers sleeping with Joe as a way to try to solidify a relationship; Jane knows that she doesn't like having sex with a man before they've defined their relationship or at least chatted about what's going on between them, so she patiently waits to see how the relationship progresses.

You will often feel a bit of nerves and curiosity in the beginning stages of dating, especially if you like someone, about when he will call and when your next date will be, but that feeling should not be all-encompassing and burdensome. Mary feels anxious not just because Joe's communication is sporadic, but because there is something off or untenable about her connection with Joe, as though she's just not good enough for him in some way. There is something she refuses to see about how she truly feels around him and she doesn't recognize these feelings as something she shouldn't be experiencing early on. She mistakenly believes that their physical chemistry is an indication of deeper connection. She clings to the idea that nobody better will come around, without stepping back and questioning his interest level or the trajectory of the relationship. Maybe she's ignoring the signs from him about what he's looking for. Maybe he doesn't want to get serious and has said as much, but Mary chooses not to listen to him, thinking she can change him. All the while, she never feels she can truly relax and enjoy herself with him.

Think about your own experiences. Have you ever felt completely on edge between dates, as if your life depended on hearing from a man? Have you ever felt not quite at ease with certain men, despite their being chemistry in other ways? Have you ever felt as though you were holding onto a new relationship that wasn't really going anywhere? (Or maybe you've found yourself rushing into a relationship before even really knowing someone?) Feelings of consistent insecurity in the early stages of dating are a sign that a man may not be the right match for you and/or ready to settle down. How can you be the best version of yourself when you are so concerned about who you have to be in order to get him or what you have to do make the connection stronger?

On the flip side, have you ever felt completely confident between dates with a man, as if you just know that he will call again? Have you felt that your connection with this man runs deeper than just superficial, external ways—ways that give you a feeling of comfort and peace that it's okay to be who you are with him? Have you felt comfortable with his and your pacing of the relationship (not too slow, not too fast)? These are the types of men worth getting to know and opening your heart to, because they are often the ones who allow you to be the best version of yourself.

A "boyfriend-material" man is interested in you for something more serious than just casual dating, hanging out, or hooking up, and he will be fairly consistent in his attentions toward you. He usually will check in a couple times a week between dates whether via text, email, or phone, and he certainly will be consistently asking you out. He's not interested in "playing games." If he goes a week or two without getting in touch and/or setting up a date, leaving you feeling confused or deflated, you probably have your answer regarding either his interest level, maturity, or desire to get serious. (See the forthcoming "LoveTREP checklist," which you can use as a reference while dating.)

Beyond general rules of thumb, though, you should absolutely be checking in with yourself when dating someone new. If you're generally a confident, happy person, and a man you've been dating has you constantly on edge, it's important to recognize and be aware of these feelings, not be dismissive of them. Start paying attention to how you really feel in his presence and when you're away from him. Do you feel confident and relaxed about the connection and bond you're forming, about who you are, and about the pace of your budding

relationship? Or do you feel anxious, on edge, and insecure about the next time you will see him and as though you're not quite good enough for this man? Own and acknowledge your feelings. Listen to your gut—it's trying to tell you something. Are you listening?

Do we value similar things in life?

Similar values are crucial for couples, but this doesn't mean someone who doesn't share all your values is not for you. It means you may have to learn to accept someone who has different values or, at the very least, get on the same page as your partner when it comes to his more deeply held values. You will get an inkling of some of your date's values on the first few outings, but other values will be discovered over time. You will be able to determine what values you can and can't live with as you invest time and energy into dating someone.

Values. Important and lasting beliefs or ideals about what is good or bad and desirable or undesirable.

But what are values?

Think about various aspects of your life. What are some things that are most important to you? Examples include: family, friends, religion, money, politics, reputation, community, career, education, and sex. This list is by no means exhaustive. Just Google *"what are personal values"* and you'll see a bunch of lists pop up to help you figure out what values are truly important to you. You may already have a good idea of what you value from having spent some time in chapter 5 thinking about who you are and what you know.

Examine your values. Let your values guide you to compatible people, but figure out what values are more deeply held versus those that aren't deal breakers for a lifetime partnership.

It is important for the person in your life to share the values that you deem most important, but less strongly held values may not have to be shared.

Get out a pen and some paper and create your list!

Here are some examples of couples who were and were not able to move their relationship forward when it came to differing values:

Couple 1:

One couple I know both grew up religious—he Catholic; she Jewish. Their respective religions were important to them, but he valued his Catholicism more than she did her Judaism and wanted their kids raised in the Catholic religion. Because they fell in love, she decided the value of raising her children Jewish was less important than the happiness she found by being with him.

Couple 2:

Another couple I know came from different monetary backgrounds. She was raised understanding the value of a buck; he was a bit more spoiled, paying less attention to his spending habits. They fell in love with one another, working through their differences on the subject. Ultimately, he became more principled and careful with his spending, because it was a value that was important to her.

Couple 3:

A third couple I know had different values surrounding family. She was very independent from her family, choosing not to spend much time with them; he wanted a ton of family time and to have her be a part of these gatherings. The amount of importance they placed, respectively, on this value ultimately made it impossible for them to be together.

Couple 4:

A fourth couple I know loved talking politics but had drastically different views. They dated for a few months, finding common ground in other areas of their lives, but ultimately the difference in the way they viewed the world was too significant a value for them to be together long-term.

Couple 5:

A fifth couple I know had different needs with regard to children. She wanted kids and he did not. She thought maybe she could get him to change his mind once they were in love and in a committed relationship. But he was still adamant about not wanting kids a year deep into the relationship. She broke up with him, because having children was too important a value on which to compromise.

Couple 6:

A sixth couple I know had differing values when it came to intellectual curiosity. He was an incredible athlete (one of the ways they bonded, because she grew up excelling at sports), but they had little to talk about when it came to the news, the arts, books, pressing societal issues. As she grew older, she began to value intellectual curiosity more than athletics. In fact, she valued it too much to spend the rest of her life with someone who didn't feel the same way.

Steady growth. In entrepreneurial terms, imagine your budding relationship in terms of the growth of a startup: *low-growth, steady, sustainable growth, and hyper-growth.* Low-growth can be problematic because you're not seeing any progress or forward motion. Hyper-growth can also be problematic because too much of a good thing too fast can blind you to certain realities and leave you feeling unprepared. Steady, consistent, sustainable growth is ideal: It allows you and your suitor to get to know each other and sort out your feelings at a reasonable, healthy pace, allowing you to determine if you are really right for each other.

Figure out the values you can't compromise on and the ones with which you can be more malleable. Maybe values surrounding, say, religion and sex are non-negotiable, but you have more flexibility with other values in your life. Maybe he's a night owl and you value being an early riser, but this isn't a deal breaker; maybe he doesn't work out all that much and you value fitness on a daily basis, but, ultimately, this isn't a major issue; maybe he's super neat and you value a more relaxed, messy home, but in the grand scheme of things, it's not a major obstacle to a long-term relationship. There are no right answers, only *your* answers.

Don't expect that a person will match up with everything you value in life, but do expect that the person you end up with will share, respect, and not ask you to change the values you hold dearest.

How is our relationship growing?

Low Growth, Hyper Growth, and Steady Growth

If you do settle into dating one person, it's important to think about the pace of the relationship. Let's look at this in terms of the growth of an entrepreneurial venture.

Low Growth: You've been dating for a few months, but things feel fairly stagnant; your relationship is progressing very slowly if at all. There's no real effort on the part of your new suitor to move things forward even though you've expressed interest in doing so.

With low growth:

- You may be settling for crumbs and unwilling to see the relationship for what it is: a dead-end. You may be compromising on what you want (your vision!), or maybe you convince yourself this is the best you'll ever get.

Hyper Growth: You've been dating for a month and your budding relationship has progressed at warp speed. Your new suitor is already planning your future, saying he loves you, and pushing your feelings along without giving you any space to decide for yourself. You get caught up in the frenzied pace of it all, without even pausing to think about your feelings or reflect on any red flags your new suitor may have displayed. When something grows too quickly too soon, you may not be prepared or ready to deal with the consequences.

With hyper (or rapid) growth:

- You may not be creating a solid foundation from which to grow with this new suitor, rushing hastily into a relationship with someone who you don't know all that well.

Steady Growth: You've been dating for two to three months and your budding relationship feels like it's growing naturally and at a healthy pace. You're taking adequate time to get to know each other and figure out your feelings for one another; there's no pressure from either person to rush things along. It feels like there is a steady upwards trajectory to the relationship.

With steady growth:

- You take the time to get to know each other. You don't rush. You get to know the man's character over time. You make sure his actions speak louder than his words. You enjoy the present moment and watch the relationship steadily progress into something you can feel proud of and safe in.

While there are certainly successful relationships that started out in low or hyper growth mode, *I encourage you to seek out steady growth.*

—⁂—

If you consistently feel good about yourself and have a general feeling of well-being with a man you are dating more seriously, if you feel good about the bond or connection that's growing between you and that the trajectory of the relationship is moving steadily upwards (as opposed to one that feels stagnant or frenzied), and if you share some deeply held values, you can feel certain that you have a strong foundation from which to build. If you are experiencing the opposite, you should really spend some time reflecting on what this relationship is doing for you. You should perhaps consider ending things so as to spend your time and energy on better-suited men.

Strong foundation. If you have a strong foundation, you can go anywhere together. And get through anything together.

Think about the questions posed in this chapter on a recurring basis, free from distraction, whether after meeting someone new or after dating someone specific more frequently. Spend some time in solitude, unplug. Learn from and reflect on, as entrepreneurs do, your thoughts and actions (in this context, the thoughts and feelings you have about your dates and time together and the actions you are taking based on those thoughts and feelings), and apply this knowledge to your experiences as you take small, smart steps forward.

Don't let these questions bog you down while on dates. You don't want to feel distracted while trying to have fun with your date. Simply put aside the questions during your time together and reflect on your experiences afterwards. Whoever is on your Board of Advisors will be there to help guide and support you and keep you on track to maintain your vision.

The LoveTREP checklist

To help guide you even further on your entrepreneurial journey, on the following pages are some checklists to use and reflect on as you are out there dating and experimenting with different kinds of men. It's wise to use these lists as a general reference. Obviously, every dating situation is unique and there's no way for a list to cover the exact context of those situations. So while you can use them to help steer you in better, healthier directions, it will be important for you to also check in with your mentor or therapist or coach to discuss certain situations. For example, if you recently started dating a man and he goes away on vacation for two weeks or his job sends him on a work assignment outside of the country or he had a family emergency, he may not "check in with you at least once a week" as referenced below in "Month One". So it will be crucial for you, at times, to examine context and talk it out with someone. These checklists are a good starting point to have continued discussions.

Also, the checklists break up your dating experience in terms of months one, two, and three, but keep in mind these guides aren't an exact science; rather, they are based on my many conversations working with clients, friends, acquaintances and other dating coaches, my

real-world knowledge in the area of dating and relationships, and, certainly, my own personal dating experiences.

Lastly, there may be overlap with each item from month to month, and not every single item will apply to you or him or your budding relationship. Again, this is not an exact science.

The first checklist applies to your new suitor; the second list applies to you.

Your new suitor

Month one:

Start date: _____   **End date:** _____

	Yes	No
Does my new suitor check in via text, email, or phone at least once a week to say hello?		
Does my new suitor ask for or say yes to dates/outings at least a couple days in advance?		
Is my new suitor interested in spending one on one time with me as opposed to group dates/outings?		
Does my new suitor express that he likes me and/or does he appear eager to see me?		
Does my new suitor seem relatively happy in his life, and does he refrain from talking about conflict in his life, whether it's about exes, family, friends, and/or his job?		

Does my new suitor refrain from judging or being critical of others too harshly?		
Does my new suitor express compliments to me easily and honestly?		
Does my new suitor refrain from sending late-night booty call texts or making late-night booty calls?		
Does my new partner appear to want to get to know me beyond having sex with me?		
Does my new suitor ask me questions, listen attentively, and remember things I say?		
Does my new suitor express sexual interest in me, but does not pressure me to have sex in any way.		
Is my new suitor geographically desirable—is he planning to stay local for the foreseeable future?		
Is my new partner available to commit to me (i.e. not going through a divorce, not recently separated, not in an "it's complicated" relationship with anyone else)?		

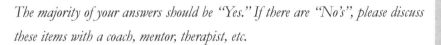

The majority of your answers should be "Yes." If there are "No's", please discuss these items with a coach, mentor, therapist, etc.

Month two:

Start date: _____   **End date:** _____

	Yes	No
Has my new suitor been treating me with consistent kindness?		
Has my new suitor been consistently reliable and trustworthy?		
If I haven't met my new suitor's friends yet, has he expressed interest in me meeting them?		
If my new suitor hasn't met my friends yet, has he expressed interest in meeting them?		
Am I continuing to do fun things together outside of spending time at our respective homes?		
Is my new suitor continuing to open up to me about his life and family? And does he appear to be emotionally available?		
Is our sexual compatibility continuing to blossom?		
Is my new suitor respecting my wishes around sexual intimacy, and is he open to taking things slowly, if that's what I ask for?		
Does my new suitor hint at the notion of me becoming his girlfriend by using the word "we" or by referencing future plans?		

The majority of your answers should be "Yes." If there are "No's", please discuss these items with a coach, mentor, therapist, etc.

Month three:

Start date: _____   **End date:** _____

	Yes	No
Does my new suitor appear to be only interested in me?		
If I met my new suitor online, has he taken down his profile?		
Has my new suitor discussed the status of our relationship or where he sees the relationship going, OR is he responsive to a conversation if/when I broach the subject?		
If my new suitor is dealing with challenging life circumstances, does he appear willing to get help or motivated to grow?		
Does my new suitor express interest in or invite me to meet his family members? Does he express interest in meeting my family members?		
If we've begun having sex, does he like to cuddle and be affectionate afterwards?		
If I have a personal emergency or am struggling with something in my life, does he want to be helpful and is he there for me emotionally.		
Is my new suitor authentically apologetic if he does something to upset me?		
Does my new suitor react calmly and maturely to challenges in both my life and his life?		
Is my new suitor increasingly responsive to my expressed needs?		

The majority of your answers should be "Yes." If there are "No's", please discuss these items with a coach, mentor, therapist, etc.

Now let's move onto you.

You

Month one:

Start date: _____   **End date:** _____

	Yes	No
Am I being authentically me on dates?		
Am I being warm, friendly, and positive on our dates? Am I avoiding hot-button topics (politics, religion, sex, race, etc.) and focusing on lighter subjects?		
Am I asking thoughtful questions but avoiding interviewing on dates? And am I listening to my new suitor attentively?		
Am I doing my best to avoid my specific early stage toxic dating patterns? (These will be individual to you; i.e. checking in too much, trying to rush things, etc.)		
Am I keeping tabs on when my limiting beliefs come up for me and practicing mindfulness – stepping into the moment when an old belief surfaces and choosing to go with my new belief?		

Am I sitting back and receiving from my suitor and not giving too much of myself too early on?		
Am I holding tight to my early stage dating boundaries (these will be individual to you)?		
Do I give my new suitor compliments, tell him thank you, and express that I enjoy his company?		
Am I refraining from talking about conflict in my life?		
Am I refraining from accepting very last-minute dates?		
Am I giving my suitor a chance to work his way into my heart? Am I giving the nice guys a chance?		
Am I refraining from judging or being overly critical of my new suitor?		
Am I refraining from sending late-night booty call texts or making late-night booty calls?		
Am I paying attention to yellow flags?		
Am I pushing myself to go outside my comfort zone (within limits, of course).		

The majority of your answers should be "Yes." If there are "No's", please discuss these items with a coach, mentor, therapist, etc.

Month two:

Start date: _____   **End date:** _____

	Yes	No
Am I continuing to have fun with my new suitor and are we exploring common interests together?		
Am I making sure that we're spending time together outside of our respective homes?		
Am I keeping my life full with activities and time with friends and family, pursuing my hobbies, etc.?		
When I do spend time with friends and family, am I making sure to be present with them and to not sit by the phone waiting for my new suitor to call or text?		
Am I approaching our blossoming relationship from a place of conscious awareness, rather than feeling drawn for unknown reasons to my new suitor?		
Am I offering to pick up or share the bill on dates or activities so my new suitor doesn't think I'm focused on his money?		
Am I suggesting date ideas and helping to plan activities for the two of us to do together?		
Am I continuing to keep tabs on when my limiting beliefs come up for me and practicing mindfulness – stepping into the moment when an old belief surfaces and choosing to go with my new belief?		

Am I starting to open up more to my new suitor and allowing myself to be vulnerable?		
Am I continuing to hold tight to my early stage dating boundaries (these will be individual to you)?		
Am I continuing to make it clear that I enjoy my new suitor's company and that he is making me happy?		
Am I allowing my new suitor to do nice things for me?		
Am I reflecting on if we share similar values?		
If I'm considering having sex with my new suitor, am I thinking about my motives?		
Am I continuing to keep tabs on and reflect on any yellow flags?		
Am I thinking about introducing my new suitor to friends? If I've already introduced him, what sort of feedback am I getting (consider who is giving you feedback and the context of their meeting)?		
If this occurs in month two: If I encounter a frustrating experience with my new suitor, am I communicating with him about it in a calm, mature, feminine way?		

The majority of your answers should be "Yes." If there are "No's", please discuss these items with a coach, mentor, therapist, etc.

Month three:

Start date: _____   **End date:** _____

	Yes	No
If I encounter a frustrating experience with my new suitor, am I communicating with him about it in a calm, mature, feminine way?		
Am I reflecting on if any yellow flags have become red flags?		
Am I continuing to reflect on if we share similar values?		
Do I feel consistently happy with my new suitor, at ease, and like I can really just be me, am the best version of myself with him? To the point where I see myself with this person long-term?		
If my new suitor doesn't bring up the status of our relationship by around the end of the third month, am I thinking about bringing up the conversation in a calm, mature, and feminine way?		
Am I considering introducing my new suitor to family members?		
Am I continuing to express my needs to my new suitor in a calm, mature, and feminine way?		
If we've begun having sex, have I expressed what that means to me?		

If I have a personal emergency or am struggling with something in my life, does my new suitor want to be helpful and is he there for me emotionally?		
Am I authentically apologetic if I do something to upset my new suitor?		
Am I reacting calmly and maturely to challenges in both my life and my new suitor's life?		

The majority of your answers should be "Yes." If there are "No's", please discuss these items with a coach, mentor, therapist, etc.

If your relationship status is still unclear after three months of consistent dating, it's absolutely time to consider having a conversation. Remember your vision of what you want to create in your life—a healthy, happy dating life that leads to a healthy, happy, committed relationship—and hold tight to your desire to create that life. Don't settle for anything less than that vision.

Up Next:

You're going out on dates, and spending time reflecting on your experiences. Now what? Well, the answer is quite simple: Take more action! Keep dating and interacting with men and continue to have more experiences from which you can learn, and then apply that knowledge thoughtfully and purposefully to future actions you take. Like with entrepreneurship, dating is about repetition and *practice*. In

this chapter, I've touched briefly on the idea of practicing, but I'll flesh out the idea in chapter 7.

I'll also discuss the ways successful entrepreneurs build their ventures through *iteration* and *incrementalism*, approaches that are based on taking small, smart steps, so that newly-gained knowledge can be incorporated into future steps.

Chapter 6 Action Steps Checklist:

- ✓ After each first date, spend time reflecting by asking yourself The Three Reasonablies. Complete the lists as outlined above.
- ✓ Depending on your answers, you may choose to go out on a second date with a certain man. After your second date, ask yourself the questions specified earlier in the chapter.
- ✓ Depending on your answers, you may choose to go out on a third date with a certain man. After your third date with a certain man and if you start dating someone more seriously, begin reflecting on (feel free to journal) how you feel about yourself and in general when you're around him, about the connection you are forming and trajectory of the budding relationship, and about shared values (don't forget to create your list), as specified earlier.
- ✓ Use the LoveTREP checklists to guide you in the dating world as you are out there taking action. Reflect

on these lists often and discuss them with members of
your Board.

✓ Don't forget about your limiting beliefs. Have you
been referencing the list you made in chapter 3? Have
you been repeating and working on your new beliefs in
the dating world? Make sure to continue to reflect on
your old beliefs and new beliefs. They don't go away
overnight. Pay them repeated attention.

CHAPTER 7: REPEAT.

(DATE. LEARN. REPEAT.)

"No man ever steps in the same river twice, for it's not the same river and he's not the same man."

– Heraclitus, philosopher

So far, I've discussed the importance of continual action and reflection in the dating world. What comes next? "I'm acting and I'm reflecting on my experiences," you say, "but now what?" Well, the answer is simple: *more action*. Dating is a repetitive, trial and error process, just like entrepreneurship. Every action a traditional entrepreneur takes gives her access to something new, whether it's new relationships or new information about the business world or new self-knowledge, which enables her to move her venture forward, step by step. The same process is true, of course, in dating and for Love TREPs: Every action you take gives you access to something new—new connections, relationships, ideas, information about the dating world, and self-knowledge.

But let me clarify: I don't mean doing the same thing over and over again and expecting different results (that's the definition of insanity).

The entrepreneurial model. Every action you take gives you access to something new, which is information you can learn from and use moving forward.

Definition of insanity. Doing the same thing over and over expecting different results.

You may have been repeating in the dating world for years but feel as though you're not getting anywhere, always back to square one, all the while wondering "What am I doing wrong, and when's it going to happen for me?" If a traditional entrepreneur just repeated her mistakes over and over again, she wouldn't be able to get her business idea off the ground, because in the uncertain business world that exists today, the rules of the game require one to learn from their mistakes, adapt, pivot, and experiment in new ways.

Sometimes, though, it's easier to *repeat blindly* instead of making mindful, purposeful changes, especially for singles. Change is hard, uncomfortable, because the act of making changes in your life is likely to stir up new, challenging questions about yourself. Some women feel safer when they're stuck in their predictable pain because to break free from that pain would force them to become vulnerable in new ways. People can be stubborn when it comes to change, even when making changes and thinking differently is in their own best interest. However, it is also true that "repeated, purposeful, and focused attention can lead to long-lasting personal evolution," so say David Rock and Jeffrey Schwartz in their article "The Neuroscience of Leadership," which discusses how attention density shapes identity.

Personal and social innovation. You will be innovating you, the way you connect with men, and the way you see and approach the dating world.

When I talk about creating change through repetition in your dating life, it is not through blind repetition; in essence, it is through *building* off the knowledge you gain from your previous actions. Let's break the concept of repetition down into two closely related but separate categories —iteration and incrementalism, known in the land of entrepreneurship as iterative development and incremental development. In the context of entrepreneurial dating, I've repurposed these

concepts to be *iterative dating* and *incremental dating*, which are, essentially, forms of innovation.

As a Love TREP, you are going to be innovating through repetition in the dating world, which will change the *way* you date and the *type of person* you bring to the dating world.

Iterative dating

Wikipedia defines the word "iterate" as follows:

The act of repeating a process with the aim of approaching a desired goal or target or result. Each repetition of the process is also called an "iteration," and the results of one iteration are used as the starting point for the next iteration.

Entrepreneurs iterate their processes constantly, experimenting on purpose, not accidentally or without forethought, as a way to build a better product or service, or even in the way they market their product or service.

Iteration. Entrepreneurship and dating are both iterative processes.

So, too, are you going to intentionally iterate as you date, drawing from the knowledge you gain from every action (i.e. your dating experiences, various interactions with men, etc.) to make subsequent actions smarter, getting closer and closer, slowly but surely, to achieving your ultimate vision: a healthy, happy relationship. In this light, you are not allowing dating to become a habitual, mindless experience where you just go through the motions; rather, you are making dating an intentional, purposeful experience. Inevitably, you will stumble, falter; sometimes you may even repeat the same mistakes. But there is

always knowledge that can be gained and put to good use from these wrong turns. When you look at your experiences in the dating world as *iterations* not failures (more on this in chapter 8), you might not be so scared of and exhausted by the process.

The point of iteration is that you're not just blindly repeating the same mistakes again and again without pushing yourself to learn from your experiences. The goal is to recognize how to not make those same mistakes again, to experiment with new ideas and possibilities. It's time to stop *mindlessly* repeating in your dating and love life.

You're going to start doing things differently by intentionally iterating on the *process* of how you date. This is what entrepreneurs do to achieve their visions in the business world, and it's a method that will work well for you in the dating world.

You won't need to iterate on every aspect of your dating life, only the ones you begin to identify are leaving you stuck, unfulfilled, emotionally exhausted, and unhappy. Surely, the knowledge you gained from the exercises and inventories in chapters 3 and 5, and what you're unearthing with the help of a therapist or coach, will help you as you iterate.

Let's look at an example.

Iterative dating in action

What follows is an example of a woman dating iteratively.

Joanna, thirty, got out of a long-term relationship that she had been in since she was twenty-five. She hardly knew who she was and what

she wanted in a man and a long-term partner after she ended it. So she spent several months being single, dating around, and learning about herself, men, and relationships. She made some wrong turns along the way, but was actively learning from those turns, pivoting and adapting (as any entrepreneur must do), and with every experience narrowing in on the man who would eventually be her husband.

Experiential Learning.

Daters can't learn solely about dating by being lectured on what and what not to do. They must go out there and *experience* it for themselves— that is how you innovate.

Let's take a look at the men she met and the experiences she had along her path to achieving her vision of a healthy, happy dating life that leads to a healthy, happy relationship:

Matt:

Joanna met Matt at a friend's party a couple months after her breakup and started dating him shortly thereafter. She liked Matt a lot and he expressed interest in her right away, but there were some qualities about Matt that she identified during her reflection time that worried her. Matt made sarcastic remarks toward Joanna that made her feel bad about herself and confused emotionally, and he argued with her about petty things. Moreover, despite having dated for two months, his communication with her was too sporadic, leaving her feeling anxious about when they would see each other again. It felt like things were always on his terms. She didn't want to see other people, yet she had no idea if he was seeing other people. Eventually, when she confronted him about this, he got very defensive and yelled at her. Joanna began to reflect on why she liked this man in the first place and realized that he had little potential for a long-term commitment. She decided to end things for good and move on.

Tim:

Joanna met Tim through Match.com. They went on three dates and had fun together but when he started contacting her every two weeks instead of once a week, she thought back to her experience with Matt and remembered that she didn't like the way this felt. She also decided that she wasn't going to put her life on hold for him or date only him, when, clearly, his actions were inconsistent with his words. So she decided that she was going to date other men and not place so much importance on Tim. He ended up disappearing completely, but Joanna wasn't as disappointed as she might have been because she had kept a better perspective throughout the time Tim was in her life.

Ben:

Joanna met Ben at a bar when she was out with her friends. Ben was incredibly handsome, charming, gregarious, and very success-ful. Joanna was flattered when he devoted his attentions to her that night and even more flattered that he asked for her number. They had the most incredible first date followed by a late-night, weak-in-your-knees make-out session. On their second date, the attraction was unbearable. She decided to sleep with Ben—her feelings of lust were overwhelming. The next day was awkward, and Ben was acting strange. She said goodbye and waited a week for him to call to no avail. When she contacted him, he was cold and short with her. She was angry and yelled at him, accusing him of using her. As she re-flected upon her experience, she didn't like what she was feeling. She felt used and sad that Ben now wanted nothing to do with her. She was especially confused because she felt their chemistry was on fire.

But there was nothing else to do other than chalk up the situation to experience, grieve a bit, learn from it, and more forward.

Luke:

Joanna met Luke at a bar during an outing with work friends. Luke was tall, dark, handsome, and super charismatic. They hit it off immediately. Luke got her number at the end of the night. They went out a few days later, and their chemistry was pretty amazing. On their third date, at the end of the night, Joanna invited Luke to come inside her apartment for a nightcap. As they got intimate, Luke asked if she had a condom. Joanna was uncomfortable sleeping with Luke so early on because of her experience with Ben. She realized from that experience (and a couple college experiences she had been reflecting on earlier) that she did not like casual sex, that she preferred to be in a relationship before sleeping with a man. In a calm voice, she told Luke how she felt and that she would love to continue to see him but that she wasn't prepared to sleep with someone before a commitment was established. She told him that however he felt about this was okay, but that she felt strongly about it. Luke responded well to her request, they kissed good night, and he went home. Joanna heard from Luke two weeks later—he sent her an email to say hello. Instead of losing her temper on him and accusing him of being a jerk, she responded to the email nonchalantly, mirroring his tone. She never heard from him again. Although she felt upset, she also felt proud of herself for setting boundaries, not backing down from them, and articulating her needs in a mature, calm way. Better that she didn't invest time and energy in someone who was not respectful of her feelings and wishes.

Brian, Dan, Alex, Steve, and Jason:

Joanna met Brian, Dan, Alex, Steve, and Jason through Match.com. Over a three-month period, she went out on first and second dates with all of them but determined they were not the right fit for her, based on her low level of attraction and differing interests and values. She felt these dates were beneficial because they were helping her to learn more about herself and what she was looking for in a partner. She even stayed in touch with Dan, becoming friends with him.

Frank:

Joanna met Frank at the dog park while walking their respective dogs. They flirted a bit and had some laughs together. Joanna had been thinking about how she wanted to try to be more spontaneous in non-sexual ways in her dating life; when Frank asked if she wanted to grab a cup of coffee, she happily accepted. Joanna and Frank had great chemistry and a couple of similar interests. After dating for three months, they became an official couple, waiting to have sex until commitment. The sex was great and Joanna was happy, but when Frank's company told him he'd be transferred from Boston to California, Joanna was devastated. They had a conversation about their status, during which she patiently, calmly, and maturely articulated her feelings and needs. Frank told her that based on his past experiences he did not want to do long distance, especially L.A. to Boston. Joanna wasn't in a position to move, so they mutually agreed to end their relationship. Although sad, Joanna felt good about the relationship she had forged with Frank, and chalked things up to bad timing and luck. She had done everything that felt good and right to her during their three months together. Although the relationship ended, she had no regrets.

Rich:

A couple months later, Joanna met Rich at a photography class she was taking at her local adult education center. Rich was friendly and cute—his temperament reminded her a little of Frank's. She liked that he was more on the reserved side; after her experiences with the gregarious Rich and the type A Luke, she felt that she meshed better with someone who didn't feel the need to dominate. Sure, Rich was not someone to whom she felt an immediate attraction, but they exchanged numbers and went out a week later. Date number one was full of good conversation and laughter. She found his passion for triathlons sexy, and his wit made her forget all about his 5'8" stature—she had always liked taller guys but with Rich she seemed not to care in the slightest. They seemed to have a lot in common, and she thought how fun it would be to explore some of those interests together. On their second date they shared a kiss. Instead of inviting Rich up to her apartment, she said goodbye to him at her doorstep. He texted the next day to tell her that he had a great time and to set up their third date, which they had at a local wine tasting due to their shared interest in wines. Joanna reflected on their time together and liked that she felt confident and at ease with Rich (aside from those early dating butterflies that were starting to build), free to be herself. She always felt confident that he would get in touch with her and it didn't feel strange for her to reach out to him. That felt good to Joanna and she noted this in her journal. They still hadn't slept together, but one night, after two months of dating, while they were hooking up, she told Rich how she felt about sex before commitment. He responded

Me, myself, and I. Iteration is about deciding what's right for YOU! Everyone will iterate differently in their dating lives. When you iterate, you give yourself room and permission to arrive at solutions that work for you in your dating and love life. Each iteration gives you access to new ideas, information, and options that you may not have considered before. In chapter 8, we will talk more about how the concept of failures in your dating and love life can be seen as productive iterations.

that he had already been thinking about this and wanted to be her boyfriend. Joanna was excited to be in an official relationship with Rich. She felt happy and at peace with Rich. Their relationship blossomed over the next several months. A year and a half after they had met at the photography class, Rich proposed.

—m—

Joanna's dating arc is a great example of someone who iterated the way she dated, employing consistent action and thought. She didn't just blindly repeat; she built on the knowledge she was gaining through her experiences. Sometimes she made mistakes, sometimes she faltered, but she used all of these experiences, especially the wrong turns, to her advantage, instead of looking at herself as a helpless victim. Instead of seeing herself as someone to whom things just happened, Joanna started to see her fate as something she had more control over, something she could shape. Eventually, she iterated her way to achieving her vision: a healthy, happy relationship.

Most importantly, this process of iteration is all about YOU deciding what's right for YOU and constantly re-evaluating how to achieve your vision as you go. If Joanna enjoyed, say, having casual sex and was able to compartmentalize her emotions when it came to no-strings sex and was capable of not using sex to manipulate a man's feelings for her, I would have supported her. In reality, Joanna did not like the way casual sex felt, physically and emotionally and had in the past tried to trade sex for love, so she learned from her experiences and created this boundary for herself moving forward in her dating life.

This book *isn't* about me giving you all of the answers (*wait 'x' months before having sex, always wait for him to call you first, never approach a man because you ruin the feminine/masculine dynamic*, and the like). No. The answers must come from YOU, from within.

This book *is* about experimenting with new ideas. It's about doing what feels right to you and being honest about that. It's about avoiding the paths that feel wrong, and, certainly, about understanding why you may go down those paths in the first place (see chapter 3) so as to make better choices in the future. When you begin to feel that *you* are the one making the decisions in your love life, that you have the agency to create your future, you will feel empowered and more confident. You will feel like an entrepreneur in your dating life, building and shaping your love story.

Now it's your turn to think about how you are using iterative dating in your love life.

If you aren't dating iteratively, what can you do to start? What can you use from your What do I know? inventory to facilitate your iterative process of dating? You must make a conscious effort to date iteratively. Make your dating intentional. Don't just repeat; make better, smarter choices from the knowledge you have at hand and from what you are learning along your journey. Be sure to journal your experiences in the dating world as I have done with Joanna.

What about you? How will you use iteration in your dating life to create your love story?

Incremental dating

To borrow once again from Wikipedia, the definition for "incrementalism" is as follows:

Iterative and incremental dating. Iterative dating = improving the *process* of how you date. Incremental dating = improving *you!*

MVP. No, I'm not talking about Mike, Vinnie, and Paulie from the *Jersey Shore* (yes, I confess, I watched the show). I'm talking about *Minimum Viable Product*: A strategy used for fast and quantitative market testing of a product or product feature.

Incrementalism is a method of working by adding to a project using many small, incremental changes instead of a few (extensively planned) large jumps.

Oftentimes, an entrepreneur starts out with what's referred to as a *minimum viable product*: Instead of spending months, years even, perfecting a product, an entrepreneur enters the marketplace with a rather lean prototype; subsequently, she collects customer feedback, learns from her mistakes, and makes small, incremental changes to her product over time. It helps her mitigate risk and create as she goes, as opposed to sticking with some rigid notion of what the product has to be.

In the context of entrepreneurial dating, I want you to view iterative dating as improving upon the *process* of how you date, and I want you to look at incremental dating as more about improving the *product*: you. That's right: *Incremental development is about improving YOU!* At this point, you can think of yourself as a minimum viable product if you wish. You'll start out with the woman you are right *now* and the knowledge you currently have at hand, launching yourself into the dating marketplace, testing and experimenting, observing yourself, paying attention to your thoughts, feelings, and behavior, learning from your experiences, and applying the knowledge you gain to self-improvement. Entrepreneurs use both approaches—they iterate their processes with regard to how they develop and deliver a product or service and they also make incremental improvements to their products and services as they bring them to market.

Please understand, though, that incremental dating is NOT about changing who you are at your core. Ultimately, I want you to love who you are, and you want the man you end up with to love you for who you are, which means all of your wonderful qualities and maybe your

not-so-wonderful quirks. The difference is that a man is more willing to accept your "flaws" or quirks once he's fallen in love with you. For example, if you are an impatient person, it will be important for you to learn how to turn the volume down on that quality, especially in the early stages of dating, because no man, let alone a healthy, whole grounded man, wants to have his feelings for you rushed. However, once you are in a relationship, your impatient nature will most likely surface in various ways, but a man will have more tolerance for this quality and will be willing to overlook your impatience from time to time, because his feelings have deepened. Indeed, this man will love you despite your flaws (maybe he'll even come to love you *for* them). (By the way, the woman I just described is ME!)

So, incremental dating isn't about changing who you are at your core, but it *is* about making yourself a better date, a better person than who you've offered to dates in the past, someone who can connect easier and more effectively with men. So while I'm absolutely not talking about personality transformations or changing your value system, I am talking about small, incremental changes or adjustments that may be holding you back from making deeper connections on dates and in the early stages of dating, changes that you make over time, by degrees, through practice and experimentation. If you date iteratively without also incrementally developing yourself, you make it harder to meet and attract men. A woman could iterate her process of dating for years, but if she's obnoxious, rude, overly snarky, desperate, needy, or whatever else seems to be turning off the men she meets, she'll likely be iterating in the dating world for a long, long time.

There are two ways to think about making personal incremental changes when it comes to your dating experiences:

Incremental dating. Improving YOU! You're not changing who you are and what makes you uniquely you, but you are looking to shine a light on some of your dating weaknesses that have held you back from making better, longer-lasting connections with men.

1) Changing your thoughts and beliefs will change your feel-ings, which affects your behavior (see chapter 3).

2) Changing your behavior will change your thoughts and beliefs, which affects the way you feel about yourself. This method is more in line with the entrepreneurial way of acting your way into thinking, but both methods are important and useful and can be used in tandem.

It will be important throughout this process for you to acknowledge and understand which of your dating weaknesses come from a deeper place. Perhaps qualities such as anger, neediness, bossiness, despera-tion, and the like, may stem from underlying toxic beliefs or uncon-scious places, and as you begin to work on changing those beliefs (chapter 3), so, too, may your attitude and the way you show up in the dating world begin to change. On the flip side, it will also be impor-tant to identify which weaknesses are ones that haven't been practiced enough (being in the present moment on dates, sustained eye contact, conversation skills, and the like), so that you can make a concerted ef-fort to change those behaviors, which will then positively affect your thoughts and feelings.

As an entrepreneurial dater, you can use both methods as you date in-crementally and start to see how they affect one another. Indeed, our thoughts create our feelings and our feelings often determine how we act, but our actions can also determine how we feel about ourselves, which, in turn, affects the way we think. Confused? Keep reading.

For instance, you can begin working on unpacking and changing an internal limiting belief, say, lack of confidence due to not feeling like you are good enough. As you work on changing your thought

processes surrounding this belief, you can affect the external way you present yourself with men (more confidence, more openness, more vulnerability)—so, changing your thoughts changes your behavior. Or you can also think of it the other way around: changing your behavior—pushing yourself to practice flirting and starting conversations with men despite not feeling confident inside—changes your thoughts (seeing successful results changes the way you think about and see yourself); in essence, if you want to look the part, you have to act the part, and then you'll believe the part.

Again, both approaches work well—addressing and replacing beliefs to help make your action more fruitful <u>and</u> taking action to help form new thoughts and beliefs. It's helpful to lean on both approaches throughout your entrepreneurial journey.

Practice, practice, practice!

Oftentimes, women enter the dating world with an entitled mindset or a closed off demeanor. Some have less than desirable interpersonal skills, such as a short attention span or lack of conversation know-how. Some are entirely too impatient and intolerant with men who aren't their perfect matches. Some have forgotten how to flirt. Some have trouble harnessing their feminine side. Some have walls up, preventing men from getting to know who they really are. And some women just aren't well-versed in dating etiquette, feeling completely inept on dates: "What do I say? How much do I share? When do I listen versus talk? What topics do I avoid?" A woman could be a great match for a man with whom she's on a date, but if she's perceived by her date as, say, closed off or too forward or an over-sharer or too cold, she'll likely not be seeing a second date.

Practice.
The key to entrepreneurship and dating is practice.

How is a woman ever going to attract the right man into her life if she has faulty beliefs, bad dating etiquette, and lacks interpersonal skills?

By using incremental development, you are attempting to shine a light on some of the ways you may be making yourself less than desirable in the dating world to potential partners. Ultimately, you want (need!) to connect with your dates, just as entrepreneurs want (need!) to connect with their customers. By incrementally improving your attitude, interpersonal skills, and dating skills, by becoming your best you through practice, you are ironing out the kinks, so that when you do meet a compatible man with whom you could envision a future, you'll attract rather than repel him.

Essentially, I am asking you to *practice dating incrementally.* You can be sure that entrepreneurs practice entrepreneurship. A lot. As Costello and her co-authors point out in their Experience Lab study of entrepreneurs, practice is by far "the most cited and most significant means of building knowledge." They continue: "This is, in part, because of the experiential nature of entrepreneurship, but also because of its complexity; it's hard to anticipate all that one might need to know. So many entrepreneurs act and learn and then repeat the cycle again. This is the obvious reason why serial entrepreneurs tend to be successful—they've literally had the chance to practice entrepreneurship in different contexts."

This is why a goal of incremental dating is to look at every date as a purposeful experience, during which you get to know someone new *and* practice your dating and interpersonal skills. By looking at dating through this entrepreneurial lens you don't go into every dating experience with an extremist attitude—that every date is a burden and

exhausting or that, fingers crossed, this date is going to be The One. The former mindset is an energy sap and the latter creates unrealistic expectations. In essence, you are finding a way to make the process of dating more pleasurable for yourself, which is especially useful when you meet a man for a date and realize it's not a match. Indeed, what if you could turn this notion of dating being a burdensome, tedious process on its face by seeing it as a tool to work on some of the not-so-pleasant stuff, such as things that don't come easy to you—things that show up as dating weaknesses?

Check yourself! A date is not a two-way audition for the next step in life: marriage and babies.

What if you could see dating and your interactions with men as opportunities to enjoy the present moment, make new connections, and work on yourself? When you incrementally date, you will use every experience you have as an occasion to not only learn about and work on yourself but also to practice dating. You can also think about incrementally improving yourself in your non-date interactions with men (for example: chatting up men at bars, parties, events, and the like).

I was able to point out the importance of practicing incremental dating to a former client of mine named Alexis. Alexis had trouble voicing her needs, because, growing up, she was taught to squash her feelings. She went out on a date with a man who she knew right away wasn't a match for her. They were supposed to have coffee at a café, but when they arrived there were no seats. Her date then asked her to sit outside on a bench so they could chat. Unfortunately, it was a really cold, windy afternoon. Alexis sat on that bench seething inside, wanting to request that they find another nearby café but not feeling comfortable doing so. She also felt less of a desire to say anything, because she wasn't interested in him. So she shut down and endured

TREP tip. When you end up on a date with a man and there is no romantic spark, you can also use this as an opportunity to practice relaxing with men, being yourself, and expressing opinions authentically. My guess is you'll notice that you end up attracting men when you are this person. Start to examine the differences between who you are with men you're not romantically interested in versus who you are with men to whom you are super attracted. Do you show up differently with people you are and aren't attracted to? This is important information that will give you a clue about a possible subconscious belief—"I have to be someone different in order to get love"— and then start unpacking that belief and working on it in your dating experiences.

the next hour feeling angry and resentful that they were sitting outside. She was also angry at him for causing her to feel this way and just ticked off in general for feeling like she needed to tamp down her voice. During one of our coaching sessions, I told her that dates with mismatches are the perfect opportunities to practice voicing her needs so that down the road she would feel comfortable doing so with men she liked. Instead of stewing with anger, I told her that the next time around something like that happened, she should speak up in a mature, warm tone and ask if they could find a spot indoors to chat, regardless of her attraction level. She could still end the date politely an hour or so later, but practicing speaking up with even the most harmless of requests would be useful for her self-growth. In the meantime, Alexis could continue to work on reframing her limiting belief about having to tiptoe around men, but she would also need to push herself to act on her new beliefs in similar dating situations in the future in order to fully overcome the belief.

You can also think about incrementally working on yourself in your interactions with men out and about, not *just* on dates. For example, while out at, say, a bar or charity gala, you can practice smiling more if that's something you feel you need to address.

Here are fifty things you can practice while out on dates and/or while interacting with men at events, parties, events, bars, cafes, and so on and so forth. Feel free to add your own suggestions to this list.

1. Conversation and small talk skills
2. Opening up and sharing stories
3. Getting others to open up to you
4. Active listening skills

5. Flirting skills

6. Eye contact

7. Giving and receiving compliments

8. Articulating your goals and dreams in life

9. Articulating who you're looking for and what you're looking for in a relationship

10. Patience

11. Friendliness

12. Warmth

13. Feminine energy

15. Generosity

16. Owning the moment, being present in the moment

17. Not being so attached to outcome

18. Empathy

19. Focus

20. Being more authentic, genuine

21. Developing presence

22. Connecting with someone's mind and heart through personal stories

23. Being playful and easygoing

24. Being vulnerable, letting your walls down

25. Being more flexible and forgiving if your date arrives a little late or does something "wrong" in your eyes

26. Setting healthy boundaries and maintaining those boundaries

27. Pushing past your insecurities whatever they may be

28. Holding yourself accountable for your actions

29. Receiving instead of giving

30. Working on stopping an old belief from taking over when you are triggered by something a man says or does, and replacing it in the moment with a new belief (see chapter 3)

31. Withholding knee-jerk reactions to something harmless your date says or does

32. Letting go and just being

33. Not feeling the need to control every moment

34. How to reject people carefully and gracefully when you're not interested in them and not feel badly about it (that's part of dating). Conversely, how to handle being rejected (it's going to happen!)

35. Not trying to impress someone with your accomplishments and achievements

36. Resilience despite a string of bad dates and thus keeping a positive attitude when your next date comes around instead of lumping him in with other men.

37. Keeping your baggage out of dates instead of dragging it with you and unloading it onto other men.

38. Not oversharing right away

39. Not making assumptions about people before you know them

40. Being adventurous and spontaneous

41. Positive body language

42. Sitting with your anxiety, frustration, or aggravation during a date

43. Not nit-picking everything your date does

44. Recognizing the humanity in your date

45. Touching your date if/when you have interest

46. Knowing when to stop talking and let your date speak, not interrupting

47. Asking questions

48. Being comfortable with awkward pauses—you don't have to fill every moment of silence

49. Stop actively looking for things that are wrong with a date

50. Having fun!

51. Bonus: Acknowledging and praising your strengths and amazing qualities before you go on a date.

The only way to get better at these things or start being the embodiment of them is to *practice them*!

Identify the items from this list or that you feel are your problem areas or certainly add any you come up with, and then commit to practicing those skills on your dates or with men you meet out and about. Whatever you feel are your dating weaknesses, I encourage you to do more focused work on them.

For example, let's say you determine you need to practice sitting in your feminine energy when you're with men, you can do research on the Internet, buy a book, or work with a coach (Allana Pratt is one of my favorites in this area to develop that skill or quality). Or let's say you need to work on your flirting skills in general, you can, once again, seek out advice from books (Rachel DeAlto has a great one titled *Flirt Fearlessly)*, attend a workshop, or seek out the services of a flirting coach. When an entrepreneur doesn't know how to do something to move her venture forward, especially in the early stages of growth, she rolls up her sleeves and starts educating herself. Remember: You are an action-oriented problem-solver!

If you need a hand identifying the areas with which you need help, consider getting feedback from those who know you. Let's talk more about this.

What about you? What things can YOU practice as you date and interact with men. Identify these things and commit to practicing them, whether on dates or interacting with men in non-date scenarios. For example, if you give off an unfriendly vibe, practice smiling more on dates or saying hello to five random men over the course of a week.

Getting feedback about you as a dater

Business consultants, especially those working with emerging businesses trying to get off the ground, will tell you that entrepreneurs are often so focused on the nitty-gritty details of launching a company that they don't have an accurate view of how they are presenting themselves to the world. This is precisely why entrepreneurs turn to consultants, because an outside perspective on strengths and weaknesses is sometimes necessary.

Likewise, many women are clueless as to how they are presenting themselves to dates or men in general. If this is the case with you, an honest appraisal not only of your strengths but also areas of improvement would be useful, so that you can leverage your strengths and improve upon some of your dating weaknesses.

Feedback. The best way to take in feedback:
- Let go of your ego.
- Listen actively and learn.

There are two ways to look at getting feedback about yourself in the context of dating and relationships. You can:

- *Ask your male and female friends* about their perceptions of you as a woman and dater, both positive and negative.
- *Directly ask past boyfriends* about their experiences with and perceptions of you, both positive and negative.

Getting both positive and negative critiques is essential. It's important in your dating and love life to build on your strengths and be conscious of and improve your dating weaknesses. Let's address why this is of importance, before I discuss how to get feedback.

Building on your strengths and the things you are doing well

By acknowledging, celebrating, and valuing your personal strengths you give yourself an extra shot of confidence and a firm foundation from which to grow as you iteratively and incrementally date. Your strengths will be your assets: As you go out into the dating world, you can play to these strengths, allowing them to attract people to you and create opportunities for you. Strengths are also important so that when you inevitably do have to step outside your comfort zone or are feeling anxious about being vulnerable, you can fall back on those qualities that make you feel confident and empowered.

Dating strengths. Acknowledge, celebrate, and build on your strengths.

Healthy self-esteem is crucial in the dating world for attracting healthy partners; part of maintaining and building that self-esteem is celebrating the wonderful qualities about you, never losing sight of them, and working to embody them on a daily basis. You'll have more motivation to date, learn, and repeat when you believe in yourself and that you have great qualities to bring to the dating process.

Take a moment to create a list of the personal strengths that you believe you can reliably fall back on when you're out there in the dating world.

My list of strengths that I brought to dates and my interactions with men were:

1. Good listener
2. Playful/witty banter
3. Empathy; desire to make the other person feel comfortable
4. Flirting
5. Positive attitude

What are your dating strengths? List them out.

What can you do differently?

This is another way of saying: What are some of your personal dating weaknesses that may be getting in the way of making better connections and how can you improve upon these weaknesses?

A common piece of advice you'll hear throughout your life is to "focus on your strengths" instead of your weaknesses. This mantra will serve you well in many respects, and I have encouraged you to celebrate and own your strengths, but at what point does ignoring your weaknesses become a personal liability? We could extend this question to any area of life. If your weaknesses aren't impeding your ability to be successful, in whatever endeavor you're pursuing, then there seems no logical reason to improve upon them. For instance, let's say you're a terrible cook, but being happy and successful in life has no bearing on your culinary skills, and therefore your weakness is not a requirement for success. But, in the context of dating and relationship happiness and success, ignoring an important social skill in which you may be deficient, such as, say, listening skills, can be problematic. If you have terrible listening skills, you're not likely to have much success with dates, because in general men want to feel like you care about and respond to what they're saying. This is the type of weakness with regard to interpersonal skills that you can learn to be more conscious of.

An entrepreneur in the traditional sense can sometimes afford to outsource her weaknesses by partnering with people who have complementary strengths. So, if an entrepreneur lacks bookkeeping skills,

Dating weaknesses. Are there things about you that prevent you from connecting more deeply to men or dates? Pay attention to how you can improve on these dating weaknesses.

she can partner with someone who has an accounting background or, if she has money to spend, pay an accountant to manage the books to fill her knowledge gaps. The dating world diverges from entrepreneurship in this way. While you can enroll others to plug your knowledge gaps and have them support and guide you (your Board of Advisors), you can't outsource your dating weaknesses to other women (unless you have a twin sister and want to play the old switcheroo—kidding). If you lack certain interpersonal and social skills that are vital for communicating and interacting with the opposite sex, you won't be getting many first dates, and certainly no second dates.

Your strengths are easy to hear about, and it's important to be told what's wonderful about you and to love yourself for who you are at your core. It's the critiques, the airing of your dating weaknesses, how you may be presenting yourself and showing up to the world that can be difficult to hear and accept. But often it's the things that you can't see but others can that will be crucial for you to be more aware of. Most entrepreneurs, if they aren't too proud to admit it, will stress the importance of listening to what others have to say when they discuss what goes into launching and building a business. Remember: The end goal is to be able to connect deeply with your customers (men!), and you can't do that unless you are aware of certain weaknesses. This is why practicing is so important.

In a speech at the 2012 Babson Entrepreneurship Forum titled "The 9 Mistakes Entrepreneurs Often Make on Their First Start-up," Bob Davis, successful entrepreneur and the Founder and General Partner of Highland Capital Founders, mentioned that entrepreneurs err when seeking only confirming not disconfirming evidence. "You want everyone to say yeah, you're great, and you're not open to

Clueless. Are you clueless (like Alicia Silverstone in the movie *Clueless*), as to how you may be pushing people away? Maybe those closest to you have some insight.

hearing the truth," said Davis. "When you get excited about your idea or company, it's hard to hear the truth, but the time to hear the truth is *now* for your business. It hurts when a company doesn't work out, because you've invested a lot of time and energy, so the time to do your homework is *now*. Be a prepared mind!"

Now that you understand the importance of feedback, let's discuss the aforementioned approaches to getting it. This is especially useful if you feel you're having a difficult time coming up with ideas on your own.

Ask your male and female friends

Your friends' feedback doesn't have to be taken as gospel. But remember these are their honest perceptions about you (and they still like you), so there's probably some truth in their assessments. Objective insight can be very valuable. It helps us deal with and respond consciously and purposefully to opportunities and challenges. Maybe, for instance, you're not an angry person with them, but your friends notice that the way you interact with other people, men especially, can oftentimes come off as being hostile. Maybe you're quick-witted but those who know you point out that sometimes this may be perceived by others as being condescending or dismissive. Sure, it's hard for friends to know exactly how you behave or come across on dates, but if they've known you for a while, they've most likely heard many of your dating stories and seen you interact with the opposite sex plenty of times. The goal is to get some useful information you can ultimately act on.

A couple years ago, a close friend who was struggling with dating had the courage to ask me if I thought she was too sarcastic with

men, understanding that by asking—especially by asking me—she might not hear what she wanted to hear. She considered that maybe this quality had been interfering with her love life. The truth is her sarcasm is one of the qualities her friends all love about her, but she also may come off as overly snarky and condescending with romantic interests. I was able to point that out to her in a friendly way, so that she was more aware of her sarcasm with men moving forward and could investigate if this behavior was coming from a defensive or protective place.

Before emailing your friends, you should ask yourself the following questions:

- What is it I want to hear?
  - Do you only want to hear confirming evidence of your positive attributes? Do you only want to hear how fabulous you are?
- What is it I need to hear?
  - Do you believe that you need to hear how you can improve yourself, your interpersonal and dating skills, or the way you come across to people?

I encourage you to be open and willing to hear the things you need to hear. If you've been struggling with dating for a while, how will you be served if you continue to be in denial or refuse to understand others' perceptions of you? Pride goes before the fall.

So get started. Send an email to your close male and female friends, asking them one, more than one, or all of the following questions:

- What are my strengths and weaknesses as a dater?
- Where did I go right and wrong with past dates or past relationships?
- Why do you think I'm still single?
- How do you think I'm perceived by men in the dating world?
- Anything else that you think will get to the heart of how men may respond to me as a dater, as a woman?

Ask your friends to be compassionate, constructive, and caring in their responses. By allowing them to suggest both positives and negatives, I think their feedback will be easier to hear. If you want, you can ask them to not focus on physical things like your appearance or weight, for example, but I will say that hearing suggestions about, say, sprucing up your wardrobe or getting a new look or hairstyle can be enormously helpful.

Similar answers? Are you getting similar feedback from friends? Maybe they're onto something.

I want you to know that it takes a ton of strength, maturity, and courage to receive criticism. You are holding yourself accountable for the way you behave and present yourself to the world, and that's not easy to do. This is a real exercise in humility. I applaud you in advance for giving it a shot. It's not easy to hear that you may come across as closed off or needy or obsessive or controlling or a pushover or a workaholic or snarky or hypersexual or distrusting or cynical or too nice or too giving or too accommodating or whatever else doesn't mesh with your self-perception. But I believe you're stronger and wiser when you attempt to examine all aspects of yourself, even the ones you'd rather not face. It may be difficult in the moment to hear certain criticisms, but those tidbits of information can prove to be useful and empowering later on.

If you start getting similar answers from different friends, maybe they're onto something? If you get lots of different answers, try sorting through them and being honest with yourself about which ones really resonate or that you instinctively feel have a ring of truth. You can always talk further with certain members of your Board of Advisors about the deeper origins of some of these qualities.

Once you've identified certain dating weaknesses, start incrementally dating to improve them.

Directly ask past boyfriends or dates

Have you ever seen the movie *High Fidelity*? Made in 2000 and based on the 1995 British novel by Nick Hornby, the film stars John Cusack as a neurotic, record-store owner who, after breaking up with his latest girlfriend, Laura, tracks down a bunch of his exes to understand what it is he keeps doing wrong in relationships. By speaking to each woman, he learns things about himself and eventually realizes that his inability to fully commit has hampered his ability to move forward with anyone. Eventually, he uses this information to help himself commit to Laura fully.

Fun fact. *Empire* magazine voted *High Fidelity* the 446th greatest film in their "500 Greatest Movies of All Time" list. It is also ranked #14 on Rotten Tomatoes' 25 Best Romantic Comedies.

I recognize that what happens in fiction is always easier said than done in real life. But if you have an opportunity to gather feedback directly from your past "customers," I encourage you to seize it. This doesn't necessarily mean tracking down former flames from your teen years who live halfway across the country and who you haven't talked to in ages or exes with whom you parted badly. But if you happen to be friendly with or still in touch with more recent exes or guys

you briefly dated, what can it hurt to send a quick email asking what his experience with you was like during the time you spent together.

Of course, I understand that sometimes two people are just not compatible, so you may get feedback from exes or past dates that serves no other purpose than to confirm the fact that you were two very different people. Again, the goal of all of this is to not mold yourself into the perfect mate or date based on the specific preferences and needs of every guy you go out with. Rather, the idea is to bring to your attention certain qualities or dating weaknesses that aren't necessarily representative of who you are, what you're all about, and what you want to put out into the world and how they hamper your capacity to form healthy bonds or connections with men, short-term and long-term.

Exploration. Think of yourself as being in exploration mode, where you are testing out and experimenting, incrementally, with new ways of thinking and different ways of behaving with men. As you create new experiences for yourself, you will take action, and learn from your action to guide future action.

A former client of mine named Alison asked Brad, a man she had dated for a few months, for this type of feedback. They parted on fairly amicable terms, mutually, but Alison was having trouble forming deeper connections with men in her love life post-Brad, so she asked him if there was any feedback he could give her about how she showed up in their short-lived relationship. Brad was thoughtful and honest in his response. He said it was difficult getting her to open up and communicate; even months into dating her, he experienced Alison as very closed off and that made dating her difficult because it made him not to want to open up either. Alison was grateful for this feedback and we worked together to understand where her anxiousness about vulnerability came from and how to start opening up slowly and courageously with new men she was meeting.

I get it: It takes a bold person to ask past dates and boyfriends these questions. Moreover, they may have no interest in responding. But if you can muster the courage and are open to receiving this sort of feedback from former flames, I say go for it. Be the star of your own *High Fidelity*.

Incremental dating in action

Now that you've identified things you can practice while dating, let's look at a couple of examples of women who employed incremental dating in different ways.

Example 1:

A client of mine named Marcy was successful in every area of her life: great job, lots of friends, awesome condo, fun hobbies. But when it came to meeting men, she couldn't seem to make things happen.

Until, that is, she asked her friends for feedback on why they thought she was still single. With compassion, her friends pointed out that she sometimes belittled men by the things she would say and the ways she would act around them. Almost as if she gave off an air of superiority. Although a bit difficult to hear, Marcy realized that this very well could be part of the reason she was still single at thirty-five.

She reflected on her past experiences and acknowledged that she did have a tendency to be overbearing, critical, fussy, and overly opinionated, especially early on in the dating process. She realized that this behavior came from a fear of being hurt. What man would want to settle down with Marcy when he feels like he is being picked apart or can't get a word in edgewise or feels unable to express his opinions without being jumped on?

So she started practicing being more relaxed on dates, allowing a man to finish his thoughts on any given subject. When she felt the urge to make a snarky comment or one-up him, she would catch herself in the moment, hold back, smile, and let it pass.

While this was difficult and took lots of practice on multiple dates, eventually she worked hard enough on it that she started seeing more success in her dating life: men feeling relaxed in her presence; more second date requests; more enjoyable dates.

Again, this isn't to say that if you are an opinionated, strong-minded woman you need to change who you are at your core. No! I am simply encouraging women to take a look at themselves in the mirror and figure out what things about them are holding them back from making better, stronger connections with men. I would never want Marcy to become bland and unopinionated, but I did encourage her to first, understand if those qualities that may be turning men off were coming from a place of insecurity and a closed heart and why that may be, and second, to find a balance between being her authentic self, which meant not going so far in one direction that she becomes unpleasant to be around and not so far in the other direction that she loses what makes her, well, Marcy.

Example 2:

After being prodded, a former client of mine in her early thirties got to the heart of some of her limiting core beliefs about men. Because Kara had been betrayed by a cheating ex, she was very distrusting of men, anticipating that all men would do to her what her ex did. Consequently, she went into the dating world cynical and guarded,

always on the lookout for the worst in men. Kara was suspicious of men even before they had done anything to deserve her suspicion. Eventually, she fessed up: "I tend to give men a hard time when I meet them."

So instead of keeping an open mind with men she was meeting and allowing connections and relationships to naturally progress and unfold, she preemptively found them guilty, sabotaging any real connection that could have been made in the process. Needless to say, that approach was turning men off. They could sense her guardedness and suspicion on dates and that made them feel uncomfortable, because they felt like they were being constantly tested and scrutinized.

As we continued to meet, Kara started working on replacing her old, limiting core belief about men with the following: "Just because I couldn't trust my ex to do right by me doesn't mean that all men are untrustworthy. I have to give them a chance. I might still meet men who are untrustworthy, but I might meet a ton of great, trustworthy guys. Those are the men I will put my time and energy into; the other ones aren't worth it."

And then she practiced her new belief by going out into the dating world and giving men her trust and an open heart until they proved otherwise. It wasn't always easy to keep her old beliefs at bay, especially when she felt triggered. For instance, when a man would ask for her number, that might have triggered her to slide back into her old belief: "I don't trust him; don't be happy because he'll never call." But she remained compassionate with herself, and during those triggering moments pushed herself to switch into her new mindset: "Cool. A man asked for my number. Maybe he'll call; maybe he won't.

Either way, dating is fun and I'm a good catch. If he doesn't call, it's not about me. The only thing I can do is control how I behave and think." This mindset became easier for Kara to step into over time, eventually becoming second nature.

Kara felt just by tweaking her mental model in this way and practicing her new beliefs while out and about, she was more relaxed, more open, more optimistic, more adventurous, and friendlier with men. In turn, she felt she was attracting more trustworthy men than ever before.

Example 3:

Let's now take a look at how Susan used incremental dating in her love life.

Susan is a twenty-nine-year-old woman who got out of an unhealthy, long-term relationship a year ago. She found the dating scene to be difficult and exhausting and was starting to become a bit jaded. She really wanted to meet someone but was having a tough time meeting anyone she wanted to go out with. In the past year since her breakup, she had only been out with three men and while she had some interest in all three, none asked her for a second date. She wasn't sure what, if anything, she was doing wrong. But she was motivated to find out. Rather than sit on her couch waiting for things to change, praying for someone to find her, she decided to employ incremental dating.

Susan accepted a date from any man that she met or with whom she was set up who seemed reasonably interesting and attractive. She also became a lot more open-minded about men on Match.com. She

signed up for a year membership and committed to spending at least thirty minutes a day searching for matches, responding to emails, and reaching out to men she thought might be good matches. At the very least, she could give her potential suitors an hour of her life for, say, a drink or a cup of coffee.

Here's a closer look at the men she met in a one-year period and what she learned along her entrepreneurial journey.

Jared:

Susan was introduced to Jared through a mutual friend. When they met for their first date, she thought Jared was cute, but he wasn't exactly her type. She thought they had a pretty good time together and was willing to go out on a second date to see what could happen, but Jared never called. She thought to herself, "Jeez, a guy who I didn't even really like had no interest in me. What gives?"

Randy and Doug:

Similar situations occurred with Randy and Doug, both of whom she met through a co-worker.

Intermission:

At this point, Susan was curious to know what her female and male friends thought about how she may be coming across on dates or with men. She asked for honest, forthright feedback. Although none of her friends had witnessed her out on dates, they had seen her interact

Learn by doing. Experiential learning is the most effective way for daters to learn and innovate in their dating and love lives.

with men at bars and various outings ever since her breakup. Here's what they had to say:

- Her body language often appeared closed off (arms folded, turned away from people).
- She tended to have a frown too often on her face when listening to people.
- She was often impatient with men she did not find immediately attractive.
- She had a negative attitude about men; she came off as jaded.
- On occasion, she could be overly snarky/sarcastic—maybe be seen as intimidating.
- She got too political too quickly with new people.
- When she did meet men she was into, she tended to share inappropriate details of her life too quickly.

Wow! Susan was shocked she came off this way. She hadn't even realized she was doing these things or that this was how she could be perceived. Many of her behaviors had become ingrained over the years for a variety of reasons, and she admitted that they could be holding her back from moving forward with men in a positive way. By shining a light on some of these behaviors, Susan was able to think more pointedly about why she exhibited those behaviors in the first place, where they came from, and, consequently, change her mindset and approach to dating. She took the constructive criticism and observations from her friends well, even though it was difficult to hear. She even made an appointment with a therapist to get a better understanding of what was holding her back. Maybe there were deeper reasons as to why she had such a negative attitude with men, and she was ready to explore those possibilities.

Back to the show:

After hearing this feedback, Susan told herself that she was going to make an effort with any and all future dates to improve her behavior and attitude. She also pushed herself to start practicing new ways of behaving toward men while out and about (bars, parties, etc.). When she felt herself slipping back into her old ways, she'd be compassionate with herself but do her best to reverse course.

Connor, Mark, Hank:

Susan decided that on her next three dates, her goals were to smile, be pleasant, and be interested in what her dates had to say, no matter what her attraction level might be. Connor and Mark were Match.com dates and she met Hank at a friend's party. On their first dates, she smiled a lot, laughed often, and was as friendly and warm as possible. She pushed herself to be interested in what they had to say, and to not jump on things they said with a sarcastic comeback. Despite her attraction levels being pretty low, she found the dates useful—she was learning how to become open and warm, and how to flirt. Post-dates, she found herself feeling a bit more confident and in control, viewing the world through a different, more entrepreneurial lens, feeling all-around more optimistic about dating.

Dan:

Susan met Dan on the subway platform. They started chatting. She thought he was nice and they had a common interest: running. They exchanged information, and, after a couple emails, set up a coffee date. On their date, she realized she didn't feel romantic

chemistry, but she did enjoy talking about their shared love of running and Ultimate Frisbee. She told herself while on their date that although there was no spark or reasonable level of physical attraction, she could use this date as an opportunity to practice her conversation skills by asking questions and talking about things that mattered to her. She appreciated the opportunity to spend time with a nice man, allowing her to practice skills she realized she needed to work on.

David:

David was another Match.com guy. She was looking forward to their date, especially because David had been making her laugh a lot over emails and text. When she met David she was shocked at how quiet he was. Could this possibly be the same man with whom she had been communicating? Although disappointed, she told herself to smile throughout the date. Susan also used this opportunity to work on her empathy skills. Maybe he was nervous? Maybe she needed to peel away a few layers before getting him to be that funny person with whom she had been communicating? Susan spent the next hour smiling, asking David questions, cracking jokes, getting him to open up, and attempting to put him at ease. It wasn't a love match, but she forced herself to see the date as an opportunity to relax, put someone else at ease, and work on herself.

Intermission:

Susan loved politics. She was a fairly conservative thinker and very opinionated on the subject, but living in New York, a very liberal state, the topic was often a source of friction. For some reason,

though, she couldn't help herself—when she met new guys she felt she had to broach the subject despite how uncomfortable it made people feel. Also, as mentioned, her friends stated that she had a tendency to share too many details about her personal life way too soon when she did meet someone she liked. After hearing this feedback, she promised herself that she would stick to less heated topics and not feel the need to tell her life story, especially on the first few dates. She contemplated that maybe she did this as a way of turning men away before they had a chance to turn her away, that she could use this as an excuse as to why they weren't right for her instead of allowing men to get to know who she was aside from her political views and family secrets. She talked with her therapist about this possibility as well.

Back to the show:

Brett and Joe:

Susan met Brett through a family friend and Joe through a work colleague. She had good chemistry with both of them within fifteen minutes of their respective first dates. Susan practiced keeping the subjects of conversation lighter and not spilling any details about her life that might make them uncomfortable. Both Brett and Joe asked for second and third dates. She gladly accepted and practiced again, getting to know these men and allowing herself to slowly open up and showcase other aspects of her identity apart from politics and personal drama.

Brett ended up moving home to another state to deal with a family issue, and she realized that despite her chemistry with Joe, he was not

at a point in his life where he was ready to settle down. But she was thankful to them both for the experiences she had. She viewed her time with both men as opportunities to work on herself and her dating and interpersonal skills.

Paul:

Susan met Paul through Match.com. They had a lot of common interests and she thought he was cute from his pictures. They exchanged a few emails before making a date for a walk in the park. Susan's dating mindset and approach had improved considerably over the last several months. She felt more confident in her abilities to relate to men, to enjoy conversations with them, to open up with dates and get them to open up to her; consequently, she was able to sit back on dates and relax more. She was looking forward to practicing all the skills she had incrementally gained during her many dates. When she met Paul, she was pleasantly surprised. While he wasn't exactly as tall as she would have liked (he never lied about his 5'9" stature), there was an attraction there that helped them off to a good start. Over the course of the next two hours, as they wandered through the park, she became even more attracted to his wit and his intelligence. She was confident in her ability to be open and warm. She flirted. She smiled. She asked questions. She stayed away from her old routine of politics and over-sharing and just let the conversation flow and meander wherever it happened to go. Susan was happy to accept a second date from Paul. A few months later they were in a serious, committed relationship, having fun together, laughing, and falling in love.

What about you? How can you use incremental dating in your dating life to create your love story?

The point, of course, of all of Susan's experiences, wasn't to become the *perfect* date so that she'd always get a follow-up date even with men

in whom she had no interest. The point was to practice becoming a *better* date, a nicer person, more open to the journey and less focused on the end result. Ultimately, she met a great man, because she worked on getting to the point where she could attract that right man to her and recognize him when he showed up. Without that practice, she might never have invited his interest.

Dating, like entrepreneurship, is a continuous learning process, during which a person evolves and grows, as their dating life grows. By incrementally working on improving yourself and your dating skills, you are practicing dating and thereby positioning yourself to eventually receive and give love to the right person.

Date. Learn. Repeat.

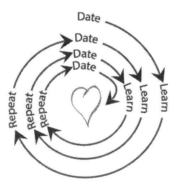

(My Date. Learn. Repeat model of entrepreneurial dating.)

The Date. Learn. Repeat. model. Dating is a continual learning process, during which you and your ideas about dating, love, and relationships evolve over time.

—⟆⟆—

It's time to stop complaining about your dating experiences and start creating better ones and that means starting with you. In an article and accompanying video for *Fast Company*, Tina Roth Eisenberg, the

founder of Swiss Miss and a serial entrepreneur, talks about living by this basic principle: creating instead of complaining. Her number two mantra is: Don't be a complainer, make things better. "If I find myself complaining about the same thing over and over," she says, "I either need to let it go or do something about it."

If you find yourself complaining over and over again about dating, about your lackluster love life, you need to take the reins and find a way to turn your negative experiences into positive, purposeful ones. Because let's face it: You'll probably have myriad dates with men you're not interested in. In fact, according to a 2010 study done by UKDating.com, the average number of dates a woman will have before she finds the man she will marry is 24. The study also found that 7 percent of women have been on between 41 and 60 dates before finding someone to share their life with. And 1 percent of women said they had been on between 61 and 80 dates before finding their match. So, considering you'll be dating a lot, how can you use those experiences purposefully? Iterative and incremental dating can aid you in this way and put the power back in your hands.

One final note about repetition: In order to have lots of experiences through which you can iteratively and incrementally date, I highly encourage you to date more than one person at a time. I illustrated this concept in several earlier examples, as the women remained open to dating other people while they figured out their feelings for a particular man and to see if he was commitment-minded and had good character.

If you are not used to dating more than one man at a time, it may feel awkward. But there's absolutely nothing wrong with this

Evolve.
Traditional entrepreneurs are constantly evolving as leaders, human beings. According to Ed Hess, author of *Grow to Greatness: Smart Growth for Entrepreneurial Businesses* and a professor at the University of Virginia's Darden School of Business, in an interview for the April 2012 issue of *Entrepreneur*, entrepreneurs become leaders through a continuous learning process. "It's more than a job. It's a personal transformation."

approach—men do it all the time and don't experience any guilt or shame whatsoever. Until you have the "defining the relationship conversation," you are not obligated to turn away other dates or stop looking and flirting with other men.

Up Next:

As you date iteratively and incrementally, your goals are self-discovery, self-improvement, and to make smarter decisions. However, undoubtedly, you *will* make a lot of wrong turns and "mistakes" on your journey. You have been used to viewing these wrong turns and mistakes as failures, but in chapter 8, which begins Part III of this book, I will discuss how to view your failures in your dating and love life as assets. I will teach you how to reframe failure and think differently about risking in your dating and love life.

Chapter 7 Action Steps Checklist:

- ✓ Start dating iteratively by identifying ways you can change with regard to the *process* of how you date.
- ✓ Start thinking more deeply about or even journaling your experiences as you *iteratively* date. By writing down and reflecting more pointedly about your experiences, you will start to see how you can use iterative dating in your love life to make better, smarter choices that work for you.
- ✓ Identify and create a list of your dating strengths and celebrate these qualities about yourself. Embody them on all

of your dates, in your various interactions with men, and in your daily living.

✓ Identify and create a list of certain dating weaknesses or skills you can work on, and then use *incremental* dating to *practice*; by creating a tangible list of skills you want to work on, you will have a better chance of holding yourself accountable. You can choose any of the suggestions from my list of fifty that you might need to work on or add any you feel are your problem areas. You must commit to practicing those skills on your dates or even with men you meet out and about. Think about delving further into specific areas of improvement by purchasing a book or attending a class.

✓ If you are having trouble identifying your problem areas/weaknesses, ask some friends and/or past boyfriends or dates for their thoughts.

✓ Start thinking more deeply about, or even journaling, your experiences as you incrementally date. Write about your progress as you date, as I have done with Susan.

✓ Don't be afraid to date more than one man at a time until you've established a committed relationship.

PART III: FACILITATING YOUR ENTREPRENEURIAL JOURNEY

TREP TUTORIAL

Let's review what I discussed in Part II of this book:

- I introduced you to the Date. Learn. Repeat. model of entrepreneurial dating, providing you with a framework from which to execute your vision.
- Within that model, I discussed the importance of taking action in the dating world (acting your way into thinking), and explained that the best supplement to the action you'll be taking is a keen understanding of yourself. To that end, I asked you to start the process of taking action by gathering the knowledge you already have at hand. You created inventories answering the questions: Who am I? and What do I know? I encouraged you to think about when to use prediction in your dating life versus taking action, and to think about how you can use both strategies together. Also, I asked you to think about what you want in a man—encouraging you to be flexible in some of your ideas, expectations, and standards—so that when you do take action, you will have additional information to help guide you. Finally, I asked you to develop powerful affirmations (your personal elevator pitch and personal brand) that you can repeat to yourself as you are taking action in the dating world.
- I showed you how to use the power of reflection to your advantage by having you think more deeply about the experiences you are currently having in the dating world. I offered you several questions to consider during your reflection time.

- I showed you how to take small, smart steps in your dating life by practicing iterative and incremental dating, so that you push yourself to date smarter.

CHAPTER 8: FAILURE IS YOUR GREATEST ASSET

"Whenever something negative happens to you, there is a deep lesson concealed within it."

– Eckhart Tolle, author and spiritual guide

In Part I, I discussed ways to prepare for your entrepreneurial journey to find love.

Failure. The condition or fact of not achieving the desired end or ends: the failure of an experiment.

In Part II, I walked you through the process of executing your entrepreneurial journey to find love.

Now, in Part III, I'll be discussing ways to facilitate your entrepreneurial journey to find love.

In this chapter, I'm going to teach you how to reframe your "failures" in dating and love as learning opportunities and how to take smart risks.

According to Professor Heidi Neck, in an article she wrote for Babson's website titled, "Reframing Failure as Intentional Iteration:

New Research on How Entrepreneurs Really Think," iteration, in an entrepreneurial context, is, at its core, a "cyclic process of prototyping, testing, analyzing, and refinement. It's a way of building knowledge through experimentation: try something, see what happens, learn from it, and then adapt or pivot." But as Neck explains, there's one major problem inherent in this iterative process, and it's one that entrepreneurs deal with often: fear of failure. Indeed, for traditional entrepreneurs, failure is a part of the game. Just look at the statistics: According to the U.S. Bureau of Labor Statistics, American businesses founded in March 2008 had a 50.8 percent five-year survival rate. That means half of all businesses don't make it past five years.

TREP failures. Treps embrace failure. They even have a conference called FailCon, a global series of conferences, at which tech treps share stories of their defeats.

Neck continues:

> There's an old catchphrase that entrepreneurs are supposed 'to fail early and often.' In other words, to be innovative entrepreneurs are told they must not only celebrate success, but also expect and embrace failure. There's an important lesson in this, but one that gets lost in translation. Businesses will fail, and accepting this, and learning from others about the experience of crashing a company are central components of being an entrepreneur. But, the predominant use of the term failure is really framing another important aspect of entrepreneurship that's little understood and discussed in entrepreneurial circles. The entrepreneur experience is rarely smooth or predictable. It requires iteration and experimentation. Yet, the language given to describe this aspect of the experience is centered around the concept of failure: setbacks, false starts, wrong turns, and mistakes. Many entrepreneurs are just not wired for iteration.

What's beneath your What If'ing? Beneath the What If's to the left lurks fear: fear of being vulnerable; fear of being lonely; fear of discovering things about yourself that you'd rather not; fear of having to overcome obstacles on a consistent basis.

Surely, the same can be said for singles' experiences in the dating world, a place that often generates as much anxiety as the business world. Many women aren't wired for failure in the dating world, because they associate it with pain, heartbreak, emotional anguish, and frustration. They fear failure so much they run from it instead of facing it head-on. In order to avoid the kind of vulnerability that comes with failure, women will erect walls, enact various defense mechanisms, self-sabotage in order to push others away before being pushed, or they might even shrink from dating entirely. Maybe you've "What If'd" yourself to death: *What if I start dating this guy and he dumps me? What if I never find the right man? What if I blow it with this incredible new guy? What if I'm just not cut out for being a girlfriend or wife? What if I fail again for the umpteenth time and feel like giving up?* And on. And on. And on.

Are you this What If'ing woman terrified of failure? Where has this approach gotten you?

A Mindshift

What if you could start to view failure in your dating and love life differently?

In this book, I have already asked you to undergo various mindshifts. Now, I want you to engage in another one about the way you see failure in your dating and love life. As a love entrepreneur, a Love TREP, I want YOU to learn how to *embrace* failure—past, present, and future—in your dating life, not fear it.

Are you a What If'er? What If'ing can hinder you from getting what you want in life, because it prevents you from taking action.

The virtues of failure. In a video on Makers.com, newswoman extraordinaire Christiane Amanpour extols the virtues of failure. Amanpour tells the audience: "I've always believed, perhaps not at the time when it was happening, but I strongly believe in mistakes, I believe in setbacks, I believe in failure to an extent because you cannot learn and you can't push forward unless you have that and I see around me, so many of the younger generation, even women, who are afraid to fail and who think that any kind of setback is a career-altering, life-altering

problem as
opposed to an
opportunity."
Amanpour could
just as easily have
been talking
about dating and
love.

Embracing failure doesn't mean you won't experience pain or heartbreak or loneliness or emotional anguish or frustration when you do fail or suffer disappointments, but it does mean you will no longer be a slave to your fears, and you will use them to push forward. As long as you're committed and have the desire to keep trying and learning so that you can make better decisions, you will be able to see your failures as purposeful steps along your journey. Often the most fulfilling things in life are ones that we have suffered for or failed at the first few times around. Your failures in your dating and love life can and will lead you to your successes. When viewed in this light, you won't be as scared to risk failure; you'll be less likely to run from it when it stares you in the face.

Consider once again the insight of Bob Davis, who said in his presentation at the Babson Entrepreneurship Forum, "Entrepreneurship is about perseverance. The life of an entrepreneur is about setbacks, disappointments, and failures, but the people who do persevere and overcome can look back and say 'Wow, I built that.' It's a real sense of satisfaction, a willingness to get knocked down, pick yourself up, dust yourself off, and keep at it." Mr. Davis very well could have been talking about my dating life. Throughout the countless rejections and disappointments, the intermittent periods of heartbreak, the nights spent crying, facing my deepest fears, I always persevered. I always rebounded, continuing to learn about myself and the world around me, from every setback. Eventually, I found someone amazing. I am now able to look back on my journey with a sense of pride and accomplishment. In a sense, I built my dating and love life.

I've worked with women who dated countless Bens or Lukes before they met their Rich (see previous chapter's section on iterative dating). Sometimes it takes repeated failures and wrong turns before a woman

figures out that she no longer wants to feel unhappy and unfulfilled, until she decides that she's going to iterate, not just blindly repeat. Surely, a woman may engage in iterative *and* incremental dating and still have setbacks here and there, but if she's committed to the process, she'll rebound and get back on track. Likewise, your entrepreneurial journey won't be perfectly linear. You're going to need to constantly reevaluate as you go until you eventually achieve your vision.

Failure in your dating and love life is the new success, ladies! Just as traditional entrepreneurs will fail, make mistakes, and go down wrong paths, so, too, will Love TREPs. Let me say this loud and clear: YOU. ARE. GOING. TO. FAIL. It's inevitable.

In fact, when you look more closely at my Date. Learn. Repeat. model of entrepreneurial dating, you'll see that the graphic looks more like this:

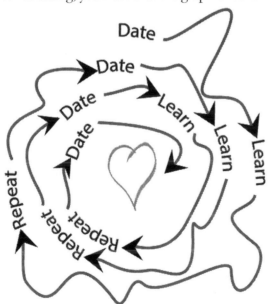

(My Date. Learn. Repeat. model of entrepreneurial

dating under a microscope.)

Divorcees POV. Learning from your failures is instrumental in self-growth. Just ask a divorced person. In a piece featured in the *Wall Street Journal* titled "Divorce's Guide to Marriage" author Elizabeth Bernstein writes: "People who lose the most important relationship of their life tend to spend some time thinking about what went wrong. If they are at all self-reflective, this means they will acknowledge their own mistakes, not just their ex's blunders. And if they want to be lucky in love next time, they'll try to learn from these mistakes." We shouldn't be waiting for a divorce to happen to engage in reflection. Most of us have had failures in our dating and relationship past we can learn from and use to make better decisions.

Ignore what you've been taught. From an early age, we have been taught to avoid failure at all costs. Failure means vulnerability and rejection—God forbid we experience these things. Remember: Our failures give us powerful information we can use. They make us stronger.

Stop running! When you run from things in your life out of fear of failure (in both business and love) you squelch innovation and creativity.

Failure—the setbacks and wrong turns and disappointments—is a part of the process of dating. Your single status and the myriad failures you've experienced can thus be seen as opportunities. What can you learn from your past and current relationships and dating experiences to help you become a better, more self-aware dater and partner?

Let's continue to break down how I want you to view failure in your dating and love life moving forward. Neck argues that to reframe failure for entrepreneurs, three things need to be done:

- de-education;
- planning to pivot;
- de-risking.

I will argue that these same three concepts, in the context of failure, can apply to your dating and love life.

De-education

Neck argues that de-education around the notion of failure is necessary for entrepreneurs to maintain a positive outlook and to stay motivated to achieve their vision. "Framed as failure," Neck writes, "entrepreneurs develop fear for this part of the experience. "Reframing [failure] as intentional iteration allows entrepreneurs to develop the skills needed to respond to the uncertainty they face."

Women who frame their experiences in the dating world purely as failures and mistakes, who refuse to learn from and see value in their experiences and their experimentation, are resigning themselves to

a powerless fate. When you reframe your failures as a series of iterations, you choose to see yourself as a change-maker rather than a victim, your mistakes as opportunities and assets rather than burdens.

One way to de-educate yourself from the concept of failure and to
begin the reframing process is to create what I like to call a "Thank
you ex-boyfriend letter."

Thank you ex-boyfriend letter

An excellent way of combating negativity in your life is by offering
gratitude and appreciation. Interviewed in the January 2013 issue of
Entrepreneur, Barbara Fredrickson, author of *Positivity* and a professor of psychology at the University of North Carolina, concurs with
this line of thinking, echoing Neck's thoughts on reframing failure.
Fredrickson believes by countering negative thoughts with positive
ones, using emotions such as gratitude and appreciation, you can effectively reframe adversity. "Positive emotions expand awareness and
attention…when you're able to take in more information, the periph-
eral vision field is expanded. You're able to connect the dots to the
bigger picture," and this is critical for anyone looking for an opportunity to solve a problem, explains Fredrickson, who co-wrote a report on bouncing back from business failures titled "Beyond Hubris:
How Highly Confident Entrepreneurs Rebound to Venture Again."
She continues: "There's really solid evidence that the positive emotions you feel today predict tomorrow's and next week's and next
month's success, health, and quality relationships, because they build
your resources and resilience." And, as article author Joe Robinson,
a work-life trainer at Worktolive.info, writes with regard to resources, "[Fredrickson's report] suggests that the resources generated by

Be an iconoclast in your love life.

New experiences can trigger the fear response. The key to pushing through, according to Gregory Burns, author of *Iconoclast*, is reframing negative scenarios. "Uncertainty always has two sides: the possibility of gain and the possibility of loss," Berns says, citing the example of a bad financial statement. "If the first instinct is, 'I'm losing money; I gotta fire someone,' that's a fear response, and that will lead to contraction of your business. Or you can look at the other side of the equation. 'Let's think about how we could increase revenue.' That's more of a positive frame."

positive emotions can help people overcome setbacks and start new ventures."

I wrote an essay once for the *Huffington Post* titled "Thank You, Ex-boyfriend," (see appendix for essay) in which I found ways to thank all of my significant exes, especially the ones who caused me pain and heartbreak. The essay showed readers how to let go of past mistakes and wrong turns and turn them into growth opportunities.

I now want *you* to take a moment to thank *your* ex-boyfriends.

- Create a list of men you deem had a significant impact on your life.
- Write down how you are thankful to them, especially the ones who caused you pain and heartbreak, and certainly the ones with whom you had positive experiences.
- If you haven't had many boyfriends, simply choose men with whom you interacted in a sexual or romantic way— men you dated, flings, one-night-stands, hookups, and the like. Even if you have had boyfriends, feel free to expand your list to men with whom you interacted in a short-term sexual or romantic way.
- If you want to expand your list beyond actual "exes," you can also thank people of both genders in your life who you feel affected the way you view yourself, men, and relationships (e.g. family members, friends, etc.)

Pain. Find meaning in your pain. Understanding and embracing it in your life can lead you to new ideas and possibilities.

By creating this list and offering your gratitude you are de-educating yourself from the concept of failure in your dating and love life. The list will show you how your experiences with exes or people from

your past weren't failures or a waste of time at all but experiments and opportunities to learn about who you are and what you want from a relationship. In fact, you can start seeing your past relationships or trysts with men as right for you at that time in your life, because they were reflections of what was going on inside of you. Moving forward, letting go of your pain, disappointments, and anger from past relationships, dating experiences, or general experiences with men who affected you, can help solidify and strengthen your vision so that you can go forth with an open heart and be an agent of change in your love life.

Reframing. Reframe your failures as intentional iterations. Doing this prevents you from being afraid to risk, to put yourself out there.

Thinking in this way empowers you to have a growth mindset—*I can grow from my experiences. I can move in a different direction based on my experiences*—versus a destiny mindset—*My path to love is fixed, so no need for learning and growth. I'm just waiting for that perfect person to come into my life.* It makes it easier for you to risk failure moving forward, because you instinctually know that whatever happens, it's an iteration not a failure, an opportunity to gain some sort of knowledge from the experience.

When a former client of mine named Alison did this exercise, she commented how liberating it felt to offer gratitude, especially to those who had hurt her. She was holding onto so much anger and taking that anger into the dating world, piling it on to new men she would meet. But when she was able to see men from her past in a different light, as human beings who had something to teach her, she felt her anger shift to something more positive, productive.

In agreement. The best, most successful treps agree: Failure is a necessary ingredient in the recipe for success. As a dating coach/ expert, I echo this sentiment. The good times and happy moments...that's the easy stuff; it's the failures that get you where you want to go.

Traditional entrepreneurs also need to let go of certain failed ideas, concepts, or initiatives in order to move forward with better clarity and purpose, in order to be more innovative. As Tim Ogilvie, CEO of

Pivoting. I've talked about the importance of not being so hard-headed and inflexible in your ideas of men who might make compatible matches, your expectations of the dating process, and your approach to dating. Life rarely goes according to plan. That's why treps and daters learn to adapt and be flexible in response to what comes their way. What's your Plan B?

Peer Insight, an innovation consultancy based in Washington, D.C., explains when it came to one of his failed businesses, in a January 2013 *Entrepreneur* piece titled "Epic Fail," "Now we look at it and say that first business was the scaffolding we put up to build a reputation in the market and a body of knowledge around innovation. And the scaffolding is always ugly. You have to say, 'Wait, behind this is something that's really beautiful.'"

As you engage in iterative and incremental dating, and move away from the concept of failure, you will start to see men not as the enemy but as teachers who can help you grow and eventually reach your vision. And as you begin to de-educate yourself in this way, you will feel less scared of dating, less afraid of making mistakes but also more empowered to try to make smarter decisions and let go of bad habits and toxic beliefs that are really a result of your fear of failure and vulnerability. In an entrepreneurial context—be it business or love— when people consistently drag their old, unproductive habits, beliefs, and behaviors into their venture, they run a risk of stagnating any sort of forward motion. They have to unlearn and move beyond certain habits and limiting beliefs from their prior experiences in order to move their venture to new heights.

Planning to Pivot

Entrepreneurs can predict an ideal path to success in their heads but rarely does idea or company growth happen the way they've imagined, which means it's essential to be prepared to *pivot* and be flexible when the unexpected happens.

To illustrate what it means to pivot, consider the case of Carissa Reiniger, founder of Silver Lining, a Manhattan-based consulting business dedicated to helping small businesses succeed. Profiled in the May 2012 issue of *Entrepreneur*, Reiniger explains how her first product launch, which she spent a year developing, was an abysmal failure, turning little profit. Soon after the launch, she realized she needed to *pivot* immediately by changing her model. As the article's author Jennifer Wang points out, "Reiniger realized her site shouldn't be the place to close the sale; rather, it should be a funnel to gather information and drive sales to where her team was far more effective: offline." After pivoting, Reiniger's business took off. Her ultimate vision of helping small businesses was still intact but how she delivered that help changed: instead of selling an impersonal business program obtained directly through her site, she would generate leads through her site, prompting her team of coaches to reach out directly to customers to explain and sell the program.

Neck argues that every venture starts off with an idea that will change and develop, and a major pitfall in the entrepreneurial journey is the temptation to overly commit or stick with a particular idea even in the face of certain setbacks. This is why it's important, for both traditional entrepreneurs and Love TREPs, to believe in their overarching vision, but not be so attached to specific ideas of what they think they know, especially at the outset; rather, the focus should be on taking action, experimenting, creating as you go, reflecting, and learning along the way what works and doesn't work.

In chapter 2, I talked about the importance of vision for both entrepreneurs and daters. I explained that the route to achieving a vision may change over time: What kind of a man you want and need, what

Be prepared. Be prepared for your wants and needs to evolve and develop over time. Be prepared to do things that might make you a little uncomfortable or anxious. Be prepared to change your mindset and adapt to more flexible notions about dating and love. Without this flexibility and adaptability, you'll have a more difficult time finding what you're looking for, and you'll come to resent the opposite sex and the process of finding love.

you want in a relationship, and how you think you can get there will evolve as you go through this process, but your overarching mission or vision will remain the same: finding a healthy, happy dating life that leads to a healthy, happy relationship. Neck stresses this kind of vision and adaptability in her work with entrepreneurs: "Entrepreneurs often talk about the importance of identifying a mission that is likely to stay consistent even while the scope changes as the venture grows, as customers engage with it, and as it is influenced by the ecosystem. Developing a mission and guiding vision that is malleable enough to accommodate and even anticipate inevitable pivots is critical for success. All ideas change, and entrepreneurs need to keep an open mind toward their capacity to pivot."

A 36-year-old client of mine was adamant about not dating a man who had children from a previous marriage or relationship. Her overarching vision was, of course, to find love with a commitment-minded, kind-hearted man, but she was stuck on this idea that she couldn't possibly find that with a single dad. I encouraged her to let go of such strict ideas of who could make a great partner for her, to let go of her fantasy ideals she'd dreamed up in her head—ideals that hadn't been serving her well all these years, anyway—and give single dads a chance. I asked her to turn the mirror on herself. What if she had a child from a marriage or relationship that didn't work out? Would she want men not to even consider her as a potential partner because of her circumstance? The fact was my client was 36, and a decent amount of the men looking to meet 36-year-old women were divorced men with young children. Although my client's ideal partner was a man without kids, she embraced the *reality* of her situation and pivoted— she broadened her ideas of who the man in her vision could be, and agreed to pivot accordingly when she met a single dad

online or out and about. As she started dating men with kids (taking action), she slowly began to understand that a connection and shared values was more important than the fact that a man happened to be a dad.

Also, with regard to pivoting in your dating and love life, it's important not to become so attached to the outcome of your dates ("This has to work out, because I'll just die if it doesn't!"), particularly in the early stages of dating. When you stop yourself from getting attached early on to the outcome of your experiences, before you know anything about who a man is or what he's looking for or before you even understand your own feelings, you give yourself room to *pivot* if things don't work out.

By learning how to adapt and pivot in your dating and love life when things don't go exactly as you'd like them to or when you become more aware of who you are and what you want, you begin to see your experiences less as failures and more as experiences, intentional iterations that help shape your journey. Look at Joanna's iterative dating arc in chapter 7 as a wonderful example of how someone adapted and pivoted multiple times when curveballs, disappointments, and self-knowledge forced her to do things differently.

Remember your Affinity List from chapter 5?

In Chapter 5, I was adamant about keeping your Affinity List short fluid, flexible, and not extremely specific. The wider you cast your net, the more options you give yourself. The same strategy works for a traditional entrepreneur. For example, a woman who develops, say, a mobile app for people who like dance raves in Boston puts herself into a

Evolution. Treps understand that to evolve is part of the game. This doesn't mean, however, that they throw fate to the wind and see where they end up. Their choices are not undisciplined or random. There is a sort of planning going on behind the scenes, even if there are no set or firm plans. Indeed, I have asked you to undergo a similar sort of planning in your dating and love life, through completing various exercises, inventories, and action steps in this book, while simultaneously being flexible in your plans, expectations, and approach.

very narrow, one-dimensional business model; her options are limited, and thus she's more likely to fail. But let's say instead that she develops a mobile app directed at young professionals who like to go out to bars and clubs in the metro Boston area. With the latter app, she broadens her base of customers, giving herself more options and ability to pivot in her entrepreneurial journey. Likewise, a single woman who has *very* specific limitations about what and who she's looking for and how she wants to get there doesn't give herself much room to pivot in the dating world. When she's more flexible, open-minded with her requirements, and not immediately focused on the outcome of her dating experiences after the first couple of dates ("Our chemistry is amazing, I have to *get* him to be my boyfriend!"), she casts a wider net and takes the pressure off, thereby giving herself more options.

Risky business. Treps don't risk blindly or without forethought. (That's just a myth.) Neither should daters.

De-Risking

Entrepreneurs accept the fact that they will fail and make mistakes and take wrong turns. But the truth is, entrepreneurs don't plunge headfirst into ventures without an element of forethought. Successful entrepreneurs start with the resources or means they have at hand and then use both action and thought to take small, smart steps forward based on knowledge that was gained from their previous step. Each action instructs the next action. Repeat until desired effect achieved. Sure, they may be failing or making mistakes by taking an action that eventually proves wrong for their venture, but each action is usually measured and purposeful. This is how entrepreneurs de-risk.

My entrepreneurial journey: Instead of quitting my job to grow my business full-time, I held on to a steady, 9-5 job that allowed me to fund my growing business and have nights and weekends to spend on coaching and various entrepreneurial-related activities.

It's a myth that entrepreneurs risk everything to achieve their vision, that they "bet the farm," max out all their credit cards, quit their safe,

stable day jobs, or go through their life savings to start their businesses. These are, however, the popular stories we're told. Let's face it: They make for great news items and magazine articles. Although we may know an entrepreneur "who went for broke," so to speak, most entrepreneurs do not operate in this all or nothing world.

The reality is that successful entrepreneurs take careful, smart risks, because, as Schlesinger and his co-authors write in *Action Trumps Everything*, "Entrepreneurs are people, too." The authors continue: "They have lives, families, and financial obligations. They don't say 'to hell with financial security' on a whim. They commit after careful thought, and even then they don't bet everything they have."

Jeffry Timmons echoes this sentiment in *New Venture Creation* in a section about dispelling the common myths of entrepreneurs, writing "Contrary to popular wisdom, entrepreneurs are *not* gamblers. Often they slice up the risk into smaller, quite digestible pieces; only then do they commit the time or resources to determine if that piece will work. They do not deliberately seek to take more risk or take unnecessary risk, nor do they shy away from unavoidable risk."

Of course, there is some unavoidable risk inherent in the dating process. You will get hurt, be confused, and feel like pulling your hair out at times. There are many things you can't control, especially in today's uncertain dating world. *But there is a difference between engaging in unnecessary risk and necessary risk.* You don't need to operate in the extremes in either entrepreneurship or dating.

Good risk vs. bad risk. There is a difference between engaging in unnecessary risk and necessary risk.

Engaging in unnecessary risk repeatedly without learning from your actions, without figuring out how to break the cycle, and conversely

refusing to take risks at all are both unproductive strategies for achieving your vision. To illustrate this concept, let's return to an earlier example: A woman who does not like having casual sex but still has it repeatedly with new suitors before establishing the status of where the relationship stands, in the hopes that he will commit to her, is engaging in unnecessary risk. This woman is not reflecting upon and learning from her experiences and paying attention to her needs and boundaries, committing the same unnecessary risk over and over again. On the flip side, if she holds tight to her boundary —waiting to have sex until she is in a committed relationship and maturely communicating that need to a man—and the man disappears on her or breaks up with her suddenly, she can be certain that she engaged in a smart, necessary risk. Despite holding the line on her boundary, she risked becoming vulnerable by voicing her needs and showing vulnerability which are necessary components of the dating process.

Failing smarter. If it's inevitable that you will fail in your dating and love life, the question becomes, how do you fail smarter?

Ultimately, entrepreneurs must take risks in certain ways, and by doing so they set themselves up for the potential to fail; often, they do fail. So the question then for entrepreneurs becomes: *If it's inevitable that I will fail, how do I fail smarter?* Specifically for daters that question becomes: *If it's inevitable that I will fail in my dating and love life, how do I fail smarter?* The Date. Learn. Repeat. entrepreneurial model of action, reflection, and more iterative and incremental action will help singles in this regard. But it is also helpful to look at failure through the lens of what entrepreneurs call "affordable (or acceptable) loss" —a way to think about de-risking before risking. In essence, before taking a step within a venture, entrepreneurs must ask themselves the following question: *If I take this step, what can I afford to lose?*

Affordable (or acceptable) loss

Successful entrepreneurs have developed ways to limit potential losses when starting new ventures, despite what you may read about their risk-taking habits. They do this, according to Schlesinger and his co-authors, by "adhering to the basic principles of risk management: If you're going to play in a game with uncertain outcomes, 1) don't pay/bet more than what you expect as a return, and 2) don't pay/bet more than you can afford to lose. Both of these ideas can be summed up with the phrase 'affordable loss,' a concept where you calculate the potential downside of whatever risk you are about to take ... and put on the line no more than you can afford and are willing to lose."

In other words, when it comes to dating and love, what can you realistically afford to lose by taking the next step should that next step not work out?

Affordable loss is going to mean something different for everyone. What I am willing to risk in my dating and love life may not be what you're willing to risk. And, surely, it will mean something different at different ages. What a twenty-something is willing to risk may not be what a forty-something is willing to risk. But once you know what you are willing to lose, risk no longer gets in the way of your decisions to take action.

We can look at this concept in two ways:

- Affordable loss from a macro view
- Affordable loss from a micro view

Affordable loss. The things one can afford to lose in her venture. A way of limiting potential losses. This depends on the individual and varies from person to person.

Affordable loss from a macro view

In this *overarching* entrepreneurial venture of finding love, what are you willing to risk?

Macro.
Adjective: large-scale; overall.
What are the macro level risks for you?

In Neck's article on embracing and re-defining failure for entrepreneurs, she mentions a woman named Laura, founder of an online marketplace for Twitter tools, who described a primary business failure strategy as that of de-risking. As Laura is quoted in Neck's piece: "An entrepreneur's job is to dive headfirst into a really, really risky undertaking and systematically de-risk it. Identify what are the six main ways this could fail, and what can I do about it. … OK, three of them I can't control, but these three I can. Let me make progress toward that. … And so, I just kept working all the angles of, well, I can't do anything about this risk, but I can do something about this." Neck concludes that "by identifying all the ways her venture might fail," Laura was "recognizing which of these she had some control over, and then incrementally working to address those issues, she was able to reduce her risk and learn about her product and market iteratively."

As a single, by dating, learning, and repeating you are indeed risking a number of things. So let's put Laura's excellent strategy to use in the context of the macro dating world to determine what you can and can't control and therefore how you can de-risk.

Using Laura's template:

- Identify several general risks that you might have to face on your journey to find love.

- List one or two things within these general risk categories that you can and can't control.

Here's my sample list:

- *Heartbreak* – I'll most likely get hurt along this journey. Am I willing to have a heavy heart, feel sad, disappointed, and lonely from time to time?
  - o Control: I can control my process of dating and who I let and don't let into my life, based on iterative dating.
  - o Not control: Sometimes I'll make mistakes and let people into my life who might end up hurting me. Sometimes, I can do all the things that feel good and right to me but still end up getting hurt by someone who changes, deceives me, or disappears on me.
- *Frustration* – I'll most likely get annoyed, aggravated, and confused along this journey. Am I willing to feel this way from time to time?
  - o Control: I can learn how to control my own reactions to frustrating experiences. I can refrain from constant self-judgment.
  - o Not control: I can't control how others will behave or act. I will undoubtedly encounter people along the way who do frustrating things.
- *Pride* – I'll most likely have to swallow my pride along this journey by doing things that might make me uncomfortable and anxious, such as accepting dates from people to whom I might not normally be attracted, or trying online dating and sticking with it for, say, a year, even though I feel awkward or silly about meeting people this way. Am I willing to swallow my pride to try new things and be open-minded?

o   Control: I can control how I perceive my actions and decisions. I can control how seriously I take myself. I can control how open-minded I will or won't be. Just because I never imagined something happening a certain way in my love life doesn't mean I can't embrace a different reality.

o   Not control: I can't control what others will think about my choices or how I go about taking control of my love life.

- *Vulnerability* – I'll most likely need to be vulnerable on this journey. Am I willing to embrace all that I discover along the way as I spend time reflecting? Am I willing to open myself up to others? Am I willing to be kind to myself?

  o   Control: I can control how vulnerable and open I am through incremental dating, as I pursue new opportunities and meet new people. I can be kind to and compassionate with myself.

  o   Not control: I can't control how someone will respond to my vulnerability or what he will do with that vulnerability. I can't make others want to be vulnerable and open if they don't want to be.

- *Time* – I'll most likely be dedicating a significant amount of time to this journey. Am I willing to risk spending some of my free time looking for love? How much time? Maybe an hour each night sorting through and responding to online dating emails? Maybe an hour for a cup of coffee with a guy who isn't my ideal? And so on and so forth.

  o   Control: I can control how much of my time I choose to dedicate to dating or dating someone. I can choose my priorities.

o   Not control: I can't control the way others view time, and I certainly can't control or manipulate their time-lines as far as how long it takes them to commit or settle down.

- *Energy* – I'll most likely be devoting a significant amount of energy to finding love. Am I willing to risk putting energy into this venture, even when I'm tired or make mistakes or meet a string of men who aren't matches?

o   Control: I can control the amount of energy and positivity I put into this process.

o   Not control: I can't control the energy and positivity of my dates.

- *Money* – I'll most likely need to spend some money on this journey. Am I willing to risk investing some of my hard-earned money on myself and on various opportunities that might help me to meet people?

o   Control: I can control how much money I'd like to put into this venture of finding love (even if I don't have a lot of it). I can prioritize where I choose to spend my money.

o   Not control: I can't control the costs of various dating events, online dating sites or other opportunities to meet people (charity galas, for example), or the rates that professionals such as therapists or dating coaches charge.

Now it's your turn.

- Create a list of macro-level affordable losses.

Maybe *your list* looks similar to mine. Maybe it has some differences. Everyone has unique challenges and fears even within macro-level categories, so everyone's list will look a little different and mean something different to them. If you have desire (as we established in chapter 2), your answers to the questions you create within the general risk categories should be YES. If you have desire, you will be more willing to take action in the face of certain types of loss, and you will accept the things you cannot control as you go out into the dating world.

I want you to believe that the reward of finding a healthy, happy relationship is worth risking all of the items on your list (and mine!). Remember: You have to have some skin in the game if you want to reach your vision. You can, of course, reduce your risk of experiencing some of the items on your list over time if you reflect pointedly on ways to act smarter in accordance with what you're learning from your experiences. That's why reflection time is so important to this process—it helps you lower your risk, and therefore spares you from dedicating time, emotions, and energy on the wrong men any more than necessary. And by thinking about what you can and can't control as you risk, you create necessary boundaries and let go of unnecessary boundaries for yourself, thereby making it easier for you to risk freely, without hesitation or fear of failure.

Micro.
Adjective: small-scale. What are your micro-level risks?

Affordable Loss from a micro view

You can also view affordable loss in the form of more specific, individualized actions you take in the dating world (a micro level), as opposed to thinking about this in general macro themes like some

of the aforementioned ones (time, money, energy, vulnerability, and so on). Surely, you will see how using prediction (chapter 5) as opposed to action and experimentation can be useful when considering affordable loss from a micro view. In fact, leaning on prediction when thinking about affordable loss from a micro view can, ultimately, empower you to act and experiment in different, healthier, smarter ways.

Let's employ Laura's risk analysis to micro scenarios. Here are a few examples:

Casual sex:

Let's say a woman has had three negative experiences in a six-month period, during which she slept with men before determining their relationship status, only to see them disappear and have her heart broken. She might want to think about delaying the act of intercourse until she's had a chat with a man about where they stand. She can then promise herself that she'll hold her ground and wait to see if this is the type of man that will stick around and get to know her as a person (and not just her vagina). Now that's empowerment, ladies!

o   Control: She can control what she decides to do about staying true to her needs and what feels right to her.

o   Not control: She can't control how men will respond to her needs. Even if a man agrees to her needs and enters into a relationship with her, he may still disappear or end things. But at least she can feel she stayed true to her boundaries and needs.

Don't get bogged down. The point of thinking about affordable loss from both macro and micro perspectives is not to get bogged down making a pros and cons list every time you act. The point is to engage in a brief reflection period as you move forward in your dating life so that you prevent yourself from taking unnecessary risks.

Real intimacy:

Or let's consider the case of a woman who really wants true intimacy and a relationship but seems to always fall for men who live far away and ultimately end up breaking her heart. The next time she meets a man who doesn't live within, say, an hour's commute, she asks herself the following question: *Am I willing to risk getting involved and potentially getting my heart broken for a man who doesn't live near me, and has no plans to move here?*

- o Control: She can control, geographically speaking, the types of men she pursues and puts time and energy into.
- o Not control: She can't control that she may meet men like this when she goes out, say, to a bar.

Non-committal men:

Or how about the woman who says she wants to find a healthy, happy relationship but keeps going after men who tell her they are not ready or too busy to settle down into a relationship with her. The next time she meets a man who says as much, instead of pretending not to hear him, she listens to what he's actually telling her, consequently, deciding to put her time and energy into someone who is looking to settle down.

- o Control: Again, she can control the types of men she chooses to put her time and energy into. She can control what she hears when a man tells her where his head and heart are at.

o   Not control: She can't control that she may meet a slew
of men who just aren't ready or are too busy to settle
down into a relationship.

In any of those three scenarios, the woman has to measure and calculate her risk. She can reflect on her past experiences and say to herself
either "I am willing to risk again in this situation, even though I've
been disappointed many times in the past going down this particular
road, and if I do risk again in this way, I'm willing to accept and face
the consequences," or "I'm not willing to take these risks, because
I can't afford it anymore as far as my time, physical and emotional
health, vision for my love life, and general well-being is concerned,
and I'd rather risk and experiment elsewhere and in different ways
with different people."

Now it's your turn.

• Create a list of micro-level affordable losses based on your
past and current experiences and patterns.

Over time, a woman learns that she can engage in selective risk-taking in her dating and love life—that is, she can risk while de-risking
by taking time to think through her affordable losses on both a
macro and micro level. It is important to ask yourself when beginning this process and constantly throughout it what you are willing
to lose/risk to find love, and how you can get smarter about your
risks as you move forward. It's not that I don't want you to experiment and take chances in the dating world. Of course I do—that's
what much of this book is about! But I also want you to understand
that *you* can make choices to think and act smarter in your dating

and love life than you've been used to doing, embracing risk in the process.

—⁂—

Your entrepreneurial journey will not be straight and narrow. It will not be linear. You will make wrong turns. Undoubtedly, you've already made many.

But if you can learn to turn the concept of failure on its head, to de-educate yourself from what you've been taught about failure, if you can learn how to pivot and adapt in the face of wrong turns and setbacks, if you can learn how to intelligently de-risk your risks so that you can take smarter, healthier, more informed, more productive risks, you will put yourself in an excellent position to achieve your vision in a way that doesn't make you feel drained, demoralized, and damaged. You will feel empowered by and confident about the risks you do decide to take, and, certainly, the ones you decide to leave behind, and you will not be as frightened anymore by the prospect of future failures.

Learn to see your failures in the dating world as assets, opportunities, experiences that have the power to teach and inform. Your failures humble you; they help you to understand what it takes to build a business and, of course, a healthy, happy dating and love life. From here on out, I want you to frame anything resembling a failure or misstep—past, present, and future—as knowledge that will help you date iteratively and incrementally in your entrepreneurial venture to find love.

Amy Cosper, editor-in-chief of *Entrepreneur*, having lived through a major fire that destroyed her home and, momentarily, her spirit, puts it brilliantly when she sums up how to move past fear and failure in the Editor's Note of the September 2012 issue: "The bottom line is this: No matter what life tosses your way, do these things and do them in this order: Fall to your knees and cry, stop crying, dust yourself off, go buy some new clothes and start over. Reintegrate. Whatever your ashes are, emerge from them as a better version of yourself."

Up Next:

Part III of this book is focused on facilitating your entrepreneurial journey. In this chapter, I have showed you how to look at failure and risking differently in your dating and love life to facilitate a more em-powered, informed dating process. In chapter 9, I will show you how to use your networks to your dating advantage, and how to nurture and build current and new networks.

Chapter 8 Action Steps Checklist:

✓ Create a list of men you deem had an impact on your dating and love life and write down how you are thank-ful to them, as outlined earlier. What did they teach you? You can extend this list to women, if you feel there were women in your life who had an impact on the way you view yourself, dating, relationships, and love.

✓ Re-visit your Affinity List that you created in chapter 5. Have you pivoted? Have any of the items on this list

shifted or changed at all? If you want to delete some and add new ones, please do so, but remember to keep the list at about ten.

✓ With regard to thinking differently about risk from a macro view, identify several general things that you might have to risk on this journey to finding love. Within these categories, list one or two things that you can and can't control. Reflect on your list. Did you answer "yes" to the questions you posed to yourself about what you are willing to risk?

✓ With regard to thinking differently about risk from a micro view, identify specific, more personal ways that you can de-risk, based on your past and current experiences. These will be great boundaries for you—boundaries that you might have already thought about in the iterative dating section in chapter 7.

✓ Revisit chapter 3. Are there any other obstacles to finding love from the ones you've identified that you can begin to overcome using the same processes as outlined in that chapter?

CHAPTER 9: NETWORKING

"The currency of real networking is not greed but generosity."

-Keith Ferrazzi, author and founder/CEO of Ferrazzi Greenlight

At this point, you may be saying to yourself: "OK, I've got desire, a problem-solving mentality, and a vision, I'm working on my internal and external obstacles, I've surrounded myself with supporters, I understand and am ready to implement the Date. Learn. Repeat model of entrepreneurial dating, and I've learned how to view failure differently, but *how on earth do I get the darn dates?!*"

Once again, we can look to entrepreneurs for solutions.

Indeed, successful entrepreneurs understand the power of networking and use it to their advantage. They understand that a network of people to draw from and rely on is an indispensable resource when building a venture. They see everyone who comes across their paths as potential customers or collaborators, people who can help make their visions come to fruition.

Consider, once again, the story of Suzanne Sengelmann and Mary Jo Cooke (see chapter 5), the entrepreneurial leaders who successfully

The means at hand. When you are faced with uncertainty in the dating world, the quickest way to get started is to access the means or resources you already have at hand. In chapter 5, I talked about accessing self-knowledge (Who am I?; What do I know?); now I will focus on accessing who you know.

brought Clorox's Green Works product line to market. Leveraging their personal networks, they forged a partnership between Clorox and the Sierra Club, a powerful environmental group. As part of the partnership, the Sierra Club logo would appear on the Green Works label and the Sierra Club would receive financial compensation. A win-win.

Although we as a society often embrace the fables of self-made millionaires and billionaires, entrepreneurs rarely get to the top strictly on their own. Their success is often dependent upon a web of support, ideas, and networks. As Hoffman and Casnocha argue in their book *The Start-up of You*, entrepreneurial success is not an "I" vs "We" scenario. It's both: "I^{WE}," as they put it.

We all understand the concept of networking in the professional sense. It's a word that's been thrown around *ad nauseam* for much of our adult lives. By meeting people you gain access to their knowledge, resources, and networks. The process expands your opportunities. It's a proactive rather than reactive approach. You never know who will introduce you to whom.

Networking is networking is networking. We should view networking in our dating lives in the same way we view it in our professional lives.

The same concepts can certainly apply to dating. Without a network of people, dating can be a lonely and unproductive venture. This is precisely why I want you to start networking like an entrepreneur in your dating and love life.

In chapter 5, I discussed the three simple questions that Schlesinger and his *Action Trumps Everything* co-authors suggest entrepreneurs ask themselves when starting a venture of any sort: Who am I? What do I know? Who do I know? Well, now it's time to address the last question: *Who do I know?*

In chapter 10, Opportunity Identification, I'll be asking you to start branching out, meeting new people, forming new networks, and creating your own opportunities, but in this chapter I'll ask you to start with the people in your already-established networks, the people you *already know.*

So…who do you know? And how can you access these networks to help increase your chances of achieving your vision: a healthy, happy dating life that leads to a healthy, happy relationship?

You may not think you know that many people or that many people who can help you in this specific area. But that's where you're mistaken. The truth is everyone in your network is capable of introducing you to eligible men, whether directly or indirectly, *and* you probably know a lot more people than you think who can aid you in this capacity—you've just never thought to see these people as part of your "network," no less your dating and love network.

Primary and Secondary Love Ambassadors

I want you to create a complete inventory of the people you know. Sort this list into your:

- *Primary network*:
  o Your primary network is comprised of people who are closest to you: good friends, family members, and perhaps some members who are on your Board of Advisors.

Your network.
You know more people than you think you do. And you know more people who would be willing to help you in this area of your life than you think you do.

- *Secondary network:*
  - o Your secondary network includes everyone else with
       whom you interact on more of a surface-level but
       reasonably consistent basis: acquaintances, neighbors,
       friends who aren't super close but who you still see
       or go out with from time to time, current and former
       co-workers, business contacts, service providers (hair
       colorists, personal trainers, etc.), and so on and so forth.

As Hoffman and Casnocha write, "the best professional network is
both narrow/deep (strong connections) and wide/shallow (bridge
ties)." I would argue that the same goes for a dating and love network.
Both your primary and secondary networks have their advantages
and disadvantages, which is why accessing, strengthening, and maintaining both are important.

People in your primary network will become your:

- *Primary Love Ambassadors (PLAs)* – these are people who
  are more likely to be committed stakeholders in helping
  you in your venture to find love and will be more prone to
  actively introducing you to and setting you up with potential romantic interests.

People in your secondary network will become your:

- *Secondary Love Ambassadors (SLAs)* – these are people who
  are on the periphery of your network and, more than
  likely, contributing less frequently and more passively to
  your venture. They are, however, great resources.

Your ultimate goal is to enroll as many love ambassadors as possible into your total network. In essence, these people become co-creators with regard to your vision.

Co-creators.
The people in your life who you reach out to for help will co-create your vision with you. Not only are the people on your Board of Advisors your co-creators, but the people within your networks can function in this way, too.

I'll use myself as an example, pretending I am creating this list in the months before I met Dave. I am not listing exact names, but you should do this when creating your list.

Neely's Primary Network:

- Closest friends in Boston and elsewhere who I see or keep in touch with on a regular basis. [List names here.]
- Family members (parents, brother, sister-in-law, grandmother, sister-in-law's sister, cousins). [List names here.]
- Mentor.

Neely's Secondary Network:

- Other Boston friends. [List names here.]
- College and high school friends not in primary network. [List names here.]
- Current and former work colleagues. [List names here.]

- Service providers (my massage therapist, personal trainer, hair colorist). [List names here.]
- Neighbors. [List names here.]
- Squash club acquaintances. [List names here.]
- Acquaintances from volunteer organizations. [List names here.]
- Current and former media contacts from my various writing and speaking gigs. [List names here.]

Note: While it is true that I met Dave through Match.com, I have drawn from and relied on both my primary and secondary networks to help me meet men throughout my twenties and early thirties.

Action Steps for your PLAs

You should contact everyone in your PLA network, whether via phone, email, or in person, and let them know you are looking to be set up on dates. Explain why dating and love are priorities at this point in your life. It is important for both traditional entrepreneurs and Love TREPs to let people who you want to bring along on your entrepreneurial journey know how much you care about your venture. Your honesty, passion, and authenticity will inspire them to take action on your behalf. Because of your strong bond to and history with people in your primary network, these are people who will probably be willing to act on your behalf already, but a genuine appeal from you for their help and honesty about what you're looking for will inspire them to action even more.

If any of your PLA's are in healthy, happy relationships, preface your request by telling them how much you admire their relationship

Help me help you. To help your PLAs help you, give them your Affinities List (chapter 5).

(assuming you do), and that you hope to emulate what he or she has someday with a partner of your own. It's also worth mentioning that if you have people within your primary network who enjoy talking about dating, sex, love, and relationships, and people who are happily in love, these are the kinds of people who will be even more inspired to want to join you in your venture of finding a healthy, happy relationship. You may even want to consider taking them out for lunch or coffee and asking them to help you brainstorm ways for you to meet people (hat tip to relationship guru and matchmaker Rachel Greenwald for this idea), instead of just asking them, "Do you know any single men?" Maybe when you sit down together, you'll discover your PLA is in a book club with lots of women and she can spread the word at meetings to her fellow club members that her amazing friend is single and looking to be set up.

You are ready! Tell your PLAs you are ready to date and find love by being upbeat and positive about your dating life and the possibilities that lie ahead.

Ultimately, you are asking your PLAs to actively keep their eyes and ears open for you on a consistent basis—essentially, to act as your ambassador. You can provide them with a short list or description of what and who you're looking for (you can use the Affinity List you created in chapter 5) to give them some direction, but let them know this list isn't set in stone and is merely a jumping-off point. The more requirements you have, the more difficult it will be for your PLAs to help you. Remember: if you are iteratively and incrementally dating, you do not necessarily need to be set up with The One from the get-go.

One final point: If your close friends and family members see you as someone who isn't ready for a relationship, complains often about men, and has low self-esteem, they'll be less inclined to want to make connections for you. This doesn't mean you can't be honest with

people in your primary network about your ideas and emotions—after all, that's what people in this network are for—but showing them that you are ready for dating, in a positive place regarding the process, and hopeful about finding love, will reassure them that their actions are worth taking.

(Note: I have included members from your Board of Advisors as part of your primary network. Some of these people you may feel belong in this network and are appropriate to act as PLAs; others would not be appropriate in this capacity. It depends on who you have asked to be a part of your Board. If you have chosen, for example, a therapist, he or she would not be part of any matchmaking activities; if you have chosen a mentor, he or she could certainly help in this way, as outlined in the mentor responsibilities in chapter 4.)

Action Steps for your SLAs

Your approach with SLAs is a bit more complicated. Because your relationship and bond with people in your secondary networks is more tenuous, they are less likely to actively help with matchmaking for you. That's not to say it can't happen, but they have more reason to help people to whom they are closer than people to whom they aren't as closely connected.

Great connections. SLAs are great connections to have. Value and nurture these relationships.

However, you can still make it known to SLAs that you're single and looking: "I'm looking to meet people, any chance you might know some single guys?" A friend of mine mentioned this to her long-time hairdresser, who just so happened to know a single guy who she thought might be a compatible match. Most importantly, she was willing to make it happen (more on *why* in a bit). They ended up going

out! While it wasn't a love connection, it was a great example of using the power of your network to meet people. Again, you're less likely to get set up through these connections, but it's worth a shot. Swallow your pride. Start talking to everyone and anyone you know in your secondary network; start telling them that you're looking to be set up.

Part of your strategy with SLAs is to simply get the word out there— even if they don't have a person or opportunity for you at that moment. The fact that they are simply hearing about your interest will put you on their radar screen if they do happen to know someone down the road who is eligible.

It's especially important with SLAs to be positive and upbeat about dating, appearing willing to try anything and meet relatively anyone. Think about it: Why would an SLA want to set up a woman who whines and complains incessantly about ex-boyfriends, the opposite sex in general, or has a laundry list of fifty requirements with someone they know? Why would they consider that kind of person for a setup, ahead of other single women who are in their own primary network? It's also important to remember that if an SLA makes the effort to set you up with a guy and that guy calls to ask you out, *always* follow through and honor that date. A close friend of mine named Kaitlin once asked another close friend of mine, Lisa, who she knew through me, to set her up. Lisa happened to know a great guy, so she decided to play matchmaker. When Kaitlin never returned the guy's calls, Lisa was upset and embarrassed, and vowed never to set Kaitlin up again.

At the end of the day, networking is about presenting the best you, so that people who can help and have the resources and motivation to do so will think and want to help you.

SLAs are also great connections for hearing about and getting invited to parties, events, and other opportunities where you can meet people directly. Again, another reason to put your best foot forward with everyone in your secondary network. You never know where an opportunity might lead when it comes to your dating and love life.

It is true that SLAs may not be your primary vehicle for direct setups (they might have women in their primary network who they would think of first), and they may not feel compelled to go out on a limb for you, but as mentioned, they are great for helping with opportunity creation. It should be noted, though, that sometimes getting certain types of SLAs to include you or tell you about parties, events, and other various opportunities can be a bit difficult, *specifically if a relationship tie is fairly weak.*

However, there are ways to increase your chances for SLAs to start involving you in their world, ways to start strengthening those ties, ways for you to inspire them to think of you even before people in their own primary networks.

What's in it for THEM? When building and nurturing your network, never go into your relationships with a "What's in it for me?" attitude. Think about how you can help them first.

The art of networking – building and nurturing relationships

Understand that there is an art to networking—especially when it comes to getting people within your networks to think of you and act for you. It helps first to look at networking in a different light; Hoffman and Casnocha prefer to view it more as relationship building, as do many other business leaders and expert entrepreneurs.

With SLAs especially, people to whom you have weaker ties than your PLAs, you'll be better off thinking about how you can build and nurture relationships as opposed to seeing them purely as vehicles for meeting your needs.

"Old-school 'networkers' are transactional," write Hoffman and Casnocha. "They pursue relationships thinking only about what other people can do for them. And they'll only network with people when they need something, like a job or new clients. Relationship builders, on the other hand, try to help other people first. They don't keep score. They're aware that many good deeds get reciprocated, but they're not calculated about it."

You have a better chance of SLAs helping, including, and thinking of you if *you* help *them* first. Your relationships shouldn't be based on what you can get from them—i.e., "What's in it for me?" The goal is to build authentic, genuine, two-way relationships. This is really a good rule of thumb in life.

Let's use the previous example of my friend's hairdresser to illustrate this point. After a couple years of getting her hair done by this woman, referring friends and family to her services, and writing good reviews for her on Yelp and other sites, the hairdresser was, of course, more than willing to help my friend with her dating and love life when she asked for the help.

As an entrepreneurial dater, you want relationship building within your networks to be less focused on the easy "gets," less calculated, and more focused on helping and relating to others with the secondary thought that your generosity may eventually be returned someday.

As Hoffman and Casnocha put it, "We're not suggesting you be so saintly that a self-interested thought never crosses your mind. What we're saying is you should let go of those easy thoughts and think about how *you* can help *first*. (And only later think about what help you can ask for in return.)" In this light, networking is a way of investing in the people within your networks.

If you can look at networking in your dating and love life this way, as something more akin to relationship building, you'll be less likely to see the process as something that's tedious, slimy, and underhanded but as something that's benevolent and—gasp!—even fun.

A note on tertiary networks

People within your tertiary networks are those who you only know or meet in passing or who you know on a purely superficial basis. There is nothing consistently tying you together. Years ago, when I was single, thinking and acting like an entrepreneur (without even knowing it) in my own dating and love life, I was under the misapprehension that anyone would be willing to help me meet people. For instance, if I was in a small retail store and got to chatting with the owner, I'd sometimes slip into the conversation that I was single and looking. Or if I overheard women nearby me in a cafe or bar talking about men or dating, I'd half-seriously, half-jokingly jump in and say: "Hey, if you know someone, I'm interested!" These types of networking approaches (that have nothing to do with building relationships but are completely transactional and one-sided), however, rarely worked and may have been seen as desperate. But there was that one time...

I was in a clothing boutique in Boston years ago. The owner was a woman about my mother's age. We started chatting and I mentioned I was single. She said that she had a son moving back from Los Angeles, that he, too, was a writer. She wanted to get my email so he could get in touch with me. At first, I was elated, but my excitement soon turned to disappointment when I learned what kind of writing he did. The shop owner's son wrote for the porn industry! You can imagine the color my face turned when she revealed his genre of writing. Still, I said he could contact me—at that point, I felt it would have been rude to say I wasn't interested. Eventually, the guy wrote me, and I confessed that after Googling his name and reading about his various exploits with porn stars and within the industry, he was not what I was looking for. But we remained friendly, and several months later I invited him to be a guest on my radio show to talk about his various sordid adventures (let's just say it was an X-rated show).

On the flip side, I was on the receiving end of a similar type of match-making request. I was in the locker room of my gym talking with an acquaintance about matchmaking for a sixty-three-year-old client I was coaching. My acquaintance said she knew a few men, prompting the fifty-something woman nearby to intervene, expressing interest in meeting some of these men. I loved her entrepreneurial spirit, and although she gave us her card, both my acquaintance and I would have considered either my client or other women within our own networks first, before this stranger.

The point I'm trying to make about people in passing, tertiary networks is that they are very unlikely to take action on your behalf. However, it is also true that you have nothing to lose by spreading the word this way; just don't expect results or let failure on this front sour

Neely's deal-breaker. While I'm all about entrepreneurial dating and not narrowing your experiences, there are lines that you should draw in the sand. For me, a deal-breaker was someone who once starred in pornographic movies.

your attitude on the process of networking. This type of networking is less likely to work for you, but it never hurts to take stabs in the dark and be open to surprises. Had the shopkeeper's son not diddled porn stars, I may have been up for a date.

Next up:

In this chapter, I've shown you how to help your entrepreneurial venture move forward by growing your networks as well as nurturing the networks you already possess. But you can't rely *solely* on your networks, which is why, in chapter 10, I'll discuss ways for you to identify your own opportunities to meet potential dates.

Chapter 9 Action Steps Checklist:

- ✓ Ask yourself the question: Who do I know?
- ✓ Create a complete inventory of the people you know and sort this list into your primary and secondary networks.
- ✓ Begin to think of these people within your networks as your Primary Love Ambassadors (PLAs) and your Secondary Love Ambassadors (SLAs), your goal being to enroll as many ambassadors as possible into your total network.
- ✓ Follow the action steps, as outlined earlier, with regard to interacting with your PLAs and SLAs.

CHAPTER 10: OPPORTUNITY IDENTIFICATION

"Ideas are like rabbits. You get a couple and learn how to handle them, and pretty soon you have a dozen"

– John Steinbeck, author

Successful entrepreneurs are adept at creating opportunity for their ventures; where others see red tape, headaches, and annoyances, they see openings. Now that you're on your way to becoming a master networker and developing opportunities through your budding and established networks, like any entrepreneur must do to build a venture, you can also proactively start working on ways to identify and generate your own opportunities.

Your total network will be an excellent resource for introductions to potential matches and invitations to various parties, events, and organizations where you can meet potential matches. But identifying opportunities on your own will also be a necessary part of your entrepreneurial journey. You need these opportunities to test out the evolving you, to practice iterative and incremental dating.

Sticky business. Are you stuck in a rut? Have you had the same weekly routine for years? Do you hang out with the same people over and over again? Do you go to the same bars again and again?

"Entrepreneurial ecosystems."

It behooves a trep to always be asking herself: Who am I surrounding myself with? Treps talks a lot about the importance of this concept, which is called an "entrepreneurial ecosystem": a supportive, inspiring entrepreneurial environment that makes it easier to launch a business, grow, learn, and succeed.

Sometimes you can get stuck in a rut, your non-work activities becoming routine and stale: gym, drinks or dinner with friends, shopping, and the like. It's no wonder you don't meet new people in this merry-go-round existence, yet amazingly you're perplexed as to why. If your regular group of friends is down on men, dating, and relationships, that negativity can affect your mentality and limit your opportunities. Upbeat, positive people are magnets for other great people who beget other great people, which can balloon your networks. You become who you hang out with.

So, as a single woman looking for love, it's often necessary to break free from your monotony, your rut, and to spend some time apart from the negative, Debbie-downer types, so that you can start identifying and pursuing fresh opportunities to meet new, positive-minded people, allowing you to maintain a hopeful, optimistic attitude about dating, love, and relationships.

Creating your own opportunities

In September of 2012 *The New York Times* wrote a story titled "Searching for a Companion, With a Smile and a Sign," about a man named Adam Orna, a thirty-nine-year-old postal worker, who was so tired of waiting for love to find him, constantly striking out through the usual approaches—bars, online dating, and the like—that he took the bold if rather peculiar action of taking to the streets with a sign listing his personal statistics – "$55,000 plus benefits, loyal, straight, marriage-minded, a marathon runner, and a vegetarian" — followed with the words "Please Date Me." In the story, a married woman by the name of Carol Dersarkissian who chatted with Mr.

Orna one afternoon told him she was married, to which Mr. Orna responded by giving her his card so that she could give it to a single friend. "There have been nights I've cried I was so lonely," he said in the piece. "You've got a good job, good hobbies, but what good is it if there's no one to share it with?" While Mr. Orna didn't seem to have much luck—more than likely being seen as desperate by most women—I had to applaud him in a way. His entrepreneurial spirit was something I could appreciate. He was dedicated to his vision and decided to take action, even on the wackiest of ideas. Successful entrepreneurs understand that sometimes the silliest, most inane ideas are often catalysts for progress (e.g. PooPooPaper, a successful line of recycled paper products made from poop!). "Don't wait for it to fall into your lap," admonished Mr. Orna with regard to companionship. "Go out and pursue it. It won't fall into your lap. Trust me."

Lest you be concerned: I am not encouraging you to strap a sign around your neck, nor do I want you to spend every second of your life strategizing about how and where to meet dates, turning into a frantic man-hunter in the process. Being excessively preoccupied and obsessed in this way can backfire (google: "The Law of Diminishing Returns"). But we can take a cue from Mr. Orna's desire to create his own opportunities and his willingness to be a little uncomfortable in the process. And who knows, an idea that seems nonsensical today may be brilliant several months down the road. In the mid 1980s when online dating was invented, there were plenty of naysayers—"Who would ever want to meet someone through a computer?" skeptics would bark. So, I am asking that when you do focus your time on opportunity identification for your dating and love life, you step outside your comfort zone as well as act and think more

Adam Orna update. In August of 2013, as I was putting the finishing touches on this book, I was curious to know what happened to Mr. Orna. Did he find love? After plugging his name into the search function on facebook, I found his profile. His relationship status said "married." I sent him a message to inquire when he got married and if his neck-sign stint was the catalyst to meeting someone. I was still waiting to hear back, as of press time, but I couldn't help but wonder if his wacky, entrepreneurial idea helped him find love. Mr. Orna: If you happen to read this, drop me a line and let me know!

entrepreneurially about opportunities than you may have been used to doing in the past.

Part of acting entrepreneurially in your dating and love life may very well mean putting more strategic thinking behind your decisions to pursue certain opportunities. There is nothing wrong with identifying or weighing opportunities based on your chances of getting to meet other singles, and there is also nothing wrong with choosing to pursue an activity that probably has a low to no chance of meeting singles. There will also be times when you just want to be adventurous and try something new, regardless of that activity's potential to meet men. The ultimate goal, however, is to learn how to *strike a balance* so that your approach to pursuing opportunities doesn't have to be all or nothing. If you always have dating and love on the mind when choosing or pursuing opportunities, you can end up feeling desperate, exhausted, and burned out. If you rarely keep dating and love on the brain, you're not really doing much at all to help increase your chances of meeting dates, and thereby decreasing your chances to iteratively and incrementally date, which is, partly, the way you figure out who you are and what you want and need.

Using creativity and "blue-sky" thinking for idea generation

Creativity.
Creative treps aren't frightened by new ideas or possibilities. In fact, they are fueled and inspired by them.

Opportunity creation and idea generation for both traditional entrepreneurs and Love TREPs takes a bit of creativity, so that you allow yourself to imagine new and different possibilities versus the old, stale ways of meeting people. It is important for you to push yourself to be more creative in the way you brainstorm new ideas and opportunities, to think more "outside the box" (to use a cliché phrase), to be open to new experiences, flexible, original, motivated, and unconcerned about failure or mistakes. As Heidi Neck writes in "Idea Generation," a chapter in *The Portable MBA in Entrepreneurship*, "The creative entrepreneur has a better ability to navigate unchartered waters, anticipate change, play offense, and create the future."

This type of creativity in the world of entrepreneurship is also known as "blue-sky thinking": Imagine looking up at an endless sky full of possibilities. Blue-sky thinking in your dating life is all about breaking boundaries, pushing past self-imposed constraints and limits in terms of how and where you can meet men. As you're looking up at this crystal-blue sky, ask yourself: "How might I break free from my predictable, status quo dating existence?" The higher in the sky you look, the wackier, sillier and more inane the idea should be.

Entrepreneurs engage in these types of blue-sky brainstorms and often find that not being limited by current thinking or beliefs helps stimulate the kind of creative thinking needed to come up with novel, reality-based products and services.

Consider the story of a group of Amherst College (my alma mater) students who were commisioned by Fritz Van Paasschen, CEO of Starwood Hotels & Resorts, to study marketing and branding trends as they pertain to young adults. By the project's end, the students were expected to present new ideas to Starwood executives. As the four-member group delved into project research, they let their imaginations run wild. One of the students, Danielle Amodeo, suggested a rather outlandish idea: a fleet of Lamborghini's available for guests to drive. While her teammates brought her back down to earth, Amodeo remarked, "That crazy dream scenario made it possible for me to think of the hotel as an interface for other things."

Ultimately, her blue-sky thinking led her to a more grounded and plausible idea: "The Closet." The concept was to enable guests of Starwood Hotels to rent or borrow clothing items when they're traveling. "What if a tourist had an option to wear—but not buy and take home—a sari in India or a Burberry coat in London? What if a business traveler could use an extra suit jacket?" As it turns out, of all the ideas presented to Starwood executives, "The Closet" was the one that resonated the most and made sense for two of the hotel's brands, the W and Aloft.

How can you make blue-sky thinking work for you in your dating life? Think as big as you can. Imagine that there are no barriers whatsoever in your way, that anything is possible. Whatever resource you need is available to you (time, money, personality traits, networks, abilities, and the like). Move beyond your assumptions and limiting beliefs of what is possible. What new, adventurous ideas can you come up with? (You'll be creating lists in just a moment.)

Again, I'm not saying that you have to strap a sign around your neck (like Mr. Orna) to meet people—that's an idea that worked for one person but it won't work for 99% of the population. *But* maybe there are new ideas and possibilities that *you* can explore, ideas that seem a little nutty to you because of the limits you've placed on yourself, ideas that make you step outside of or expand *your* comfort zone. Those ideas could be anything from joining a niche online dating site to going out to an event or the local pub by yourself to joining a co-ed sports league as a free agent to hiring the services of a friendly "wingwoman" for the night (if you're in the Boston area, check out Hire a Boston Wingwoman), and so on and so forth.

Blue-sky Thinking. What bold ideas for meeting men can you come up with that scare you a little? More than just ideas to meet new men, how can you extend blue-sky thinking to new ways of communicating with men, new ways of risking with men, and news ways of thinking about yourself?

Neck believes that it is "easy for us to feel paralyzed at times when asked to do something perceived as creative. All of a sudden our thinking becomes limited and we get stuck based on what we know, and have trouble embracing what we *could* know." She maintains that fear is by far the most significant roadblock to moving forward creatively and entrepreneurially. She uses the example of a recently graduated MBA student, Josh, who was asked to brainstorm ideas with his creative development team at his new job. His disbelief in his ability to be creative held him back.

> "By habit he self-screened every idea that entered his head. The group encouraged him to just throw out any idea that came to mind, no matter how big, small, funny, or mundane ... His biggest fear at this juncture was that he could not generate any ideas ... Not only was his brain blocked by fear, disallowing new ideas to emerge, but his mind's eye had already jumped minutes ahead into the future, seeing the potential outcome after sharing an idea, any idea."

Josh's story is a perfect illustration of how a lot of daters approach brainstorming dating opportunities. Many play it safe with their ideas, are immediately dismissive, and unwilling to think of ideas that are different than what they're used to or comfortable with. "What if's" plague their brains: *What if I go to this event and there's nobody there my age? What if I attend that party and it's a waste of my time? What if I'm not attracted to anyone at this activity? What if this turns out to be a terrible idea? What if other people think I'm stupid for going to this event? What if I go to this event/bar/party by myself and look stupid?*

Boxed in. Break free from that box you've created around yourself. Push yourself to feel a little uncomfortable. It's during the uncomfortable moments when real growth happens and when opportunity presents itself. Remember: Treps break the mold. They create the future by shaping opportunities, especially when the future is unpredictable.

As you generate ideas for yourself, don't be afraid to be uncomfortable. Don't be afraid to try something different. Don't always play it safe. Stop the What If'ing and start the blue-sky thinking!

Shaping ideas into opportunities

The purpose of this chapter is to brainstorm ideas that you can turn into opportunities for yourself, opportunities to have fun while meeting new people. When brainstorming opportunities, it's important to remain open, playful, and imaginative. Don't be predictable all the time with your ideas. Break your own boundaries.

Below are three suggestions on how you can begin the process of brainstorming ideas and shaping them into opportunities. But don't let *my* suggestions limit *your* creativity, especially with the first and second bullet points. The third point offers general ideas that I have identified as opportunities most singles could benefit from. Feel free to think of bold ideas, perhaps more bold than what I have listed. You may not have any wild and crazy ideas like Mr. Orna, but push the envelope, allowing yourself to think freely and be unobstructed by doubts, "What If's", and your particular fears; maybe that idea you happen to think is wild and crazy or the one that scares you a little could actually prove to be quite fruitful.

Three ways to think about opportunity identification for your dating and love life:

1. Opportunities based on your interests.
2. Opportunities based on trying new things completely unrelated to your self-stated interests.
3. Opportunities based on already-identified, high-percentage ways to meet men.

1. *Opportunities based on your interests*

The best way to feel like you're pursuing opportunities to meet people without trying so hard, which can sometimes make you feel desperate and drained, is by simply choosing activities that really interest or excite you in some way. Remember, that's an effective way of enrolling others into your entrepreneurial venture: Present people with an opportunity that is personally exciting to them. You can apply the same principle here: To get yourself excited about meeting new people, you should pursue opportunities you enjoy, opportunities you would pursue even if you weren't looking for love. It's a win-win.

In order to start identifying opportunities for yourself, outside of the help from your network, it will help to make a list of your interests and hobbies, and any activities you'd like to pursue in the future. Sometimes when you have so many competing ideas in your head, it helps to get them down on paper. You may have all sorts of interests you've been thinking about pursuing but not know how to choose amongst them. Writing them down allows you to create a tangible list on which you can take action.

Below is a list of interests and hobbies I enjoy. When creating yours, try to be specific if applicable. For example, don't write: "I love creating things." Instead, specify what you love creating: "I love creating poetry."

Interests and hobbies:

- I love discussing and debating politics and current affairs.
- I love playing tennis, squash, and all racket sports.

Brainstorm.
Brainstorm ideas.
Be creative.
Silence your
doubts. Shape
your ideas
into specific
opportunities.
Try to take
advantage of
two to three
opportunities per
month.

- I generally enjoy athletic endeavors and competitions of all kinds.
- I enjoy drinking wine, going out to bars, and having drinks with friends.
- I love food of all kinds.
- I love fashion and style.
- I enjoy volunteering and connecting back to the community.
- I enjoy writing of all kinds (non-fiction, fiction, blogging, screenwriting, etc.).
- I enjoy listening to talk radio and radio hosting.
- I love the ballet.
- I love going to the movies, and I especially enjoy foreign films.
- I enjoy reading of all kinds (books, magazines, newspapers).
- I love to laugh and make people laugh.
- I enjoy keeping up with and staying involved in my alma mater.

<u>Activities for the future:</u>

These are interests, hobbies, or self-improvement activities you are considering exploring in the future.

- I'd like to learn how to cook.
- I'd like to learn how to play Ultimate Frisbee.
- I'd like to learn how to improve my singing voice.
- I'd like to get over my fear of dogs.
- I'd like to get better at public speaking.

Now, for every item listed in these inventories, get even more specific by listing two corresponding activities.

- I love discussing and debating politics and current affairs.
  o Volunteer on a mayoral or gubernatorial campaign.
  o Join a young professionals political organization.
- I love playing tennis, squash, and all racket sports.
  o Join a tennis or squash league or tennis or squash club.
  o Teach or volunteer with an inner city tennis or squash organization.
- I generally enjoy athletic endeavors and competitions of all kinds.
  o Join an athletic league, competition, or organization.
  o Take part in a Beirut or Cornhole competition.
- I enjoy drinking wine, going out to the bars, and having drinks with friends.
  o Go to wine tastings.
  o Join pub crawls.
- I love food of all kinds.
  o Enroll in a cooking class.
  o Attend food festivals.
- I love fashion and style.
  o Check out fashion shows.
  o Go to store openings.
- I enjoy volunteering and helping those less fortunate.
  o Sign up to be on a planning committee for an annual gala.
  o Sign up to be a big sister.
- I enjoy writing of all kinds (non-fiction, fiction, blogging, screenwriting, etc.).

Become a more interesting person. A benefit of creating and pursuing opportunities is that you become a more interesting person to be around. You have more to offer conversations with others while out on dates or interacting with men; you have more chances of connecting with others; you bring new and different perspectives to your dating interactions.

- o   Take a writing class.
- o   Go to a writing conference.
- I enjoy listening to talk radio and radio hosting.
    - o   Go to one of your favorite local radio station's events.
    - o   Attend a broadcaster's conference.
- I love the ballet.
    - o   Volunteer for a ballet organization.
    - o   Take an introductory ballet class.
- I love going to the movies, and especially enjoy foreign films.
    - o   Join a film lover's club/network.
    - o   Attend film festivals.
- I enjoy reading of all kinds (books, magazines, newspapers).
    - o   Join a book club.
    - o   Check out book signings and readings.
- I love to laugh and make people laugh.
    - o   Go to a stand-up comedy festival.
    - o   Take an improv class.
- I enjoy keeping up with and staying involved in my alma mater.
    - o   Check out NESCAC events.
    - o   Attend Amherst College events in Boston.
- I'd like to learn how to cook.
    - o   Take a cooking class.
    - o   Join a food enthusiasts group.
- I'd like to learn how to play Ultimate Frisbee.
    - o   Join an Ultimate Frisbee league.
    - o   Go to the park and join up with other Frisbee enthusiasts.

- I'd like to learn how to improve my singing voice.
  - o Take a group singing class.
  - o Open mic night.
- I'd like to get over my fear of dogs.
  - o Volunteer at an animal shelter.
  - o Go to the local dog park and interact with the dogs.
- I'd like to get better at public speaking.
  - o Join a public speaking group.
  - o Take an acting class.

Once you've identified two general ideas associated with your interests, hobbies, and future activities, go another layer by getting *even more* specific, in order to really start shaping your ideas into specific opportunities. So, it's not just "take a cooking class at the Boston Center for Adult Education," which is a great idea, but it's going a step further by identifying a specific class that piques your interest the most: "The Art of French Cooking, four Mondays, 7:30–10 p.m., starting January 7, 2013." Identifying these precise opportunities will take some effort on your part. You can inquire within your networks and/or do Internet research. Facebook and Twitter can also be good sources of information.

It's also important to consider diversifying your portfolio, so to speak. Let's use my love for food and wine as an example. For both interests, you could choose to take a class at Boston Center for Adult Education (BCAE). However, I recommend branching out a bit —maybe you write down taking a wine class at BCAE but a cooking class with ArtEpicure Cooking School, in Somerville, MA. This way, you don't get burnt out on one organization; you keep your options new and fresh.

Facebook idea. Looking for fun ways or cool events to meet people? Try publishing a status update to your Facebook friends asking for their suggestions. It's amazing how people will write the most embarrassing notes about their exes or personal dating life on Facebook, but shy away from asking for help in this way. Go ahead, give it a shot!

Here's how I took my list, which I compiled in the summer of 2012, and drilled down deeper:

- I love discussing and debating politics and current affairs.
  - o Volunteer with a political campaign or organization.
    - ▪ Sign up to volunteer with Massachusetts Women's Political Caucus: http://www.mwpc.org/get/volunteer.php
  - o Attend a politically-oriented event in your city/town.
    - ▪ Debate Watching Meetup.com group – October 16, 2012, 7:30–11:00 p.m., Jose McIntyre's bar.
- I love playing tennis, squash, and all racket sports.
  - o Join a tennis or squash league or tennis or squash club.
    - ▪ Contact Diane, membership coordinator, at the University Club of Boston to inquire about application process.
  - o Teach or volunteer with an inner city tennis or squash organization.
    - ▪ Squashbusters, volunteer squash coaching, Saturdays, 8:00-10:00 a.m. and/or 10:00 a.m. – 12:00 p.m.
- I generally enjoy athletic endeavors and competitions of all kinds.
  - o Join an athletic league.
    - ▪ Social Boston Sports, kickball co-ed fall league, free agents team, starts September 7, 2012, six weeks. Sign up via website.
  - o Take part in a Beirut or Cornhole competition.
    - ▪ Boston Cornhole, Tuesday nights beginning October 23, Great American Tavern, North Reading, 7:00 p.m.

- I enjoy drinking wine, going out to the bars, and having drinks with friends.
  - o Go to wine tastings.
    - ▪ Museum of Fine Arts, wine tasting, Wednesdays ("Winesdays") at Bravo restaurant (the MFA restaurant), 5:30–7:30 p.m.
  - o Join local pub crawls.
    - ▪ Happy Hour Halloween PubCrawl Boston, Friday, October 26, 2012, 5:00 p.m.
- I love food of all kinds.
  - o Enroll in a cooking class.
    - ▪ BCAE, Pizza and Calzones: Wednesday, 6:00 p.m.–9:00 p.m., one session October 31, 2012.
  - o Attend food festivals.
    - ▪ Taste of WGBH: Food & Wine Festival, September 13–15, 2012, WGBH, One Guest Street, Boston.
- I love fashion and style.
  - o Check out fashion shows.
    - ▪ Boston Fashion Week, Opening Night Gala, The Tent at Boston Fashion Week, Thursday, September 27, 7:00 p.m.–11:00 p.m.
  - o Go to store openings/promotional events.
    - ▪ Ted Baker, Newbury Street; Ted's Fall Folly in-store event, Ted Baker London store in Boston, Wednesday, September 19, 2012 from 6:00 p.m.–9:00 p.m.
- I enjoy volunteering and helping those less fortunate.
  - o Sign up to be on a planning committee for an annual gala of a charity you like:

- Steppingstone Foundation annual gala, apply for volunteering opportunity with planning and executing events at www.tsf.org/volunteer.php
  o Sign up to be a big sister.
    - Apply on www.bigsister.org to become a big sister.
- I enjoy writing of all kinds (non-fiction, fiction, blogging, screenwriting, etc.).
  o Take a writing class.
    - Grub Street: The Art of Column Writing, Friday, October 19, 10:30 a.m. –1:30 p.m., at Grub Street headquarters.
  o Go to a writing conference.
    - 2013 AWP Conference & Bookfair, Hynes Convention Center & Sheraton Boston Hotel, March 6 p.m.–9 p.m., 2013.
- I enjoy listening to talk radio and radio hosting.
  o Go to one of your favorite local radios station's events.
    - Meet WBUR Hosts At The Boston Book Festival, Saturday, October 27 – 10:00 a.m.
  o Volunteer for one of my favorite radio stations.
    - WBUR volunteering, email volunteer@wbur.org or call (617) 353-8155.
- I love the ballet.
  o Volunteer for ballet organization.
    - Boston Ballet, for more information on how to get involved email volunteers@bostonballet.org.
  o Take an introductory ballet class.
    - Boston Ballet, Open Adult Classes, no experience necessary, Boston studio. Beginner Ballet,

Mondays and Wednesdays, 7:00 p.m.–8:30 p.m. Drop in classes, no pre-registration needed.

- I love going to the movies, and especially enjoy foreign films.
  - o Join a film lover's club/network.
    - ▪ Join "Movie Date: Boston" on Meetup.com, for singles who love movies.
  - o Attend local film festivals.
    - ▪ Boston Underground Film Festival, March 2013, buy tickets at www.bostonunderground.org.
- I enjoy reading of all kinds (books, magazines, newspapers).
  - o Join a book club.
    - ▪ Join "20ish & 30ish Boston Book Club" on Meetup.com.
  - o Check out local author book signings and readings.
    - ▪ Brookline Booksmith, 279 Harvard St., Brookline MA, Writers & Readers Series, Thursday, October 18 at 6:00 p.m., Chris Elliott, Emmy-award-winning comedian, *SNL* alum, *The Guy Under The Sheets: The Unauthorized Autobiography*, Coolidge Corner Theatre, Tickets on sale 9/1 for $5 each.
- I love to laugh and make people laugh.
  - o Go to a stand-up comedy festival.
    - ▪ Boston Comedy Festival, September 13–22, buy tickets at www.bostoncomedyfest.com.
  - o Take an improv class.
    - ▪ Improv Boston, Improv 101, Saturdays 3:00 p.m.–5:00 p.m., starts 10/13.

- I enjoy keeping up with and staying involved in my alma mater.
  - o Check out NESCAC events.
    - NESCAC+ Alumni Club of Boston 2012 Annual Boat Cruise,
      Thursday, August 23, 2012, 8:00 p.m. –11:00 p.m.
  - o Attend Amherst College events in Boston.
    - Amherst Association of Boston, Amherst-Williams Football Telecast, November 12, 2012.
- I'd like to learn how to cook.
  - o Take a cooking class.
    - Stir Boston, Autumn Beer and Cheese, 10/21. Sign up on website at www.stirboston.com.
  - o Join a food enthusiasts group.
    - Join "Food Lovers" on Meetup.com, next event on Thursday, October 25, Sushi Night, Fugakyu Japanese Restaurant, 1280 Beacon Street, Brookline, MA, 7:30 p.m.
- I'd like to learn how to play Ultimate Frisbee.
  - o Join an Ultimate Frisbee league.
    - Social Boston Sports, Tuesday Night Ultimate Frisbee League, Co-Ed All Levels, starts June 26, six weeks.
  - o Go the park and join up with other Frisbee enthusiasts.
    - Boston Common, Sunday afternoons.
- I'd like to learn how to improve my singing voice.
  - o Take group singing class.
    - BCAE, Voice Workshop, class open to beginners as well as students of all levels, 6:30 p.m. –8:00

p.m., 8 sessions starting September 11 ending October 30.

- o Karaoke night.
    - ▪ Sissy K's bar and restaurant; karaoke, Sundays–Thursdays, 8:30 p.m–1:30 a.m.
- • I'd like to get over my fear of dogs.
    - o Volunteer at an animal shelter.
        - ▪ Animal Rescue League of Boston, go to <u>www. home.arlboston.org</u> for application to volunteer.
    - o Accompany friend to dog park or event.
        - ▪ Yappy Hour at the Liberty Hotel, 5:30 p.m. until 8:00 p.m. each Wednesday through the summer and continues into fall as long as weather permits.
- • I'd like to get better at public speaking.
    - o Join a public speaking group.
        - ▪ Boston Toastmasters, all prospective members can visit club at any meetings as guest, no RSVP required, all guests can participate in the "table topics" section of meetings, meets every Tuesday at 6:15 p.m., Boston University, College of General Studies.
    - o Take an acting class.
        - ▪ Boston Acting Classes, Intro to Acting, Davis Square, Somerville, Thursdays, January 10–February 7, 2013, five weeks, 7:00 p.m. –9:30 p.m.

No excuses! By creating specific lists like the one I've created, you prevent yourself from making excuses, like "There aren't any good places or ways to meet men."

By narrowing it down to this level of detail, you will have created a robust list of different opportunities from which to choose. In shaping hazy ideas into specific opportunities you prevent yourself from making excuses, procrastinating, or becoming lazy. You now have a

tangible list of opportunities at your fingertips; moving forward, all you have to do is commit by acting on some of them.

You can always go back and add to this list as ideas strike you—just always be sure to research and write down specific activities associated with any interests you identify, so you increase your chances of acting on them.

When you do decide to act by attending certain opportunities, it is crucial that you make the most of them. That means being friendly, open, inviting, and willing to converse and flirt with new people. Say hello first, strike up conversations with men, throw them a compliment. Or if you want a man to approach you, practice sustained eye contact with a smile. Men are visual creatures, as I'm sure you've heard many times before; sometimes all they need is a friendly signal from you so that they know it's okay to approach.

At this point, you can begin sorting through your list and choosing the opportunities that excite you most. However, there are ways to get even more strategic about which opportunities you ultimately decide to pursue:

Diversify your portfolio.

Short-term opportunities and long-term communities both have pros and cons. Why not have a mixture of both?

- Short-term opportunities versus communities
- Male-oriented activities.

Short-term opportunities vs. communities

From the list you create, there will undoubtedly be a slew of short-term opportunities. Using my list, a few of these would be: the Ted Baker in-store clothing event; the BCAE's Pizza and Calzones

cooking class; and the Taste of WGBH food and wine festival event. In other words, these are one-shot opportunities: You go to the class or event once and that's it.

Given your interests, these will be fun opportunities for you to pursue, at which you also might meet single men. On the flip side, they do not allow you to become a deeper part of a network where you can start building and nurturing relationships, as discussed in chapter 9. Using my list, a few of these types of opportunities would be: volunteering at WBUR; becoming a member of the University Club of Boston; and joining the Movie Date: Boston club on Meetup.com. These opportunities allow you to build deeper connections with people on a longer-term basis, so that they potentially become part of your secondary or perhaps even primary networks. And if they become part of either of those networks, they can become SLAs or PLAs.

Of course, the disadvantage of becoming a member of a community in this sense, is that you'll need to commit more time and energy to being a part of it; whereas, with one-shot opportunities you have a single chance of making a connection but don't have to invest lots of time into nurturing relationships.

Both short-term opportunities and longer-term, community-oriented opportunities have their advantages and disadvantages. It's best to have a balance.

Male-oriented activities

If you're going to think strategically about the list you've created, you might start by considering what activities are probably best suited

Want to meet men? It's as simple as going where they go!

for meeting men and pursue those opportunities first. Because all of these opportunities are associated with your interests and hobbies, you're bound to enjoy the experience, but there's no harm in thinking *even more* strategically about these opportunities you've identified.

For example, if you put on your list that you love to knit, and you identify two opportunities in your area to pursue knitting, measure that activity against an opportunity that's likely to draw more men. Last time I checked, there weren't a ton of male knitters. From my list, joining a co-ed kickball team as a free agent or entering a Beirut or Cornhole competition are sure-fire ways to meet men directly (for a twenty- or thirty-something). Moreover, the kickball opportunity allows you to join a group of fifteen new people and form a community, in which you can get to know people over time, build relationships, and gain access to entirely new networks.

So take a moment to go through your list and write down the opportunities you think would be great for meeting men directly in your desired age-group. From my list, I've identified several opportunities that I think would fall into this category.

- o Join a tennis or squash league or club.
  - ▪ Contact Diane, membership coordinator, at the University Club of Boston to inquire about application process.
- o Teach or volunteer with an inner city tennis or squash organization.
  - ▪ Squashbusters, volunteer squash coaching, Saturdays, 8:00 a.m.–10:00 a.m. and/or 10:00 a.m. –12:00 p.m.

o   Join an athletic league.

- Social Boston Sports, kickball co-ed fall league, free agents team, starts September 7, 2012, six weeks. Sign up via website.

o   Take part in a Beirut or Cornhole competition.

- Boston Cornhole, Tuesday nights beginning October 23, Great American Tavern, North Reading, 7:00 p.m.

o   Go to wine tastings.

- Museum of Fine Arts, wine tasting, Wednesdays ("Winesdays") at Bravo restaurant (the MFA restaurant), 5:30 p.m. –7:30 p.m.

o   Join local pub crawls.

- Happy Hour Halloween PubCrawl Boston, Friday, October 26, 2012, 5:00 p.m.

o   Sign up to be on a planning committee for an annual gala of a charity you like:

- Steppingstone Foundation annual gala, apply for volunteering opportunity with planning and executing events at www.tsf.org/volunteer.php.

o   Go to a writing conference.

- 2013 AWP Conference & Bookfair, Hynes Convention Center & Sheraton Boston Hotel, March 6–9, 2013.

o   Join a film lover's club/network.

- Join "Movie Date: Boston" on Meetup.com, for singles who love movies.

o   Take an improv class.

- Improv Boston, Improv 101, Saturdays 3:00 p.m. –5:00 p.m., starts 10/13.

o   Check out NESCAC events.

  ▪ NESCAC+ Alumni Club of Boston 2012 Annual
    Boat Cruise,
    Thursday, August 23, 2012, 8:00 p.m. –11:00 p.m.

o   Attend Amherst College events in Boston.

  ▪ Amherst Association of Boston, Amherst-Williams
    Football Telecast, November 12, 2012.

o   Join a food enthusiasts group.

  ▪ Join "Food Lovers" on Meetup.com, next event
    on Thursday, October 25, Sushi Night, Fugakyu
    Japanese Restaurant, 1280 Beacon Street,
    Brookline, MA, 7:30 p.m.

o   Take a cooking class.

  ▪ Stir Boston, Autumn Beer and Cheese, 10/21. Sign
    up on website at www.stirboston.com.

o   Join a food enthusiasts group.

  ▪ Join "Food Lovers" on Meetup.com, next event
    on Thursday, October 25, Sushi Night, Fugakyu
    Japanese Restaurant, 1280 Beacon Street,
    Brookline, MA, 7:30 p.m.

o   Join a public speaking group.

  ▪ Boston Toastmasters, all prospective members can
    visit club at any meetings as guest, no RSVP re-
    quired, all guests can participate in the "table topics"
    section of meetings, meets every Tuesday at 6:15
    p.m., Boston University, College of General Studies.

o   Take an acting class.

  ▪ Boston Acting Classes, Intro to Acting, Davis
    Square, Somerville, Thursdays, January 10–
    February 7, 2013, five weeks, 7:00 p.m. –9:30 p.m.

It's important to note that while *all* opportunities have the potential to create value for your dating and love life, some may be more directly fruitful than others (Cornhole versus knitting). But they all have the power to create opportunity. Let's return to the knitting example. You could sign up for a knitting class because you are dying to learn how to knit. Now, as far as meeting men is concerned, this is, as I mentioned, probably not the best direct route, but you could certainly meet other women there, build relationships with them and eventually be directly set up with someone in their network or be invited to, say, a party or event where you could meet someone.

2. Opportunities based on trying new things completely unrelated to your self-stated interests

You may also want to think about new activities that are completely unrelated to all of the interests you mentioned when creating your first list ("opportunities based on your interests"). If your friend invites you to an activity or event that sounds like something totally opposite of what you're interested in, be adventurous and say YES.

Years ago, a friend invited me to a play in the suburbs of Boston. I had (have) no interest in plays—they bore me—let alone driving thirty minutes to get to the venue. But that particular night, it was either go to the play or sit on my couch for the second weekend in a row. So I got off my butt, went to the play, and ended up meeting a guy during intermission. We exchanged numbers and went out a week later. It wasn't a love connection, but I will always look back on that experience with fondness, remembering how an activity completely

unrelated to anything I was interested in or excited about had led me to meeting a really nice guy.

Remember: you never know where an opportunity is going to come from, so take advantage of the ones that come your way, even if they are cloaked in uncertainty.

3. *Opportunities based on already-identified, high-percentage ways to meet men*

As someone who was in the dating world up until my early thirties, and as someone who has written and spoken about dating and relationships for more than a decade, I know a thing or two about high-percentage opportunities to meet men. You certainly may have other ideas to add to this list, based on your experiences and geographical location, and you should certainly pursue those ideas. My list is just a jumping off point, a catalyst to help you start thinking about your own list of these types of opportunities. You may want to try some or all of these suggestions, or maybe you're not into any of them. If you are the type of person that doesn't deal well with the type of chaos that might arise by doing a summer house with other people, then that's not the right opportunity for you. Remember, though, try being open to new ideas.

Here are my suggestions:

- Online dating
- Singles events, activities, or professional matchmakers
- Summer or ski vacation house with others
- Friends of friends' parties, activities, or outings
- Charity balls, galas, and events
- Sport and social clubs/organizations

Online dating

I met my fiancé on Match.com, so obviously I'm biased. But I truly believe online dating should be a tool in every single person's dating tool belt. It's not the only avenue you should explore for meeting men; rather, it's one option. It's also a proven way to arrange dates, during which you can practice your dating skills. If you're employing iterative and incremental dating, you shouldn't be consumed by the idea of immediately meeting the perfect man who you'll marry and have babies with, anyway. It's great if you meet that person on your very first date, but for 99 percent of the population it doesn't work that way. Many of you reading this book have been out on tons of dates and you're still looking. Remember the statistic I quoted in chapter 7 about the average number of men a woman dates (24!) before she finds her man? That's just the way it goes sometimes in the dating world. And the sooner you accept the reality that your experience will probably be a lot of trial and error, the sooner you give yourself permission to experiment and appreciate the journey.

Another bonus of online dating is that many (not all) of the site's subscribers are interested in actually getting to meet and know people. With online dating, you can email a few times back and forth with someone and set up a date, as opposed to meeting men at bars, where you have no idea who you're meeting, what they're thinking, or what their relationship status is. On top of that, if you give a man your number, you have to wait for him to call to initiate a date (unless you want to experiment with getting his number and calling him). Online dating puts hundreds (thousands) of men at your fingertips, allowing you to be more action-oriented, to take control of your dating and love life in a more relaxed environment than places like bars and clubs.

Niche dating.

Online dating sites targeted to a very specific audience.

The best part about online dating in the 2000's is the multitude of site options. Beyond just the generic fee and non-fee sites, such as Match, eHarmony, OKCupid, PlentyofFish, and the like, there are all sorts of niche dating sites, many of which are free. If you're into running, you can join Runningsingles.com to meet fellow joggers; if you enjoy the work of author Ayn Rand, you can sign up for Atlasphere.com to meet other Randian enthusiasts; if you're a vegetarian, you can become a part of Veggiedate.com to find like-minded anti-carnivores. And so on and so forth. If you have a passion, there's most likely a specialized dating site dedicated to it.

There are also myriad atypical dating sites, many of them free as well, such as Coffee Meets Bagel, a less hands-on service for the user that delivers one carefully chosen match every day to a subscriber's inbox; or Meetattheairport.com, a site that helps alleviate airport boredom by matching people up with nearby, fellow fliers; or Tawkify.com, online dating with a twist—a human matchmaker. By all means sign up for more than one site; diversify your portfolio.

Mobile dating.
Embrace technology. Adapt. Make your dating life fruitful by utilizing different technologies, not shunning them.

And let's not forget about all the incredibly ingenious mobile dating applications currently on the market: MeetMoi.com, a location-based service that updates subscribers' locations in real-time, so that when a match is nearby, alerts are sent to users' phones; or Skout.com, an application that identifies singles in a user's immediate vicinity, allowing the opportunity to flirt and meet up with them; or Blendr, an application that combines location-based dating with Foursquare-style check-ins. For twenty- and thirty-somethings, especially, these technologies are becoming very popular.

Whatever route you take, there are plenty of tips and suggestions on the Internet on how to create an appealing profile. Also, in addition to my coaching services and products, I help online daters create alluring, magnetic profiles. This service is especially helpful for those who find the process tedious or don't know how to put their best foot forward through the written word—check out my website for more information: www.thelovetrep.com.

Finally, please remember that it's important to give online dating time. A common complaint I hear from singles goes something like this:

Single woman: "I tried online dating. It didn't work at all for me. I didn't meet any guys I liked. And I was contacted by too many weirdos."

Me: "Really? How long were you on there for?"

Single woman: "About six months or so."

At this point I try to explain to them the folly of their complaint. How can you be so critical of something to which you've devoted so little time?

The truth is people who usually make these complaints don't want to try online dating in the first place. They go into the process with a negative mindset, which affects the way they experience it. It becomes a self-fulfilling prophecy: *I'm not going to like it. I'll try it but not put in any real effort or be skeptical about it.* Then when they have negative experiences, they tell themselves they now have evidence to support their original perception (also known as confirmation bias). When

ePatience. I was on and off Match.com for years before I met Dave. Give online dating time, just as you give other opportunities to meet people time.

Picture Time! If you sign up for an online dating site, think about hiring a professional photographer to take some photos of you for your profile. The difference between using

some run-of-the-mill amateur shots versus professional photographs can mean all the difference in the world. Men are visual creatures! Get them to click on your profile by piquing their interest with your spectacular pictures.

their subscription comes to an end, they can triumphantly reassure themselves that their suspicions were right all along: *I knew I wouldn't like online dating.* There are also the people that go into online dating with the polar opposite mindset: that a site is going to lead them to their Prince Charming within three to six months. Inevitably, both mindsets set daters up for disappointment.

Go into online dating with a positive approach, but understand that, realistically, it may take more than six months; it may even take two to three years. Think about it: You've been trying the traditional routes to meet people (bars, setups, parties) for years upon years (how many times have you been hit on by a drunk guy at a bar?!), and you still have faith in those opportunities, so why would you magically expect online dating to work for you in a mere six months? Give online dating time. But also be sure to make an effort with it—that means carving out, say, thirty minutes to an hour each day to look at profiles, reach out to people, and respond to emails. I was on dating sites on and off for several years before I met Dave.

Without a doubt, online dating is one of the best ways to create your own opportunities, and sometimes not in the ways you would even expect. Just ask a former client of mine named Julia. She went out on two dates with a guy named John who she met on Plenty of Fish. She liked John, but, unfortunately, he did not share her affections, sending her a note after their second date that he just didn't feel the romantic spark. Feeling defeated, Julia emailed me for support. While I understood that she felt disappointment, I encouraged her to turn this setback into an opportunity. I suggested that she reply to John saying that she respects his feelings, enjoyed his company, would love to introduce him to her single friends, and then to ask if he knew

of any single guys who might be a good match for her. While a bit uncomfortable with this approach, she eventually sent the email and received a wonderful reply from John the very next day that he did indeed have a friend to whom he could introduce her. Julia's email was such a delight to John, because it showed how confident and comfortable Julia was in her own skin, how well she handles disappointment, and how willing she is to rebound in the face of vulnerability.

Remember: Look for the opportunities in your setbacks and in the face of uncertainty.

Singles events, activities, or professional matchmakers

These are opportunities that have a very specific purpose: to meet other singles. There is no other reason to attend these events. Examples include, speed dating, cocktail mixers, singles cruises, and the like. Depending on your age, you might be more or less open to attending these types of events. But remember: Entrepreneurs see opportunities in just about everything, especially the ideas that frighten them or make them step outside their comfort zones. Sometimes that's where the best opportunities lie.

You also may want to consider professional matchmakers. The downside is that they can often be pricey; the upside, of course, is that they are totally devoted to helping you find compatible matches.

Summer or ski house with others

I've met numerous men by joining a group of people in summer and ski houses. The first two summers after graduating college, I joined

Opportunity knocks.

Years ago when I was doing online dating, I met a man and we went out twice. The romantic feelings weren't there for either of us, but we remained friends. A few months after our second date, he invited me to a party he was having at his home, at which I met a man who I dated for a year!

a group of people (some of whom I knew and some of whom were strangers) in renting a Newport, Rhode Island, house for the summer. We'd all pile into cars every Friday after work and drive off to our house, returning home on Sundays. Not only did I have a ton of fun during those summer weekends, but I forged new relationships, and met a bunch of guys.

I also joined a Stowe, Vermont, ski house one winter in my late-twenties, organized by one of my high school friends. I knew only a couple of the people going in on the house, but I got introduced to many of my high school friend's college friends. Although I didn't ski, I had a blast getting to know new people and exploring Stowe. I ended up meeting a guy at The Matterhorn, a popular, local watering hole, one weekend when I bumped into a co-worker. My co-worker was friends with the guy who, in the coming months, I dated a bit. While it didn't last due to the distance (he lived in DC), I will never forget the experience I had and the friendships I made that winter at the ski house.

Friends of friends' parties, activities, and outings

My guess is that going to your friends' parties (dinner, birthday, seasonal, theme, and so on) is a big part of your social life already. This can certainly be a good way to meet people, because you're gaining access to all the people your friend knows. But an even better opportunity is going to a party of a friend's friend, because you are gaining access to even more extended networks of people who you've never met before. For instance, compare a friend's theme party to a friend of a friend's theme party. At your friend's party, let's say there are thirty people. You may know about twenty of those people. If you get invited by a friend to go to her

or his friend's theme party, at which there are thirty people, you'll most likely be meeting twenty-nine new people. I'm not advocating blowing off a friend's party for a stranger's party, but if you have the option of going to the movies with a few friends (even though this is exactly what you did last weekend) or going to a friend of a friend's party, consider which opportunity is more likely to help you meet potential dates.

Prioritize and seek out these types of opportunities in your life. Breaking out of your inner circle from time to time is crucial. Your close friends are wonderful to have by your side for so many reasons: support, comfort, companionship. But when you are hanging out with the same people all the time (probably going to the same, tired bars), you'll be less likely to meet new people and have new experiences. You need to break free every now and then from your comfort zone and seek new experiences, new opportunities that will give you access to new faces, new networks.

Charity balls, galas, and events

I have found galas and charity balls to be an excellent way to meet men. Not only are you spending money on worthy causes, but you also get to dress up, enjoy great food, and dance the night away. Moreover, you have built-in conversation starters at your disposal:

- "How did you hear about the event?"
- "Are you involved in the charity at all?"
- "Are you going to bid on any of the silent auction items tonight?"
- "I love your tux/tie."

Sport and social clubs/organizations

In the Greater Boston area, there are several organizations dedicated to providing sports leagues, social events, ski trips, and adventure travel for over thousands of socially active professionals. Joining one of these organizations can be great for your social life, not just for meeting men but forging new friendships as well.

—◊—

So, what would you put on your list of high-percentage ways to meet men, based on your experiences or observations?

The lists you create may be completely different than mine. I've simply listed opportunities that have worked for me in the past as well as opportunities that I know have great results for many singles. Again, if you hate going to large-scale galas, you're probably better offer taking advantage of other opportunities first. It's up to you to decide!

Design Thinking

"Always design a thing by considering it in its next larger context,
a chair in a room, a room in a house, a house in an environment,
and environment in a city plan"
– Eero Saarinen, Architect

Another way to think about creating your own opportunities in your dating life is through something called *design thinking*. Many new and seasoned entrepreneurs begin an entrepreneurial journey by engaging in design thinking exercises.

Design thinkers design products. Look at a product in your home: a piece of furniture or an electronic gadget. In order to design that product, a designer (and/or a design team) goes through a design thinking process that seeks to understand the customer, the person who will be using that product.

As a Love TREP, one of your goals is to understand the "customer"—in this case, men—better, so that you can identify opportunities and new ideas for interacting and connecting with them. You can use design thinking to do just that. (I'll talk even more about understanding your customer in chapter 11.)

Here's the design thinking model, conceptualized by the design firm IDEO, that you can follow to create opportunities for your dating life:

Please read through this description carefully and refer back to it when you do this exercise.

Step #1:

<u>Defining the Challenge</u>

Your challenge: As a Love TREP, your challenge is to create new ideas, possibilities, and opportunities for interacting, engaging, and connecting with men.

Step #2:

Observations

The next step is to observe those people with whom you want to make deeper connections and understand better (men!). You have to observe and listen to men in order to relate to, understand, and connect with them. Without this knowledge, you might end up making *assumptions* or developing misperceptions about men and thus create solutions in your dating life that lead you in the wrong direction.

I want you to start observing men wherever you go. To create new ideas and perceptions about men, it's important to observe them in a variety of environments, and where and how they live and socialize.

What are observations?

- Observations are facts without judgment. Oftentimes, we think we are making observations, but we are inserting our bias into what's happening.

How does one observe?

- When observing, focus on the facts; don't let feelings or opinions get involved.
- Don't let your assumptions or preconceived notions about men, which are based on experiences and images from your past, taint your observations. Separate observations from your interpretations (or you may miss something).

- Describe what you see (don't interpret) as it's happening even if you don't know why or what the importance of the observation will be.
- Observing and collecting facts without immediately judging those facts is difficult, but it's critical to developing useful *insights*. Just record the facts and avoid temptation to *interpret* the facts for now.
- Look at body language and facial cues to add more context to what you are observing. But don't interpret what you see; just observe and record.
- Also, remember to keep an eye out for things that surprise you.

Don't just observe one place—observe different men in action in different spaces. Tell me what you see men doing, how they are behaving, what you hear them saying. Just the facts!

Here are a couple of ideas you can choose from with regard to observing men:

Places:

- Cafes/restaurants
- On the street/sidewalk
- At bars/clubs
- At stores or malls
- At the park/dog park
- At events around town
- At food markets

- At parties or events
- At family gatherings
- On unscripted TV shows
- In videos (wedding videos in particular can be illuminating)

With whom:

- Observe them alone
- Observe them with family
- Observe them with friends
- Observe them with animals/pets
- Observe them hitting on and flirting with women
- Observe them with girlfriends/wives
- Observe them talking on the phone
- Observe them with service personnel

Examples of observations:

1. *Observation*: Men frequently order beer at bars. Men talk with other men about different kinds of beer and the beer-making process. Men attend beer festivals. Men crack a cold beer when they get home from work.

2. *Observation*: A single man is alone at a bar despite many women around him. He pulls out his phone and starts checking Facebook.

3. *Observation*: A group of five women, despite being dressed up and not wearing engagement rings aren't approached by men all night at a bar. Some men look over at their group but never walk over.

4. *Observation*: A woman sits alone at a bar with a glass of wine and a magazine. She turns her chair outward toward the crowd. She smiles and appears open and friendly. A handful of men approach her to say hello.

5. *Observation*: A woman in a café comments on something a man at the table next to hers is eating. Man smiles and answers. Man and woman begin conversation. Man asks questions, cracks jokes.

Step #3:

Form Insights

- From your various observations, you will form educated, useful insights about men.

- It doesn't mean your insights will be 100% correct, but your insights will help you develop and refine your ideas about how men think, feel, and live.

Examples of creating insights from my observations:

1. *Observation*: Men frequently order beer at bars. Men talk with other men about different kinds of beer and the beer-making process. Men attend beer festivals. Men crack a cold beer when they get home from work.
    a. *Insight*: Men enjoy bonding over beer.
    b. *Insight*: Men love talking about and learning about beer.

2. *Observation*: A single man is alone at a bar despite many women around him. He pulls out his phone and starts checking Facebook.

    a.   *Insight*: Although he would enjoy a woman saying hello and chatting, he is embarrassed because people might think he's alone and therefore a "loser" or "creepy."

3. *Observation*: A group of five women, despite being dressed up and not wearing engagement rings aren't approached by men all night at a bar. Some men look over at their group but never walk over.

    a.   *Insight*: Men are intimidated by a gaggle of women and prefer not to face rejection in front of other women.

4. *Observation*: A woman sits alone at a bar with a glass of wine and a magazine. She turns her chair outward toward the crowd. She smiles and appears open and friendly. A handful of men approach her to say hello.

    a.   *Insight*: Men find it easier to approach women when they are alone and won't be judged by or have to compete with a woman's friends.

5. *Observation*: A woman in a café comments on something a man at a nearby table is eating. Man smiles and answers. Man and woman begin conversation. Man asks questions, cracks jokes.

    a.   *Insight*: Men love when women approach.

    b.   *Insight*: Men are looking to meet women everywhere.

    c.   *Insight*: Men aren't that scary and intimidating or think they're better than women, and, in fact, may be scared to come up to us.

Step #4:

<u>Framing Opportunities</u>

What does it mean to frame opportunities?

- The process of translating insights into opportunities is about moving from the current state to envisioning future possibilities. [per IDEO+ExperiencePoint—see bibliography]
- Opportunities are the launching pad for ideas and possibilities.
- It helps to frame your opportunities by starting with: "How might I…?"

Examples of framing opportunities from my insights:

1. *Observation*: Men frequently order beer at bars. Men talk with other men about different kinds of beer and the beer-making process. Men attend beer festivals. Men crack a cold beer when they get home from work.
   a. *Insight*: Men enjoy bonding over beer
   b. *Insight*: Men love talking about and learning about beer
      i. *Framed opportunity*: How might I connect with men over beer?
2. *Observation*: A single man is alone at a bar despite many women around him. He pulls out his phone and starts checking Facebook.
   a. *Insight*: Although he would enjoy a woman saying hello and chatting, he is embarrassed because people might think he's alone and therefore a "loser" or "creepy."
      i. *Framed opportunity*: How might I engage with a man when he is standing alone at a bar?
3. *Observation*: A group of five women, despite being dressed up and not wearing engagement rings, aren't approached

by men all night at a bar. Some men look over at their group but never walk over.

   a. *Insight*: Men are intimidated by a gaggle of women and prefer not to face rejection in front of other women.

      i. *Framed opportunity*: How might I break apart from my friends?

4. *Observation*: A woman sits alone at a bar with a glass of wine and a magazine. She turns her chair outward toward the crowd. She smiles and appears open and friendly. A handful of men approach her to say hello.

   a. *Insight*: Men find it easier to approach women when they are alone and won't be judged by or have to compete with a woman's friends.

      i. *Framed opportunity*: How might I start creating opportunities to go out on my own?

      ii. *Framed opportunity*: How mignt I start making myself appear more open and approachable when I do venture out by myself?

5. *Observation*: A woman in a café comments on something a man at a nearby table is eating. Man smiles and answers. Man and woman begin conversation. Man asks questions, cracks jokes.

   a. *Insight*: Men love when women approach.

   b. *Insight*: Men are looking to meet women everywhere.

   c. *Insight*: Men aren't that scary and intimidating or think they're better than women, and, in fact, may be scared to come up to us.

      i. *Framed opportunity*: How might I approach men and engage with them more often in a friendly way?

    ii. *Framed opportunity:* How might I go into my dates and interactions differently with men now that I see them differently?

Step #5:

Brainstorm Ideas

How do you brainstorm ideas?

- A productive brainstorm requires you to give yourself permission to think without constraints. It allows for silly or impossible ideas so as to spark relevant and reasonable ones.
- Brainstorm rules: no bad ideas, plenty of time to judge them later; encourage wild ideas; go for quantity.
  [per IDEO+ExperiencePoint]
- Brainstorm rules: no criticism, no order to getting ideas out there, no "buts", get lots of raw ideas out there so you can experiment and test them.

Examples of brainstorming ideas from my framed opportunities:

1. *Observation:* Men frequently order beer at bars. Men talk with other men about different kinds of beer and the beer-making process. Men attend beer festivals. Men crack a cold beer when they get home from work.
    a. *Insight:* Men enjoy bonding over beer.
    b. *Insight:* Men love talking about and learning about beer.
        i. *Framed opportunity:* How might I connect with men over beer?

- *Brainstorm ideas*:
  - ✓ Join beer-related groups on Facebook or meetup.com;
  - ✓ Attend beer festivals, new beer restaurant openings, beer-related events (a new brewery debuting their beer flavors);
  - ✓ Attend beer workshops or classes to gain more knowledge about beers and to meet men;
  - ✓ Ask a man his opinion on different beers at a bar, market, or liquor store;
  - ✓ Ask a man at a bar what kind of beer he's drinking and the difference between that beer and other beers.

2. *Observation*: A single man is alone at a bar despite many women around him. He pulls out his phone and starts checking Facebook.

   a. *Insight*: Although he would enjoy a woman saying hello and chatting, he is embarrassed because people might think he's alone and therefore a "loser" or "creepy."

      i. *Framed opportunity*: How might I engage with a man when he is standing alone at a bar?

         - *Brainstorm ideas*:
           - ✓ Position myself closer to him to make it easier for him to say hello;
           - ✓ Smile at him and give sustained eye contact when he looks up;
           - ✓ Comment on his phone;

    ✓ Ask if he's waiting for his friends;

    ✓ Ask if he's ever been to the bar and/or if he likes the bar;

    ✓ Make a playful joke about him standing alone.

3. *Observation*: A group of five women, despite being dressed up and not wearing engagement rings aren't approached by men all night at a bar. Some men look over at their group but never walk over.

    a. *Insight*: Men are intimidated by a gaggle of women, and prefer not to face rejection in front of other women.

       i. *Framed opportunity*: How might I break apart from my friends?

         • *Brainstorm ideas*:

           ✓ Go out with one or two friends maximum (two preferably so if I meet someone my friends can talk to each other);

           ✓ Hire a "wingwoman" from a wingwoman service to accompany me out one evening so the focus is on me and meeting new people;

           ✓ Break free from the group intermittently to go to the bathroom;

           ✓ Offer to buy drinks so I can go alone to the bar.

4. *Observation*: A woman sits alone at a bar with a glass of wine and a magazine. She turns her chair outward toward the crowd. She smiles and appears open and friendly. A handful of men approach her to say hello.

a. *Insight*: Men find it easier to approach women when they are alone and won't be judged by or have to compete with a woman's friends.

    i. *Framed opportunity*: How might I start creating opportunities to go out alone?

- *Brainstorm ideas*:
  - ✓ Go out alone to local, neighborhood bar where it feels more comfortable to fly solo;
  - ✓ Befriend bartender at a bar so I will have someone to chat with when sitting alone;
  - ✓ Make sure I look approachable with my body language and remain open to the crowd;
  - ✓ Tell friend to meet me at the bar at 9:00pm and get there at 8:00pm;
  - ✓ Order dinner at a low-key bar and bring a magazine, but look up often at those around me.

    ii. *Framed opportunity*: How might I start making myself appear more
open and approachable when I do venture out by myself?

- *Brainstorm ideas*:
  - ✓ Take a flirting class;
  - ✓ Watch your friends who are good at flirting and connecting with men and emulate them;

      ✓ Take off my ear buds and put away my iPod when walking in populated areas;

      ✓ Practice smiling at strangers, and make sure my head isn't focused downward when walking in public places.

5. *Observation*: A woman in a café comments on something a man at a nearby table is eating. Man smiles and answers. Man and woman begin conversation. Man asks questions, cracks jokes.

    a. *Insight*: Men love when women approach.

    b. *Insight*: Men are looking to meet women everywhere.

    c. *Insight*: Men aren't that scary and intimidating, and, in fact, may be scared to come up to us.

        i. *Framed opportunity*: How might I approach men and engage with them more often in a friendly way?

          • *Brainstorm ideas*:

            ✓ Consider starting more conversations with men I meet out and about;

            ✓ Relate to men about what they are doing—I don't have to create an experience, I can simply relate to what they are currently experiencing (if a man orders a ham sandwich, I can comment on his choice or ask him a question about it);

            ✓ Smile more at men when out and about and make eye contact to encourage them to come up to me.

       ii. *Framed opportunity*: How might I go into my dates and interactions differently with men now that I see them differently?

- *Brainstorm ideas*:
  - ✓ Repeat mantra before dates that men are not better or worse than me; they are my equals. I am not above or below them, and many of them are looking for the same things as me;
  - ✓ Try asking them different questions than what I'm used to or talk about me in a different way than I'm used to (don't focus on my job but talk more about passions and interests).

Step #6:

Try Experiments

Why try experiments?

- Experiments help us answer specific questions in order to evolve ideas. Multiple experiments may be necessary.

How do I experiment?

- Start *testing* out the ideas that were brainstormed.
- You may need to try experiments with multiple men to test your ideas. You may need to try different approaches. Maybe some men respond well, others do not, but if your experiment works with some, it opens you up to the notion that this idea *can* work and gives you courage to keep trying.

- Continue to experiment and refine the way you test your ideas. *Example*: Maybe I start by saying hello to a man. Then I refine that idea to commenting on something he's doing or a shared reference in our environment. Then maybe I do this with men who aren't typically my "type". Then maybe I work on simply smiling and sustained eye contact to get a man to come to me.

- What questions do you still need answered so your idea can succeed? *Example*: Do I need to ask a few men if they like when a woman approaches or starts a conversation with a man to know that my insight was right and to therefore give me the confidence to go do it? (More on talking to and getting feedback from men in chapter 11.)

With each of the examples *you* come up with when you go through the design thinking process, the same steps apply.

Slow down and take the time to observe men in the world around you. You will be amazed at what you begin to see once you start paying attention. There are opportunities and possibilities everywhere— the world is bursting with them and it's waiting for you to find and act on them!

Other strategies for you to consider

Here are ways for you to make your opportunities more fruitful.

Ordinary →
Extraordinary.
Don't
underestimate
the opportunity
to meet someone
organically
through
everyday,
outings/errands.

Make the Ordinary Extraordinary

I hope the design thinking exercise convinced you that even ordinary outings to cafes, markets, and shops can be great opportunities to meet men. Not only is it important to study and understand men, but it is also crucially important to make yourself approachable when out and about. That means taking your headphones off, being willing to make eye contact, smiling, and flirting.

I've met guys in all sorts of ordinary places where I had no intention of meeting anyone, simply because I made myself available for conversations, eye flirting, and being approached. I've met several guys at cafes and eateries, just by hanging out with my laptop, working on writing projects—curious as to what I was writing, they'd make eye contact and inquire. One time, I met a guy in line at a bakery. We made eye contact, I smiled, and he complimented me on my shoes. We ended up going out for dinner and bowling. We never became romantically involved, but we're friendly to this day. Another time I met a guy outside a mall. I had noticed him in one of the stores; when we crossed paths again outside the mall, I smiled and kept walking. About ten seconds later, I looked back at him and smiled again as he looked back at me. That's all it took for him to come after me. He got my number and we went out on a date. Never underestimate the power of eye contact and a smile.

These are just a few examples of how I was able to take ordinary, everyday occasions and create extraordinary opportunities for my dating and love life. Men are dying for you to flirt with them, for you to smile at them, for you to start a conversation with, say hello to, or compliment them. So go for it! On the flip side, if you want them to

come up to you, give them positive affirmations that it is indeed okay to approach. As I mentioned earlier, men are visual creatures and will respond well to smiles and sustained eye contact; in fact, they need you to give them these signals.

Sometimes you may not feel like smiling, or maybe you're just not naturally good at doing it. A flirting expert once told me that when I listened to or looked at others my lip line was too flat, potentially giving off an uninterested or uninviting vibe. I've always remembered that critique, if not for the hilarity of it (who knew I had a flat lip line?), but also because it had the potential to decrease opportunities to meet people or draw them in. To this day, when I catch myself in the flat lip expression (or lack thereof), I remind myself to curl my lips upward a bit. If you're not adept at smiling or giving good eye contact, go out to cafes, bookstores, museums, and the like and just start practicing. Sometimes the solution is simply to fake it until you make it, until it becomes natural and authentic. So get out there and smile at every man who meets eyes with you and hold your eye contact for just a bit. Try doing this on the sidewalk with passersby. The next week, start saying hello to people you walk by. The next week, throw out a few compliments to different men with whom you're standing in line. It's a lot simpler than you think. When you practice in this way, you also make it easier to smile at, flirt, converse, and hold eye contact with men at the more specific opportunities you decide to pursue (galas, events, parties, classes, and the like).

Fake it until you make it. Research has shown that the simple act of forcing a smile has the power to change your attitude.

Ultimately, you have a choice. You can go out into the world and keep to yourself, or you can make your opportunities fruitful by pushing yourself to flirt, smile, and converse with new people.

Sorry, I'm taken. When nothing's on the line, it's easier to risk. Adopt the attitude of a taken woman and see the men flock to you.

Pretend You're Taken

Here's a technique you might consider trying when pursuing opportunities, especially if you find yourself jaded about dating and men.

Have you ever noticed when you're in a relationship, men seem to flock to you or it somehow feels effortless drawing them in to you? It's true that when it rains it pours in this sense, if only because of your shift in attitude. You don't feel pressure when interacting with men or overly worried about how they will perceive you. You take risks by saying hello first, engaging them in conversation, or harmlessly flirting, because you have nothing to gain (or lose) from interacting with them. A woman in a healthy, happy relationship often radiates confidence and warmth. She is friendlier and more easygoing. She's not focusing on what she doesn't have or what she can get from an interaction. She doesn't care whether a man she's interacting with or men around her are potential suitors or marriage material. No doubt, others can sense this attitude; it's often the reason why a woman in a relationship seems to feel all the men come out of the woodwork when she's taken and why men are attracted to women who are taken. When I compare attempting to meet guys at bars as a single versus helping my friends meet them when I've been in relationships, the contrast is vivid. As a taken woman, I have no problem introducing myself to or having conversations with men who, if I were single, I'd probably shy away from, simply because as a coupled person I couldn't care less about *their* interest level or if *they* reject me in any way. It's like liquid courage without the actual alcohol.

It's sort of a cruel irony, but you can learn from it by taking on the mentality of a taken woman. When you pursue any opportunity, think

about carrying yourself as a woman in a healthy, happy relationship would carry herself. When you start to doubt yourself or feel insecure or get caught up in the should-I-or-shouldn't-I game or feel yourself harden, adopt the attitude of a taken woman in a healthy, happy relationship: You're friendly; you smile; you converse easily regardless of who you're talking to; you say hello and introduce yourself; you don't care so much about rejection or what others will think of you.

Long-term strategic thinking

I want to encourage you to start thinking strategically in the longer-term sense as well.

For example, I know women who take multiple girl vacations every calendar year to random locations, where the chances of meeting eligible, local men are slim to none. Each trip probably costs upwards of $1000–$1500 when all is said and done. If they take three of these types of vacations each year, that's more than $4000 on trips that have little opportunity for their love lives. Am I saying not to go on trips with your girlfriends ever? Of course not! Sometimes you need to get away and have girl time. Absolutely. But if you're committed to seeking opportunities to meet people, perhaps you can take $1000 from your girl vacations budget (by taking a pass on that third vacation to some obscure Mexican resort) and, say, buy ten $100 tickets to various charity galas (prime singles spots) where you have much better odds of meeting local, single men.

Or consider the dilemma of the self-proclaimed, cash-strapped woman who wants to sign up for a subscription-based online dating site but says she doesn't have enough money for a year subscription.

Cash-strapped? Prioritize your money strategically. Cut back on the pricey lattes each week and save yourself $50/month – that's $600 for the year that you could put toward opportunities for your love life.

My bet is that she could find a way to fund a subscription (around $300 for the year) by prioritizing what she spends her money on. This woman could cut back on the number of alcoholic beverages she consumes each month when out at bars, or reduce the amount of Starbucks coffees that she drinks each week and easily be able to afford a yearly subscription to, say, Match.com.

Think longer-term. Prioritize your love life.

Be Resourceful. Bootstrap Your Love Life.

Bootstrapping. Stretch the resources you already have at hand and get out there and experiment. You can bootstrap in your love life just as treps bootstrap in their businesses.

In the course of building my dating coaching business, I've had to be resourceful by creating my own opportunities and learning through experimentation. In the land of entrepreneurship, they call this boot-strapping: a way to stretch the resources that you already have at hand and gradually experiment your way to success. By living in the trenches, so to speak, you have a much better opportunity to learn and grow than if all the answers and wealth are given to you from the get-go. For example, when starting my coaching business, I did not have a ton of money to throw around, but I realized that the primary way I was going to learn about the business (both from a coaching and marketing standpoint) was building from the ground up and penny-pinching. I used the resources I had at hand by tapping into my already-established networks: my friend Dave took professional photographs of me for almost no cost; my boyfriend's friend created my website for a reduced price; my friend Sarah's friend helped me register my trademark for The Love TREP at a substantially reduced cost; my various contacts in the dating industry that I had forged over the years helped publicize my business for free, and gave me

free legal and marketing advice. Furthermore, I realized that the best way to get started was just to get out there and test ideas frequently: I experimented and prototyped my ideas to see which ones worked with clients and fans and learned from the roads that did not prove to be fruitful; I offered free coaching sessions to get feedback on my content and delivery; I gave interviews and practiced talking about my coaching philosophy to anyone and everyone who was curious (and probably to some who weren't!). I used the bootstrap model by being resourceful with my networks, by shaping my own opportunities, and by framing failure as a positive, productive force that would help build—not hurt—my business.

Creating opportunity, though, takes commitment and effort; rarely do entrepreneurs and singles have opportunities magically placed into their laps. While media outlets, as I already mentioned, tend to focus on the sexier narratives of entrepreneurs—so-and-so sold her house, maxed out her credit cards, lived on Ramen Noodles and water, and quit her day job to pursue her entrepreneurial venture, eventually becoming a successful millionaire—they often do the same with love stories—in *Eat, Pray, Love: One Woman's Search for Everything Across Italy, India and Indonesia*, Elizabeth Gilbert, at thirty-four, reeling from divorce and another relationship gone awry, leaves her home, family, and friends, in search of herself and romance, and eventually finds love with a Brazilian man. The majority of people, however, in business and love have much more normal stories about how they achieved their goals and visions. For example, an entrepreneur keeps her day job, so she doesn't have to go into debt and live on preservative-laden, cheap noodles, or a single decides to stay local and practice dating instead of escaping to fantastical faraway lands to find herself and create the perfect environment for The One to magically

Be a doer!
"When you *do something* you stir the pot and introduce the possibility that seemingly random ideas, people, and places will collide and form new combinations and opportunities."
– James Austin, entrepreneur.

step into her life. Gilbert's declaration that she wasn't rescued by a man but "was the administrator of my own rescue," is a noble one; unfortunately, the rest of us don't have the opportunity or resources to travel the world for a year in pursuit of spiritual and emotional awakening.

I am asking you, in a sense, to *bootstrap your love life*. Be resourceful with the resources you have at hand to create and shape your own opportunities; seize on and experiment with new ideas and learn from the ones that don't work; draw from your networks but also create new ones. Think outside the box when it comes to matters of the heart. Get creative. Be playful. Don't be content to sit and wait for opportunities to come your way; go out there and pave your own path.

Truly, your fate is what you make

The one thing I can guarantee about identifying and pursuing opportunities is that many of them might not lead anywhere as far as meeting dates. You might take a class or attend a gala and strike out with both. Love TREPs recognize that they may pursue a lot of dead ends, so to speak, understanding that the more they put themselves out there, the greater their chances of meeting people and extending their network, which ultimately increases their chances of eventually meeting someone special.

In *The Start-up of You*, Hoffman and Casnocha call this approach "courting serendipity." They write: "The key is to raise the likelihood that you stumble upon something valuable —namely, by courting good randomness and seeing the opportunities that reveal themselves." You may know someone who always seems to

have dates. I can tell you that it's not because she's lucky in that she happens to choose all the right places and events for meeting people; it's more about the fact that she puts herself out there and creates opportunities for herself: She says yes to dates with a lot of different men, even those who might not be her exact type, she nurtures and builds her networks, she doesn't let failure get in her way, she pushes herself to be social, even when she's tired, and so on and so forth. In summary, she courts or designs her own serendipity. According to Hoffman and Casnocha, "serendipity involves being alert to potential opportunity and acting on it." They continue, paraphrasing entrepreneur James Austin: "When you *do something* you stir the pot and introduce the possibility that seemingly random ideas, people, and places will collide and form new combinations and opportunities." By being in motion, Hoffman and Casnocha believe you are "spinning a web as wide and tall as possible in order to catch any interesting opportunities that come your way."

My mom always used to say to me, "Neel, you're never going to meet anyone lying on the couch," to which I'd usually respond with an eye roll and a gnashing of the teeth. In retrospect, her advice was simple and spot-on. My mom taught me that I have to get off my butt, create opportunity for myself, and make the most of those opportunities, so that "serendipity" has a chance to be set in motion.

In other words, your entrepreneurial journey to find love has little to do with luck; it has so much more to do with creating your own opportunities and then making the most of those opportunities. In the words of Linda Hamilton in *Terminator 2*, one of my and my brother's favorite movies, "Our fate is what we make."

Throughout the course of my life, both personally and professionally, I've had plenty of missteps, wrong turns, and dead ends. But I've
also had myriad successes. As an entrepreneur both in the traditional
business sense and within my dating and love life, I learned to create
my own opportunities, seize the ones that came my way, and bounced
back from the ones that led nowhere. I learned to make my own fate.
And that's what you must do as a dater—create, build, and shape your
fate, your love story.

—m—

A common complaint I hear from clients, friends, or overzealous
Facebook posters is that "There are no good single men out there."
My response to this gripe is simple: You're nuts. They are everywhere! They're walking next to you on the sidewalks; they're eating
by your side at cafes; they're browsing a couple rows down from you
at bookstores and drugstores and gadget shops; they're enrolling in
self-improvement seminars and Cornhole tournaments; they're joining movie lover and political groups; they're volunteering and taking
cooking classes; they're getting dressed up and going to charity events
and galas. Men, *good men*, are all around you. Meeting them can be so
much simpler and easier than you imagine it to be in your head.

On an epsiode of NBC's *Shark Tank*, a woman who invented a treat
for dogs called "Puppy Cakes," made her pitch to the sharks, explaining that she needed their money to grow the business, that she
believed in her idea but wasn't a good saleswoman. Mark Cuban responded that he was "out" (meaning he would not be funding her
business), saying to the lady: "You find the excuse rather than find
the opportunity." When none of the sharks decided to put money

into her entrepreneurial venture, the woman, when later interviewed, realized her misstep: "My biggest mistake was saying I wasn't a good saleswoman. Don't let excuses get in the way of making yourself successful." Indeed, successful entrepreneurs, in dating and business, don't accept excuses. Because when you stop accepting or making excuses, you start looking for solutions. Take advantage of opportunities that come your way and create your own. Don't make excuses.

Again, there's no exact science to identifying and creating the perfect opportunities for your dating and love life and you'll inevitably choose activities or events that disappoint you as far as making connections, but that's no reason to stop creating, pursuing, and making the most out of opportunities. The sooner you accept and embrace the possibility of disappointment, the sooner you give yourself permission to experiment with new ideas, and not beat yourself up for the ones that lead nowhere. Gordon MacKenzie, consultant and author of *Orbiting the Giant Hairball: A Corporate Fool's Guide to Surviving with Grace*, a business cult classic, argues that attachment is the biggest obstacle to creativity for businesspeople. "As soon as you become attached to a specific outcome, you feel compelled to control and manipulate what you're doing and in the process you shut yourself off to other possibilities. Creativity is not just about succeeding. It's about experimenting and discovering."

Don't be so attached to the outcome of your opportunities that you lose sight of enjoying the present. Most importantly, make the most of all your opportunities by flirting, exuding warmth and friendliness, making eye contact, engaging in conversations, and smiling. Push yourself to be a little uncomfortable as much as possible. From each opportunity, you'll learn something new, making pivots accordingly

Attachment to outcome. Don't be overly attached to outcome of the opportunities you pursue. Enjoy the journey and the desired outcome will happen eventually.

and then experimenting some more. All the while, you'll be keeping the spirit of a creative, action-oriented, thoughtful, purposeful entrepreneur alive and well.

Up next:

In this chapter, I have offered you suggestions as to how to identify opportunities on your own, as opposed to relying solely on your networks. To further facilitate your entrepreneurial journey, in the final chapter, chapter 11, I discuss how to think of men as customers and why "customer feedback" is crucial to your experience in dating and love. I touched on this idea in chapter 7, when I discussed incremental dating, but I will now go into more detail about understanding the way your customers view and experience dating and love. I will encourage you to put more thought into considering your customers' experience by asking you to think about the following questions: What do men in general care about when it comes to dating, sex, love, and relationships? What are their needs? What do my dates care about? What can I offer as a woman, as a dater, as a human being, that makes my customers' experience more enjoyable and meaningful?

Chapter 10 Action Steps Checklist:

- ✓ Create a list of your current interests and hobbies, and a list of activities you would like to do in the future.
- ✓ Once compiled, list two corresponding activities associated with every item on your list.

✓ Once compiled, get even more exact by listing two specific opportunities happening in your area in the near future so that you begin shaping your ideas into definite opportunities.

✓ Be open to opportunities that may not fall exactly within your area of interests. Experience new things.

✓ When choosing which opportunities to pursue, think strategically: short-term opportunities versus communities; male-oriented activities.

✓ Brainstorm opportunities that you believe to be high-percentage ways of meeting men in your geographic area, or consider the ones I've listed: online dating; singles events; matchmakers; summer or ski house; friends of friends' parties/outings; charity galas/events; sports and social organizations.

✓ Think about making your opportunities in the dating world more fruitful: make the ordinary extraordinary; pretend you're taken; long-term thinking.

✓ Of all the specific opportunities you identify, commit to doing at least two to three per month. In conjunction with online dating, this plan will enable you to create many dating opportunities during which you can practice iterative and incremental dating.

✓ Be resourceful—bootstrap your love life. Remember: Your fate is what *you make.*

CHAPTER 11: CUSTOMER FEEDBACK

"If you don't have a passion for your customers, you won't create a company, you'll create a job."

– Dan Martell, serial entrepreneur and CEO/Founder of Clarity

The final element of this experience that will help facilitate your entrepreneurial journey is *customer feedback,* an extremely important part of the entrepreneur's experience, without which a venture cannot grow.

At the heart of venture growth is the needs of the customer. If a company offers a product that doesn't meet current and future customers' needs, why would customers spend time, energy, and resources investing in it? The customer would simply look elsewhere—to the competition. As a dating entrepreneur, a Love TREP, you have to care about your customer; you have to empathize with him. This venture to find love can't *just* be about you. In the worlds of dating and entrepreneurship, you cannot exist in a vacuum; you cannot arrive in the marketplace, announcing, "This is who I am and this is what I'm going to do" without *any* regard for the customer. In chapter 7,

Not just about you. This experience can't *just* be about you. Treps have to care about where the other person is coming from. You cannot lose sight of the fact that there is another human being involved.

Empathy. People high in empathy tend to report higher levels of relationship satisfaction. Nurture and cultivate your curiosity about men; start being open to seeing the world through their eyes.

TREP talk. "We wasted $1,000,00 on a company that never launched. We were perfectionists so we built the best thing we could without even understanding what our customers cared about." – Hiten Shah, Co-Founder at KISSmetrics.

I discussed becoming an iteratively and incrementally better dater to work on the way you date and on your dating and interpersonal skills so that you improve your dates' and men's experiences with you, but I want to use this chapter to dive deeper into your customers' (men's) needs.

The best entrepreneurs spend time understanding their customers, developing *empathy* for them, getting into their heads: who they are, what they're looking for, and what they care about. Entrepreneurship is not *just* about having a product or idea, but it is *also* about seeing what needs there are from your potential customers and becoming aware of the environment in which you live. By paying attention to customer needs you differentiate yourself from the pack; you become a person that *creates value for others.* In a popular product design and development course at Babson, students are taught that in order to fully recognize an opportunity for a product or service, they must understand the user experience. To do that, they must go out into the "field" and have discussions with consumers. One year, students in the course were trying to understand the water fountain opportunity space better. They engaged in discussions, observational research, and had interactions with consumers and key stakeholders. "As the team developed their deep understanding of how individuals used water fountains," write Sebastian K. Fixson and Jay Rao, in chapter 2 of *The New Entrepreneurial Leader,* "they recognized the opportunities for improvements relative to existing water fountains, in terms of both functionality and appearance."

In the dating sense, a woman shouldn't spend *all* her time trying to get into the heads of men, worrying incessantly about what men are looking for and why a man would want to date her, but she should

dedicate *some* thought to it. A balance should be struck between the value a man is creating for a woman—*Why do I want to date this man? What does he have to offer me? How is he making my life better? Why should I choose him over the thousands of other men out there?*—and the value a woman creates for a man —*Why would this man want to date me? What do I have to offer him? How am I making his life better? Why would he choose me over the thousands of other women out there?* Surely, traditional entrepreneurs need to ask themselves these types of questions in the context of the product or service they're offering. And if more women asked themselves these types of questions while dating, answering them honestly, I believe their choices in a partner would be better and the type of person they offer to a partner would be better.

Businesspeople and singles who fail to seek customer feedback are less likely to have success in their respective ventures. As Karl Stark and Bill Stewart, co-founders of Avondale, a strategic advisory firm focused on growing companies, wrote in a piece for *Inc.* magazine titled "How Attractive Are You to Potential Suitors?", "While any good businessperson understands that you need to understand and meet the needs of the customer, it was surprising how some of these experienced business leaders were so fundamentally off in this regard. One team came in with a lot of assumptions and asked few, if any, questions about our client's business. Essentially, they assumed that the needs of their customers fit with their own goals and objectives. The best company, in our view, took time to understand the goals of the customer and, more importantly, was open to learning more during the process."

How many times have you made *assumptions* about men? How many times have you lumped men together based on your past experiences,

Don't ass-u-me. Never assume because you make an ass out of u and me (goes the Benny Hill quote). Don't assume that you are offering what a man needs by, say, giving all of yourself to him or by trying too hard with him. That behavior actually comes from an insecure place of trying to control getting love from another person.

assuming that they are all guilty by association of the same gender? How many times have you sought to control a situation thinking only of your needs?

A former client was anxious to get into a relationship after being single for many years. She was a self-proclaimed "Type A" personality, admitting that she had a tendency to come off as rigid and particular. These qualities may have served her well in her career, but in the dating world they had the opposite effect. Indeed, she often found herself trying to rush a man's feelings for her and rush the dating process itself. Once she understood that a man, especially in the early stages of dating, doesn't like having his feelings manipulated or forced, that he wants to come to his own choices and decisions independently, without pressure, she was able to take a step back and understand her "customer" a little better, which enabled her to alter her behavior accordingly. Now that's an entrepreneurial dater!

So, in much the same way, a business would founder if it ignored the experience of its customers. You, a Love TREP, must care about what your customers care about. If you're only focused on your own needs and objectives, your venture to achieve a healthy, happy relationship will probably feel more like a job, a one-sided end unto itself rather than an enjoyable, evolving journey that leads you to a loving partnership with another human being.

In chapter 5, I had you ask yourself What do I know?, in order to mine your past experiences so that you could start taking action in your entrepreneurial journey from a place of knowledge. But beyond self-knowledge, a Love TREP must understand, be aware of and

responsive to the context in which she is operating. So What do I know? becomes not just personal knowledge, but it becomes about developing a social awareness of the group of people with whom you are trying to connect. Take another look at your inventory. Can you glean anything constructive about men from your past experiences that might shine a light on men's deeper needs?

When your ideas about men have become entrenched over the years (*men just want sex, men don't have feelings, men don't want commitment,* and the like), it can be impossible to see the world through their eyes, to engage in what's called "outrospection." This is why it is important to confront your own mental map of how you think men *should* be by opening your mind (suspending judgment) to how men actually experience women and dating and relationships. Doing so enables you to appreciate any differences *and* establish strategies for how to respond to these differences.

In the context of dating and love, do not *assume* that your needs, wants, and goals are always going to be the same as your customers' needs, wants, and goals. Your journey will be that much more fruitful if you develop social awareness—an understanding of where men in general are coming from, which thereby helps you understand where men you are dating may be coming from. Your goal is to collect customer feedback in this regard.

Obviously, every man is unique and has different wants, but as you start talking with men, asking them questions, as I'm going to ask you to do, I believe you will uncover general themes across most men's answers about their *deeper* needs that you can draw from as you move forward in the dating world.

To consider customer feedback in this context, I encourage you to *talk to men* (i.e., the customer) about what they are looking for in women, on dates, and in relationships. Essentially, you want to understand what they care about when it comes to women, dating, and love. Are *you* offering the customer what *he* cares about?

Let's examine this concept a bit more.

Talk to men about dating, love, and relationships

One way you can approach getting feedback is by (gasp!):

- *Directly asking men* (friends, family members, acquaintances, strangers, etc.) and *listening purposefully* to their feedback and conversations about dating and relationships to uncover their deeper needs.

Directly ask men and listen purposefully

Keep yourself in check. If you find yourself formulating answers or comebacks in your head while someone is speaking, you're not *really* listening.

It's important for you to actively hear and understand feedback from men about what they are looking for in women, on dates, and in relationships. If you cannot hear them or understand what it is they care about when it comes to dating and love, you'll only be coming at this research from one angle, your angle. That just won't cut it, because dating and love, like entrepreneurship, is a two-way street. As Erika Napoltano explains in the January 2013 issue of *Entrepreneur*, in an article titled "Listen and Learn," "Flexibility in business begins with listening—really *listening*—to your customers so you can match their desires with your capabilities while also keeping your own business goals in mind." Her interview subjects,

brothers Butch and Jerry Milbrandt, owners of Milbrandt Vineyards, concur: "When you talk to your customers and become avid fans of feedback, it's amazing what your business can become when you use that information wisely," says Butch. Finally, consider the sage advice of Andy Smith, co-author of *The Dragonfly Effect: Quick, Effective, and Powerful Ways to Use Social Media to Drive Social Change,* when it comes to listening to the customer. Quoted in the January 2013 issue of *Entrepreneur,* he opines, "When you listen to and create discussions about the problems [the customers] are having, you can progress toward becoming the person or having the product that addresses that problem."

You cannot be so locked into your world and your way of doing things that you aren't receptive to feedback and open to making changes based on what you find out. Entrepreneurs sometimes make this mistake: they live and breathe their business to the point that they're not thinking about the value to the customer. If you're someone who lives and breathes *only* for yourself, you're not giving any consideration to the value you would bring to someone else's life. *Ultimately, a man falls in love with a woman when he realizes his life is better with her in it.* There needs to be a willingness to put yourself in his shoes, to consider the world from his point of view from time to time (not just in the early stages of dating but deeper into relationships as well). When you align yourself with your customers in this way, you have a better chance of making better connections.

As you attempt to get customer feedback, you are looking for general themes. As I mentioned, each man has very specific wants and needs based on who he is as an individual, but I guarantee as you start gathering feedback, you'll also start to see general themes emerge from

Remain true to who you are. The point of collecting customer feedback is *not* to mold yourself into what every man wants you to be. Ultimately, you want a man to fall in love with who you are, but you also want to respect a man's needs and understand where he's coming from, too.

TREP talk.
"I spent six months building a product I wouldn't use very often, in a market I wasn't familiar with, for users I didn't understand—big mistake." – Sandi MacOherson – Editor-in-Chief, Quibb.

men's answers. You can use what you learn from this feedback to become a more compassionate, empathetic person, woman, and dater, someone in whom a man wants to invest his time and heart.

But I want to make the following very clear: *The point of collecting customer feedback is not to mold yourself into what you think every man wants you to be.* Absolutely not! The majority of this book is centered on you—getting clarity on who you are, your needs, doing what feels right to you. You want to make this sort of clarity a priority in your life, to recognize your worth, and to fall in love with yourself, rather than becoming what you think men want you to be and ignoring your voice and needs (which is perhaps what you've spent years doing). *However*, it is also imperative to get a general understanding of what the other half of the equation (in this case, men) think and care about. You want to uncover what qualities men are attracted to and repelled by, so that you increase your chances of connecting with them.

So ... if you want to know what men want and need, try asking them.

Sounds like a pretty simple idea, huh? You'd be surprised how many women have never asked. Don't just read articles or blogs on the Internet to understand men's perspectives; go out and ask them directly; listen to them with your own two ears. Any insights will be much more potent and real when you are face-to-face with someone as opposed to reading what some random commenter on the Internet a thousand miles away from you has to say.

Send an email to male friends or family members, and/or the next time you are out at a bar or event or activity where men are present, strike up a conversation, asking them the following question:

- "What do you think men truly value in a woman when it comes to dating and relationships?"

It's actually a great conversation starter, one that I've used in variations at bars, parties, and various events during my time as a single and as a dating coach. You can, of course, phrase the question in different ways or create offshoots (e.g., "What general qualities do men look for in a woman when they first start dating her?" "What makes a man want to commit to a woman?"); just be sure you don't inject your personal bias into the phrasing of your questions. You will be surprised how willing men are to answer. After spending so much time trying to figure out what it is women want, they appreciate a woman trying to understand what it is they want, a woman who cares enough to inquire.

I want you to really listen to men's answers. Leave your ego at the door. Don't fight back or argue or try to offer a woman's perspective. You are engaging them in a dialogue not lecturing them on what and how they should think. Simply take each answer in and understand where the respondents are coming from. You'll probably get a bunch of different answers; men may even start to talk about specifics from their own past dates or relationships as opposed to offering generalizations. Your goal will be to take all of the answers you get and fit them into general categories so that you are uncovering men's *deeper needs*. For example, if a few men comment that they don't like women calling ten times a day or having to be together 24/7, you might understand that to mean that a man's deeper need is for his partner to not be so needy and to display independence and trust.

Here are some answers that I've heard men give in response to this type of question:

Buy a book! Or what about a workshop or class? There are plenty of books out there by male dating coaches—coaches who share what's going on in the male brain when it comes to women, dating, and relationships. Although I recommend speaking to men directly, these books can also help you understand your customers' experience. A dating workshop or class hosted by a man can also be eye-opening.

- "My last girlfriend got offended if I wanted alone time to go read a magazine in a separate room. That was difficult for me."
- "I wish women didn't get so hung up on the little things."
- "When we're first dating, I don't want to feel like she's already picturing our wedding and picking out children's names. A man doesn't want to feel pressured into things."
- "If I didn't call her three times a day she got upset with me. That was frustrating. We had nothing left to talk about at the end of the day."
- "Women are so picky sometimes; I feel like I can't measure up."
- "I'd like women to understand that I am an emotional person, too. I'm sensitive and have feelings."
- "I can't stand the games and power struggles."
- "I want her to feel comfortable and be open and trusting. In bed I like a girl who is confident and a little wild."
- "I would like a woman not to play games and to be logical, reasonable, fun, and not to bring drama."
- "I want less uphill battles, not more."
- "I want to be loved for who I am, not for who I could or should be."
- "I want to feel like I can be myself around her."
- "I appreciate an independent woman. But not too independent that I feel like I'm not needed."
- "Support. There's nothing better than knowing that your woman has your back and is there for you when times get tough."
- "A man wants a woman who is trustworthy to a fault"
- "If you ask me a question or for advice, really make sure that you want the answer."

- "I don't need a woman to tell me how to run my business, who my friends should be, or how to live my life."

- "I want a woman who enjoys sex and affection."

- "We don't necessarily care where a woman went to college or what her *specific* dreams are as long as they exist. An impressive goal doesn't have to fit the mold of a woman aspiring to work her way to the top of a law firm. It could be as simple as raising a nice family."

- "In our relationships, we want to have equal input on situations showing that our opinions are valued. We want to feel that we are being listened to and understood. More importantly, we want to be allowed to make big decisions, even if we are just being humored."

- "Our primary concern in the relationship is that the women we marry will not hold their careers over our heads, bring career dominance into the relationship and will not make us feel as if we are replaceable."

Honesty. Men will be honest with you when you ask them for honest answers. That can be a blessing and difficult. Be prepared to hear some things that might not gel with your view of things as a woman.

Certainly, you can email men you know if you aren't comfortable discussing these issues face-to-face, although I encourage you to start chatting men up in person. As Stephen Deets and Lisa DiCarlo write in chapter 9 of *The New Entrepreneurial Leader*, "It is difficult to fully appreciate differences in context and perspective until one confronts those differences in person." But, at the end of the day, no matter how you gather feedback, I guarantee many men will be more than happy to respond, with honest, genuine answers no less.

If I were to categorize the answers I've heard from men over the course of my life on the topics of dating, love, and relationships into men's deeper needs with regard to women, love, and relationships,

Empathy. TREPs need to develop empathy for their customers. The best way to develop empathy for your customers is to walk in their shoes, to understand a different perspective than your own.

I'd say that in general emotionally available, commitment-minded, boyfriend-material men appreciate:

- Women who, for the most part, will be easygoing, fun, warm, and nice. The less drama, game-playing, or emotional roller coasters the better. (Note: This doesn't mean silencing your voice and needs, but it does mean interacting and communicating with men in an emotionally mature way. Men respect when a woman owns her feelings and presents them in a measured, reasonable way.)
- Women who don't try to control or change them.
- Women who are positive and upbeat and don't carry around anger at men.
- Women who don't rush relationships prematurely.
- Women who allow a man to be a man, whatever that means to that particular man.
- Women who set boundaries and have self-respect.
- Women who will respect a man.
- Women who will love a man for who they are, making him feel a sense of peace and safety.
- Women who they can trust, who are loyal.
- Women who enjoy sex and affection.
- Women who can be independent and have passions of their own and allow a man to have his independence when he needs it.
- Women who make them feel needed in some way.

It's natural to question others' perspectives as you test them against your own, and, more than likely, as you talk to and gather insights about men, you *will* experience frustration or other unwanted

emotions. As Deets and DiCarlo write about a course they teach at Babson called "The Enlightened Entrepreneur," the participating students often respond angrily to differing viewpoints (especially those from different cultures) by asking rhetorical questions such as: "Why aren't they more rational?"; "Why aren't they like us?" Only through further reflection, the authors write, do the students "realize how they have privileged their own perspective—that their beliefs and behaviors may not be 'right' but simply one set among many. It is then that the students are on their way to becoming 'enlightened' entrepreneurial leaders."

Undoubtedly, you've experienced anger and frustration in your experiences with men. Sometimes it may feel as though they exist on an entirely different planet. Is it no wonder that John Gray's book *Men Are From Mars, Women Are From Venus* was a worldwide bestseller? Men and women certainly experience each other in ways that feel completely foreign, which is why it is crucial to put yourself in the other gender's shoes from time to time.

Men, for instance, often say that women are full of drama. I'm sure you've heard this before. While we women may balk at such a characterization, believing that our feelings and way of communication is the right way, how often do we really stop to understand or empathize with the male perspective? When we can understand their context a bit better, we can consider how to deconstruct and reconstruct our own behaviors in useful, enlightened, more mature, more cooperative ways. For example, men's relationships with each other are less verbally communicative, less touchy-feely, less focused on direct eye contact than in female relationships—perhaps a result of both biology and culture. Understanding this generality might help women to

come up with new and more effective ways of communicating with men.

Am I saying that because men communicate differently that it is *always* up to the woman to change her preferred mode of communication? No. The hope is *both* man and woman will learn to understand each other's perspective and make compromises accordingly. When you become mature enough to want to empathize with your customer and do what you can to see the world from his perspective, you're more likely to attract a mature, good, open-hearted man. And that type of man, in response to your empathy, will do everything he can to see the world through your eyes, too. And when both partners are willing to investigate and empathize with the other's world, you have a recipe for relationship success.

By understanding men better, you give yourself more information that you can use in the dating world (and beyond) to your advantage. If, for instance, you discover that in the early stages of dating, you tend to be an exceptionally needy person—wanting constant attention from a man and lashing out when he can't give you what you want—having a better understanding that men value time alone and with friends might prompt you to learn how to deal with your neediness in other, more productive ways. Maybe you work with a therapist to understand where your neediness comes from in the first place or maybe you divert you needy energy into personal projects and hobbies.

Does this mean you empathize with a man when he treats you disrespectfully? Does it mean you put up with bad behavior? Does it mean you make excuses when a man ignores your fundamental needs? No.

Empathizing and understanding the needs of men doesn't require one to become a doormat. It simply means that on a reasonable level, you are exploring different perspectives, so that you can approach dating and men in more useful, enlightened ways.

As you're out there in the dating world, working on yourself, do not lose sight of the fact that an entrepreneurial venture must have some sort of understanding of the people for whom it is creating. So get out there and find out what men are saying. Don't just take my word for it; understand and listen for yourself to what the customer is saying about these topics. Observe and hear them without inserting your own biases or feelings. You might have a visceral reaction to something a man says, but that is how he feels and it might very well be indicative of how a lot of men feel. Once you've started to get feedback, you can begin to form *insights* about your customer (as I have done earlier in the chapter).

I think you will discover for yourself some interesting knowledge that you can apply to your own dating experiences. If, in the early stages of dating, you offer your customer the type of woman who appeals to a broad spectrum of men, you cast a wider net of potential mates. Consequently, YOU put the power in your hands to narrow down your suitors to the ones *you* are really interested in getting to know, as opposed to being a woman who picks a man because he picks her.

The point of getting customer feedback *is not* to make you dizzy with advice. I don't want you going into your dating experiences with an enormous amount of feedback muddying up your head so that you can't be present and authentic on dates. Moreover, I can't stress enough that caring about your customer *does not mean* becoming

someone you are not simply to get a man. Don't become *so* focused on other people's needs that you lose yourself in the process. The goal *is* to take in what you are hearing from men and objectively ask yourself:

> *Based on what I'm learning about what men care about in the context of dating, sex, love, and relationships, how am I presenting myself in the early stages of dating? Am I likely to either make a man feel like his life would be better with me in it or more stressful with me in it? How is my life an inviting place for a man to be? How do I enhance a man's life?*

Take some time to really think about those questions and answer them honestly.

Think about how you comport yourself in the early stages of dating. Do you give a man space? Are you into playing games? Do you communicate your feelings openly, gently, and maturely? Do you push a man on his feelings too soon? Are you overly needy, clingy, or bossy? Are you overly demanding of a man's time because of your insecurities? Do you punish a man or hold things over his head? Do you never let your guard down and make yourself vulnerable? Do you overact, nag, and try to change or fix a man? Do you carry around anger and resentment toward men and take it out on them? Are you able to freely trust men?

Considering your customer's needs in the later stages of dating

Thinking about customer feedback will be handy in the early stages of dating as well as the later stages. If you've begun to date someone exclusively, you should always be asking yourself: "What does

this man I'm now with care about? And how can I continue to care about his deeper needs the way I would like him to care about mine?" Surely, it's important that your values and interests match up in the way I discussed in chapter 5, and you certainly need to feel a man is a compatible partner for you and is responsive to your needs, but you also want to think about how *you* are going to be someone who can fulfill his needs on a longer term basis, so that, together, you are sharing love, as opposed to approaching love from a selfish or needy place. If you realize after dating a man for a while that, despite an attraction for each other, you still can't fulfill his more specific needs and he can't fulfill your specific needs, then you're probably not a good match for each other.

I'll offer a couple personal examples.

Before I met my husband, I dated a man for about a year. As we moved deeper into our relationship, I realized that he was headstrong and set in his ways. He needed someone who was more willing to go with his flow, someone who was more reserved—that is, partly, what he cared about. I realized after several months of dating that despite our initial chemistry, I couldn't give him what he needed long-term in this regard. I had too many alpha qualities myself; we ended up butting heads far too often and I knew from my experiences and conversations that to try to change a man was counterproductive and not a good foundation upon which a relationship grows.

With Dave, my husband, I discovered during the dating stages that he is an introvert at heart. We get along well, have similar interests and values, and love each other dearly, but I need to remember that he cares about having his alone time, his introverted time, and not push

Continue to care. It's never time to stop caring about the needs of your customer, especially when you become a couple.

him to be someone he's not. As we started dating more seriously, I knew to respect that. Fortunately, it was something that I was able to accommodate. In turn, I believe he fell more deeply in love with me because of my ability and desire to make him feel safe about who he is, that I am capable of accepting some of his more specific, deeper needs.

Thinking about your customers' needs does *not* have to end after the early stages of dating have given way to a more established relationship. Your customer's needs may change in nature somewhat—on the surface, perhaps—but he will always have deeper needs, and, as a partner, it's important to keep striving to identify, understand, communicate about, and respond to those needs.

Chapter 11 Action Steps Checklist:

- ✓ In order to start getting feedback from men about their needs when it comes to dating, love, and relationships, start talking and listening to them. Talk to male friends and family members. Ask men questions when you go out. And certainly consider purchasing a book or two; maybe even attend a workshop or class offered by a male dating coach.
- ✓ Do you see general themes emerge from the feedback you are getting? If so, what are they? Put them into categories. How can you use this feedback to become a better dater, woman, and partner?
- ✓ Can you identify ways that you comport yourself in the early stages of dating that may not gel with what you are

finding out about men's deeper needs? Create a list. Start working with a therapist or a coach or on your own to understand where this behavior comes from and then work to change your thought processes and corresponding behaviors. You've already been doing much of this work in earlier chapters.

✓ Revisit your Affinity List. Do you want to change any of the items on your list?

✓ Have you identified any other internal or external obstacles that you'd like to work through?

CONCLUSION: STAYING "AGILE" IN YOUR LOVE LIFE

"The unexamined life is not worth living"

- Socrates, philosopher

Dating and entrepreneurship are more similar than most people would ever assume. By reading this book, I hope you can appreciate how effective the lessons from entrepreneurship can be when they are applied to the dating world. Also, I hope the framework I've presented in this book, which is based on the principles and spirit of entrepreneurship and the ways successful entrepreneurs think and act, will help you break down into digestible pieces the experience of dating and finding love.

Looking at dating through the lens of an entrepreneur gives you access to a whole new arena of ideas and possibilities for your love life. My deepest wish is that these pages motivate and excite you to start thinking of yourself as an entrepreneur, a Love TREP, creating, building, and shaping something of value in your life, namely your love story.

See it through.
"You have to
have the courage
to see [your
idea] through
to the end. The
ideas are just the
start." – Gregory
Bruns, author of
Iconoclast.

Now it's up to you to do the work. Don't give up on your vision. Your journey won't always be easy, but if you keep working at your dating and love life, good things will come your way.

In summary, *Skin In the Game* has taught you:

- To think of yourself as a natural-born entrepreneur with an ability to think and act like an entrepreneur. That entrepreneurship is not an exclusive club; rather, it's a life skill that can teach all people how to think and act in unknowable, uncertain situations, and you can use that template to move forward in your dating and love life.

- How to create and maintain a vision for your dating and love life, and how desire and a problem-solving mindset can keep that vision burning bright.

- How to embrace uncertainty and pivot when your dating life throws you curveballs (which it will!), how to move forward and adapt in the face of unknowable environments, and how to become a more evolved person in terms of the ideas that lead you to achieving your vision.

- Why identifying your internal and external obstacles is crucial to your entrepreneurial journey and how to go about removing them.

- That it is important to enroll others in your journey and not go it alone, to have supporters by your side who help guide you and believe in you.

- How to use the Date. Learn. Repeat. model of entrepreneurial dating to achieve your vision.

- How to use action and experimentation in the dating world, how to use prediction based on reflection and past

experiences, and how to know when to lean on one approach over the other or use both together.

- That getting started in taking action is as simple as drawing from the means you have at hand and then taking small, smart steps.
- How to practice dating, iteratively and incrementally.
- How to view failures as your greatest assets.
- How to risk intelligently in your dating and love life.
- How to look at your networks differently, how to harness them to help you find love, and how to build and nurture the relationships within these networks.
- How to create and shape your own opportunities.
- How to see the world through your customers' eyes.

To simplify even further, the entrepreneurial journey to find love is as follows:

1. See your self as an entrepreneur in your dating and love life.
2. Have desire, a problem-solving mindset, and a vision.
3. Confront and remove obstacles.
4. Enroll others.
5. Take action (Date.)
6. Reflect on your actions (Learn.)
7. Act again (Repeat.)
8. See failures as assets.
9. Network.
10. Identify and seize on opportunities.
11. Understand your customer.
12. Stay agile.

While I have referred to your entrepreneurial venture to "find" love countless times throughout this book—heck I even use the word "find" in the title—the truth is that you are doing so much more than finding it; you are *making* it, *creating* it, *shaping* it through a very thoughtful, purposeful, entrepreneurial approach. You are *building* your love story.

One final pearl of wisdom.

The most important thing you can do throughout your entrepreneurial journey in dating and relationships is to stay *agile*.

I never would have guessed in a million years that the land of software development would provide me with this particular piece of inspiration. Then again, you may never have thought the land of entrepreneurship could inspire you to create your love story.

In the software world, the three most popular design methodologies for creating and innovating products are known as *waterfall, scrum,* and *agile.*

The *waterfall* method is a predictive, sequential, stage-like, and linear process, progressing steadily downwards, like a waterfall. So developers come at the design process saying, "let's figure out everything upfront that will happen in the system and design everything around that." When one stage of development is completed the next stage begins. Considerable time is spent designing and planning. The advantage is it allows teams to compartmentalize the work to be done; the downsides are rigidity and inflexibility.

Scrum is also a more rules-based, precise approach to software design and innovation. It is based on radical transformations in a short amount of time. Scrum is considered less risky than waterfall and agile in that fully-tested *features* of a product are developed in a regimented manner and then delivered piecemeal to the marketplace for testing and iterations. However, while scrum exposes waste and any other issues in the design process very quickly, it has a rigid cycle for the development process.

The *agile* design method hews closely to the entrepreneurial method that I have asked you, throughout this book, to apply to your dating life. Of all the software design methods, agile is the most fluid, adaptive, evolving one. It draws entirely from iterations and incremental improvements. There are no prescribed rules; ideas can take many shapes and forms. Testing the product and receiving customer feedback occur simultaneously. It is approached from the mindset of "we don't know what will come up, so it's better to have a flexible process so that once we see what things happen, we can talk to the customer and make improvements from there." In the software world this adaptive method is known as "beta testing": a company releases a product for customer use in test mode so that bugs or issues can be ironed out as they're discovered and reported by programmers and customers alike. Google's Gmail was famously in beta mode for five years, collecting feedback and experimenting with various features, from when it launched in 2004, before exiting beta in 2009.

As Bruce Eckfeldt, CEO of Cyrus Innovation, a software development and consulting firm, explained in a Babson Center for Information Management Studies presentation titled "Lean and Agile: A Powerful

TREP talk. "One of the biggest mistakes we've made at Moz was to repeatedly build "big bang" projects that required many months of development time without much visibility into progress. Don't be like us—use agile development, have lots of visibility into progress..."
- Rand Fishkin – Ceo of Moz and Co-Founder of Inbound.org.

Combination": "Being Agile isn't always easy, but it's a way of getting better at software. It's not a bar you reach. It's never-ending, an on-going process, and you get more and more agile, more mature, over time."

More than just applying this agile approach to your dating life, though, consider that *staying agile once you've found love* is crucial. Because people who prescribe to an agile philosophy are ultimately more responsive to those around them and more perceptive of their own and their partner's needs; they broaden their view and don't get locked into rigid, self-serving ways of thinking and acting. They recognize that there is *no finish line to personal development*. They don't get complacent; they keep striving for personal growth and growth within the relationship. And that is a good model to follow moving forward.

By the end of this experience, it is my hope that you've empowered yourself to find a healthy, happy dating life that leads you to a healthy, happy relationship with a wonderful man. Congratulations a hundred times over if you've found someone! But, please understand, your journey is far from over. As Bob Davis opined in his presentation to the Babson community during the 2012 Entrepreneurship Forum, one of the mistakes new entrepreneurs often make on their first-start-up is treating fundraising like it's an end, not a means. "A success-ful company is what you're looking for," he explained. "People shout 'Hooray, we raised 10 million dollars,' okay, but now what? It doesn't matter, don't get punch drunk on this; it's just one step."

For traditional entrepreneurs, starting a business is just the begin-ning. Maintaining and growing that business is the next step, and it's a step that never ends as long as the company exists. The same

is true when it comes to matters of the heart. Indeed, being happily coupled doesn't mean you have to stop learning and growing. Now you just have someone to learn and grow with, alongside you—you are beginning an entrepreneurial venture with someone else to find lasting love together.

Your love life is a lifelong commitment. Never stop growing, evolving, and adapting. Enjoy the journey. Stay agile. Push forward, especially when times get tough and disappointments come your way. Don't be a victim. Don't be a cynic. Don't let your situations define you. Instead, be hopeful. Be persistent. Be resourceful. Be a doer. Be a creator of your future. Be an entrepreneur.

Be a Love TREP.

ACKNOWLEDGEMENTS

I'd like to thank the following people for helping me on my entrepreneurial journey to start my coaching practice, The Love TREP, and to write this book: Professor Heidi Neck, your expertise and initial feedback were instrumental; Stephanie Carter, you're the best friend a gal could ask for; Dave Hansel, photog extraordinaire; Shela Dean, for your excellent legal advice; Danna Katz Steinberg and Sharone Jeldon, for your comments and feedback; Professor Joel Shulman, for the title suggestion "Skin In the Game"; Sharon Sinnott, Director of the Speech Center at Babson College, for helping me to refine my pitch and work on my public speaking skills; Stephen Steinberg, my dad, for his eagle eye editing skills; Avery Managhas for her beautiful cover design; Dave, my husband, my love, for your constant support and for always coming to the rescue when various IT dilemmas threatened my sanity; my clients, who are wonderful women and inspire me to be the best coach I can be; and to all the others who I inadvertently forgot to mention on this page.

BIBLIOGRAPHY

Preface

Entrepreneurial Thought and Action® is a registered trademark of Babson College.

Greenberg, Danna, Kathleen McKone-Sweet, and H. James. Wilson. "Entrepreneurial Leadership: Shaping Social and Economic Opportunity." *The New Entrepreneurial Leader: Developing Leaders Who Shape Social and Economic Opportunity.* San Francisco, CA: Berrett-Koehler, 2011. N. pag. Print.

Introduction

Blair, Barbara Spies. "U.S. Entrepreneurship Rates Increase According to Research by Babson College and Baruch College." *Babson College.* N.p., 29 Nov. 2012. Web. 16 Jan. 2013.To access the full 2011 GEM U.S. Report, visit: http://www.babson.edu/Academics/centers/blank-center/global-research/gem/Pages/reports.aspx

Ch. 1

Costello, Christine, Heidi Neck, and Robert Williams. *Elements of the Entrepreneur Experience. Business Innovation Factory.* Business Innovation Factory, n.d. Web. <businessinnovationfactory.com/elab>.Vol. 1.

James, Kouzes, and Posner Barry. "Seeking the Elusive Credibility Factor." *USA Today,* 1 July 2012: n. pag. Print.

Timmons, Jeffry A. "1." *New Venture Creation: Entrepreneurship for the 21st Century.* 5th ed. N.p.: Irwin McGraw-Hill, 1999. 13–14. Print.

Kelly, Donna J., Slavica Singer, and Mike Herrington. "GEM 2011 Global Report." *Global Entrepreneurship Monitor.* N.p., 27 July 2012. Web. 28 Feb. 2013.

"In 1970, women-owned businesses ..." Statistic taken from: Timmons, Jeffry A. "1." *New Venture Creation: Entrepreneurship for the 21st Century.* 5th ed. N.p.: Irwin McGraw-Hill, 1999. 5. Print.

"Women own 10.6 million businesses in the United States…". *Source: Center for Women's Business Research, December 2004.*

"According to new data projections, job growth…". Source: *The Guardian Life Small Business Research Institute.*

"One in every 11 adult women in the United States…". Source: *www. bpwfoundation.org*

"Women-owned businesses now account for 50%...". Source: *Forbes*, 2012.

"Female entrepreneurs encompass approximately one-third..." Source: *www.go4funding.com*

Strobel, Tammy. "The Modern-Day Woman: How Entrepreneurship Is Saving Us From Ourselves." *Rowdy Kittens*. N.p., 8 Dec. 2010. Web. 23 Oct. 2012.

Hoffman, Reid, and Ben Casnocha. *The Start-up of You*. New York: Crown Business, 2012. Print.

Neck, Heidi M., and Patricia G. Greene. "Entrepreneurship Education: Known Worlds and New Frontiers." *Journal of Small Business Management* 49.1 (2011): 55-70. Print.

"According to the Global Entrepreneurship Monitor...". Statistic taken from: Neck, Heidi M. "What Comes Before The Business Plan? Everything." *Forbes*. N.p., 21 Mar. 2012. Web. 23 Oct. 2012.

Schurenberg, Eric. "What's an Entrepreneur? The Best Answer Ever." *Inc*. N.p., 9 Jan. 2012. Web. 16 Dec. 2011.

Kiefer, Charles F., Leonard A. Schlesinger, and Paul B. Brown. *Action Trumps Everything: Creating What You Want in an Uncertain World*. Duxbury, MA: Black Ink, 2010. 31. Print. <u>NOTE</u>: An updated version of this book titled *Just Start* was published in 2012 by Harvard Business Review Press.

Sarasvathy, Saras D. *What Makes Entrepreneurs Entrepreneurial?* pgs. 1–9. Available at SSRN: http://ssrn.com/abstract=909038

Ch. 2

Daley, Jason. "Blowin' In the Wind." *Entrepreneur* Feb. 2012: 116. Print.

Napoletano, Erika. "Power to the People." *Entrepreneur* May 2012: 21. Print.

Robinson, Joe. "Rebel Yell." *Entrepreneur* Mar. 2013: 30. Print.

Littman, Margaret. "Staying Power." *Entrepreneur* July 2012: 18-19. Print.

Ankeny, Jason. "Style Files." *Entrepreneur* August 2012: 45. Print.

Hoffman, Reid, and Ben Casnocha. *The Start-up of You.* New York: Crown Business, 2012. 101. Print.

"In a 2002 Inc Survey…". Statistic taken from: Bartlett, Sarah. "Seat of the Pants." *Inc.* N.p., 15 Oct. 2002. Web.

Jain, Naveen. "10 Secrets of Becoming a Successful Entrepreneur." *Huffington Post.* N.p., 2 Feb. 2011. Web.

Haden, Jeffry. "5 Tips From an Accidental Entrepreneur." *Inc.* N.p., 10 Jan. 2012. Web. 10 Jan. 2012.

Blanchard, Ken, and Jesse Stoner. "The Vision Thing." *Leader to Leader* Winter 31 (2004): n. pag.

Greenberger, Rachel. "Entrepreneurial Thought and Action in Filmmaking." Babson College Community Learning Day. Babson College, Babson Park. 7 Jan. 2012. Speech.

Bishop, Greg. "A French Open Title and a Career Grand Slam for Sharapova." *The New York Times*. N.p., 9 June 2012. Web.

Parkinson, Mike. "The Power of Visual Communication." *Billion Dollar Graphics*. N.p., n.d. Web.

Gordon, Michael E. "1." *Trump University Entrepreneurship 101: How to Turn Your Idea into a Money Machine*. Hoboken, NJ: John Wiley & Sons, 2007. 1. Print.

Kiefer, Charles F., Leonard A. Schlesinger, and Paul B. Brown. *Action Trumps Everything: Creating What You Want in an Uncertain World*. Duxbury, MA: Black Ink, 2010. Print.

ch. 3

Gordon, Michael E. "Introduction." *Trump University Entrepreneurship 101: How to Turn Your Idea into a Money Machine*. Hoboken, NJ: John Wiley & Sons, 2007. Xiv. Print.

Cooper, Belle Beth. "The 13 Biggest Failures From Famous Entrepreneurs and What They've Learned From Them." *Buffer App*. N.p., 5 Sept. 2013. Web. 6 Sept. 2013.

Rock, David, and Jeffrey Schwartz. "The Neuroscience of Leadership." *Strategy+business* Summer 2006: 1–10. Print. Issue 43. Reprint number 06207.

Sanders-Edwards, Carl. "JumpShift Brainstorming Workshop." Developing Entrepreneurial Opportunities Evening MBA Class. Babson College, Babson Park. Lecture. JumpShift. <www.jumpshift.co.nz>

Ch. 4

Costello, Christine, Heidi Neck, and Robert Williams. *Elements of the Entrepreneur Experience. Business Innovation Factory.* Business Innovation Factory, n.d. Web. <businessinnovationfactory.com/elab>.Vol. 1.

Cooper, Belle Beth. "The 13 Biggest Failures From Famous Entrepreneurs and What They've Learned From Them." *Buffer App.* N.p., 5 Sept. 2013. Web. 6 Sept. 2013.

Hann, Christopher. "You Can't Fight Nature." *Entrepreneur* June 2012: 26. Print.

Kiefer, Charles F., Leonard A. Schlesinger, and Paul B. Brown. *Action Trumps Everything: Creating What You Want in an Uncertain World.* Duxbury, MA: Black Ink, 2010. 87. Print.

"Advice to the Class of 2012." *Babson Magazine* Spring 2012: n. pag. Print.

Coaching vs. Therapy chart developed by Hayden and Whitworth, 1995, found on: *Relationship Coaching Institute.* "Http://

relationshipcoachinginstitute.com/professional-coaching-and-the-mft/." Chart. N.p., n.d. Web.

Wang, Jennifer. "Packing Heat." *Entrepreneur* March 2012: 48. Print.

Listfield, Emily. "The Look Good For Your Age Movement." Editorial. *More Magazine* n.d.: n. pag. *More.* Web.

Herndon, Lara Kristin. "Packaging Stimulus." *Entrepreneur* November 2012: 28. Print.

<u>Ch. 5</u>

Hogg, Sam. "Naughty, Naughty." *Entrepreneur* October 2013: 100. Print.

Kiefer, Charles F., Leonard A. Schlesinger, and Paul B. Brown. *Action Trumps Everything: Creating What You Want in an Uncertain World.* Duxbury, MA: Black Ink, 2010. Print.

Rock, David, and Jeffrey Schwartz. "The Neuroscience of Leadership." *Strategy+business* Summer 2006: 1–10. Print. Issue 43. Reprint number 06207.

Read, Stuart, Saras Sarasvathy, Nick Dew, Robert Wiltbank, and Anne-Valerie Ohlsson. *Effectual Entrepreneurship.* New York [etc.: Routledge, 2011. Print.

Greenberg, Danna, Kathleen McKone-Sweet, and H. James. Wilson. "Entrepreneurial Leadership: Shaping Social and Economic

Opportunity." Introduction. *The New Entrepreneurial Leader: Developing Leaders Who Shape Social and Economic Opportunity.* San Francisco, CA: Berrett-Koehler, 2011. N. pag. Print.

Wujec, Tom. "The Marshmallow Challenge." Interview. *NPR, WBUR 90.9.* Boston, MA, 1 Jan. 2013. Radio.

Wujec, Tom. *Marshmallow Challenge.* N.p., n.d. Web.

Greenberg, Danna, Kate McKone-Sweet, and H. James Wilson. "The New Entrepreneurial Leader: Developing Leaders Who Shape Social and Economic Opportunity." *Babson College.* N.p., n.d. Web. Article based on the Babson book, *The New Entrepreneurial Leader: Developing Leaders Who Shape Social and Economic Opportunity* (Berrett-Koehler Publishers 2011), by Danna Greenberg, Kate McKone-Sweet, & H. James Wilson.

Kiefer, Charles F., Leonard A. Schlesinger, and Paul B. Brown. *Action Trumps Everything: Creating What You Want in an Uncertain World.* Duxbury, MA: Black Ink, 2010. Print. pg. 60–61.

Wadwha, Vivek. "The Case for Old Entrepreneurs." *Washington Post.* N.p., 2 Dec. 2011. Web.

Rushdie, Salman. "The Disappeared." *The New Yorker* 17 Sept. 2012: n. pag. Print.

Tjan, Anthony. "How Leaders Become Self-Aware." *Harvard Business Review.* N.p., 19 July 2012. Web. 23 Oct. 2012.

"Where'd Julia Allison's 73-Point Checklist Come From? Her Mom!" *Bravo TV.* N.p., 19 June 2012. Web.

Ch. 6

Neck, Heidi M., and Patricia G. Greene. "Entrepreneurship Education: Known Worlds and New Frontiers." *Journal of Small Business Management* 49.1 (2011): 55–70. Print.

Deresiewicz, William. "Solitude and Leadership." Address. Address to Plebe Class. United States Military Academy at West Point Academy, West Point, New York. *The American Scholar.* Oct. 2009. Web.

Robinson, Joe. "Multiple Choice." *Entrepreneur* December 2012: 22. Print.

Ohngren, Kara. "Innovation Education." *Entrepreneur* October 2012. 102. Print.

Ch. 7

Rock, David, and Jeffrey Schwartz. "The Neuroscience of Leadership." *Strategy+business* Summer 2006: 1–10. Print. Issue 43. Reprint number 06207.

Davis, Bob. "The 9 Mistakes Entrepreneurs Often Make on Their First Start-up." Babson College 2012 Entrepreneurship Forum. Babson College, Babson Park. 9 Nov. 2012. Speech.

Reporter, Daily Mail. "The Price of True Love: How the Average Woman Will Date 24 Men and Spend over £2,000 before They Find Mr Right." *The Daily Mail*. N.p., 23 Apr. 2010. Web.

Ch. 8

Neck, Heidi. "Reframing Failure as Intentional Iteration: New Research on How Entrepreneurs Really Think." *Babson College*. The Babson Entrepreneur Experience Lab, n.d. Web. Article based on: Costello, Christine, Heidi Neck, and Robert Williams. *Elements of the Entrepreneur Experience. Business Innovation Factory*. Business Innovation Factory, n.d. Web. <businessinnovationfactory.com/elab>.Vol. 1

Survival of private sector establishments by opening year. N.d. Raw data. U.S. Bureau of Labor Statistics, Washington, DC. Annual openings March 1994 through March 2012. Data accessed at: http://www.bls.gov/bdm/us_age_naics_00_table7.txt

Amanpour, Christiane. "Failure as Opportunity." *Makers*. N.p., n.d. Web. 23 Oct. 2012.

Davis, Bob. "The 9 Mistakes Entrepreneurs Often Make on Their First Start-up." Babson College 2012 Entrepreneurship Forum. Babson College, Babson Park. 9 Nov. 2012. Speech.

Bernstein, Elizabeth. "Divorce's Guide to Marriage." *Wall Street Journal*. N.p., 24 July 2012. Web. 23 Oct. 2012.

Robinson, Joe. "Emotional Rescue." *Entrepreneur* January 2013: 28. Print.

Hann, Christopher. "Epic Fail." *Entrepreneur* January 2013: 34–36. Print.

Robinson, Joe. "Rebel Yell." *Entrepreneur* Mar. 2013: 30. Web.

Neck, Heidi. "Reframing Failure as Intentional Iteration: New Research on How Entrepreneurs Really Think." *Babson College*. The Babson Entrepreneur Experience Lab, n.d. Web.

Kiefer, Charles F., Leonard A. Schlesinger, and Paul B. Brown. *Action Trumps Everything: Creating What You Want in an Uncertain World*. Duxbury, MA: Black Ink, 2010. 33. Print.

Timmons, Jeffry A. "1." *New Venture Creation: Entrepreneurship for the 21sy Century*. 5th ed. N.p.: Irwin McGraw-Hill, 1999. 47. Print.

Kiefer, Charles F., Leonard A. Schlesinger, and Paul B. Brown. *Action Trumps Everything: Creating What You Want in an Uncertain World*. Duxbury, MA: Black Ink, 2010. 73. Print.

Neck, Heidi. "Reframing Failure as Intentional Iteration: New Research on How Entrepreneurs Really Think." *Babson College*. The Babson Entrepreneur Experience Lab, n.d. Web.

Robinson, Noah. "Tina Roth Eisenberg's 8 Mantras For Success." *Fast Company*. N.p., 10 Aug. 2012. Web. Video.

Cosper, Amy. "Editor's Note: A Defining Moment." *Entrepreneur* September 2012: 14. Print.

Ch. 9

Hoffman, Reid, and Ben Casnocha. "4." *The Start-up of You*. New York: Crown Business, 2012. Print.

Kiefer, Charles F., Leonard A. Schlesinger, and Paul B. Brown. *Action Trumps Everything: Creating What You Want in an Uncertain World*. Duxbury, MA: Black Ink, 2010. Print. 62–64.

Ch. 10

Vadukul, Alex. "Searching for a Companion, With a Smile and a Sign." *New York Times*. N.p., 20 Sept. 2012. Web.

Neck, Heidi M. "2." *The Portable MBA in Entrepreneurship*. New York [etc.: John Wiley & Sons, 2004. 27–52. Print.

Boutilier, Emily Gold. "The Boardroom Is Not Merrill 131." *Amherst Magazine* Summer 2013: 22-25. Print.

"Design Thinker: Experience Innovation" deck. IDEO + ExperiencePoint. Accessed while taking Babson College MBA Entrepreneurship & Opportunity class, Spring 2011.

Radcliffe, Shawn. "Quick Tip: Relieve Stress By Faking It." *Men's Fitness*. N.p., n.d. Web.

Hoffman, Reid, and Ben Casnocha. *The Start-up of You*. New York: Crown Business, 2012. 149–152. Print.

Reporter, Daily Mail. "The Price of True Love: How the Average Woman Will Date 24 Men and Spend over £2,000 before They Find Mr Right." *The Daily Mail.* N.p., 23 Apr. 2010. Web. 30 Apr. 2013.

Egan, Jennifer. "The Road to Bali." *New York Times.* N.p., 26 Feb. 2006. Web.

"Gordon MacKenzie Quotes." *Good Reads.* N.p., n.d. Web. <http://www.goodreads.com/author/quotes/13562.Gordon_MacKenzie>

Ch. 11

Gazelles, Herding. "How Attractive Are You to Potential Suitors?" *Inc.* N.p., 24 Feb. 2012. Web. 23 Oct. 2012.

Cooper, Belle Beth. "The 13 Biggest Failures From Famous Entrepreneurs and What They've Learned From Them." *Buffer App.* N.p., 5 Sept. 2013. Web. 6 Sept. 2013. Multiple quotes from this article in chapter 11.

Napoletano, Erika. "Listen and Learn." *Entrepreneur* January 2013: 23. Print.

Greenberg, Danna, Kathleen McKone-Sweet, and H. James. Wilson. "Entrepreneurial Leadership: Shaping Social and Economic Opportunity." Chapter 2: Fixson, Sebastian K., Rao, Jay. *The New Entrepreneurial Leader: Developing Leaders Who Shape Social and Economic Opportunity.* San Francisco, CA: Berrett-Koehler, 2011. N. pag. Print.

Greenberg, Danna, Kathleen McKone-Sweet, and H. James. Wilson. "Entrepreneurial Leadership: Shaping Social and Economic Opportunity." Chapter 9: Deets, Stephen, Lisa Dicarlo. *The New Entrepreneurial Leader: Developing Leaders Who Shape Social and Economic Opportunity.* San Francisco, CA: Berrett-Koehler, 2011. N. pag. Print.

Conclusion

Whitaker, Tara Lee. "Differences between Waterfall, Iterative Waterfall, Scrum and Lean Software Development." *Agilista PM.* N.p., n.d. Web. 3 Jan. 2013.

Nayab, N. "Agile vs. Waterfall — Is There a Real Winner?" *Bright Hub PM.* N.p., 12 July 2012. Web. 3 Jan. 2012.

Samuel. "Agile vs Scrum." *Bloggy Badger.* N.p., 23 July 2012. Web. 3 Jan. 2012.

Cooper, Belle Beth. "The 13 Biggest Failures From Famous Entrepreneurs and What They've Learned From Them." *Buffer App.* N.p., 5 Sept. 2013. Web. 6 Sept. 2013.

Eckfeldt, Bruce. "Lean and Agile: A Powerful Combination." Babson Center for Information Management Studies Workshop. MA, Babson Park. 25 Jan. 2013. Lecture.

Davis, Bob. "The 9 Mistakes Entrepreneurs Often Make on Their First Start-up." Babson College 2012 Entrepreneurship Forum. Babson College, Babson Park. 9 Nov. 2012. Speech.

APPENDIX

"Dating Like an Entrepreneur"
By Neely Steinberg

(Originally appeared in the *Boston Globe Magazine* in the August 1, 2010 issue.)

After almost a decade working at one of the top schools in the country for entrepreneurship, I know a thing or two about entrepreneurs. When you spend that much time in the company of the brightest, most innovative young adults in the world, you can't help but start to think like them. I'm a freelance writer in my spare time and often write about dating. Perhaps, I began to wonder, there was a way to fuse these two very different worlds of mine. Perhaps I could apply the ideas I've learned about business from our student entrepreneurs to something equally as important: love and relationships. A recent alumni panel of successful entrepreneurs gave me some valuable insight on this topic.

One of the panelists started off the discussion by comparing the creation of a business to starting a relationship; in effect, it's a marriage. Finding the right partner is crucial to your success. But more than

that: You need someone who will balance you, someone with whom you can not only argue but also respect their arguments. If you and your partner are too similar, thinking in exactly the same ways all the time, ironically, there will be too much competition; if your partner balances you, however, you can discover new ideas, new perspectives. You learn to trust each other, and trust is what ultimately carries you to the next step of both a relationship and a budding business venture.

I won't deny that my current boyfriend and I have had our fair share of spats during our time together. There have been moments when I've wished he was more like me or thought more like me, because it would make life so much easier. We'd have no disagreements and the relationship would be perfect. The more I think about it, though, the more I start to ponder how much of that fantasy really makes sense. Some of the most important ways I feel I've been able to heal and grow as an individual and a partner are in the aftermath of squabbles, because it is during these moments of respite that I force myself to engage in self-reflection. "You pay for the mistakes you make," opined a panelist, "but you learn from them and hopefully your business perseveres and becomes stronger." Sometimes I'm wrong; sometimes my boyfriend is wrong. And sometimes there is no wrong or right. But in the end, there is growth, lessons to be gleaned from the situation.

Another point that was discussed at the panel: When you start a business, proceed in small steps. Before you get to the next step, you need to make sure the business is working and viable. I've always been amazed by people who meet and get engaged after a short period of time – say, six months. I've never been that type of person, but I've certainly envied people who knew that their significant other was The One after only a handful of months.

My boyfriend and I have been together for a year, and my ring finger is still bare. If we do take that next step, it will happen on its own time, when we're ready and fairly certain that the foundation is there for long-term success.

Of course, the panelists also talked about risk. And to some degree, taking the next step in a relationship is a leap of faith, a risk we feel worth it. You can hem and haw forever about the foundation and whether or not it's solid enough, but at the end of the day, as one of the entrepreneurs said, "You need to build something with the notion that it could fail, but take the risk anyway."

If you do decide to take the plunge, to commit and devote yourself to building your life with someone, I'm a firm believer (at least at this point in my life, though I fully admit my perspective may be a tad naïve) that you need to, as one of the panelists maintained, "stay hungry, because when you stay hungry you stay excited." Furthermore, he explained, "It's not enough to think and speak entrepreneurially; you need to *take action*."

I can't imagine the day that my significant other and I aren't hungry for each other anymore. The day we stop trying with one another, the day we stop growing together and working together as a pair, the day our words speak louder than our actions, may very well be the day that our relationship files for bankruptcy.

—w—

"Thank you, ex-boyfriend"

By Neely Steinberg

(Originally appeared on *Huffington Post* on December 18, 2012.)

"Every single person who's drifted in and out of your life is a part of your Divinely chosen experience. As you move into the world of inspiration, you'll find it easy -- and even necessary -- to give thanks for all of these people, and to take serious note of what they brought you." - Dr. Wayne Dyer

(Please note: I encourage you to leave *your* thanks in the comments section below.)

In my 35 years, I've had approximately a bajillion dating experiences. I've had long-term boyfriends, short-term boyfriends, countless dates with disappearing men, blissful times, just so-so times and incredibly sad and lonely-beyond-belief times. As a young 20-something, I was inclined to see my experiences in the dating world as nothing more than wrong turns, failures and wasted opportunities. I used to wish I'd never met the guys who caused me heartbreak, or that I hadn't stayed with men I knew weren't right for me longer than I should have, including the nice guys but especially the rakes. I took little responsibility for my part in these experiences, nor did I seek to learn from them, avoiding any real introspection.

As the years passed, I put more energy into self-reflection and self-improvement. I began to see just how important all of my past relationships and dating experiences have been to my self-discovery. I like the woman I've become (although, certainly, I'll always be a

work in progress), and I am deeply thankful to all the men who have drifted in and out of my dating and love life for helping me to evolve.

As a dating coach, I encourage clients to offer similar gratitude to their exes by writing a letter titled "Thank you, ex-boyfriend." By reflecting deeply on their experiences with past boyfriends, short-term romances, flings and whoever else they select, clients empower themselves to begin letting go of the anger, hurt or apathy that may be preventing them from moving forward. They start to see these past men as teachers instead of wrongdoers or time-drains. Moreover, clients begin to realize they have the ability to take control of their dating and love lives by accepting the past, learning from it and being grateful for it. When you do this exercise (because I know you will!), you may be frightened, surprised, relieved or disappointed, among other emotions, by what you discover about yourself; just remember that whatever it is you *do* discover has the power to be instructive.

Below is *my list* of thank you's. They are based on a mix of relationships: those that were pleasant and ended fairly amicably, and those I considered more contentious, ending painfully. Some were long-term; some were short-term. I believe all types of experiences and relationships have lessons to offer. All names have been changed.

Mike: Thank you, Mike, for being my first boyfriend and for showing me that I have value and worth as a woman and human being. Thank you for allowing me to see myself as a girlfriend and partner to someone, that a man could want to put his time and energy into being with me for more than just a fling. Despite our relationship being fairly short at nine or so months and despite our ups and downs, I want to

thank you for the time you spent being kind, gentle and patient with me, despite my immaturity and lack of relationship know-how.

John: Thank you, John, for indirectly inspiring me to start seeing a therapist who could help me discover my unhealthy dating patterns, and the connections between my past and present-day behavior. Despite our emotionally draining, rollercoaster, on and off again relationship, I thank you for helping me to grow and learn. Thank you for also indirectly inspiring me to become a writer. Our dysfunctional relationship provoked me to write about dating and relationships, which led to a freelancing career, radio and Internet TV hosting gigs, an advice column and now, a career as a dating coach.

Jeremy: Thank you, Jeremy, for being the first man with whom I ever established true intimacy and a long-term relationship. In the three years we were together, I learned about what's important in relationships and got closer to understanding what kind of man would be good for me and the type of of man for whom I would be compatible. Thank you for showing me that I *am* cut out for long-term love, but that it often takes effort and commitment. Thank you for showing me that I can just "be" in a relationship, that just "being" is good enough.

Kevin: Thank you, Kevin, for definitively showing me that I don't need to chase men to get them to see my worth and that I have value to offer someone. Thank you for showing me that I don't have to try so hard all the time to deserve someone's affections.

Jacob: Thank you, Jacob, for definitively showing me that I butt heads with Alpha males. Despite my misguided desire for many years to be with a dominant, Alpha male type, I learned from our time together that I'm better-suited for a man who is more easy-going, sensitive to my needs, a good listener and allows me to shine.

To all of these exes (and the others from whom I haven't listed but have gained enormous self-knowledge), I thank you, from the bottom of my heart, for allowing me to learn and grow through the experiences we shared.

Are you *that woman* who can't see the silver lining from your past dating or relationship experiences? Do you have a friend who constantly complains about past beaus, crying foul about what she didn't get from those relationships? Remember: Your past relationships and dating experiences are not "failures"; rather, they are assets, opportunities for self-reflection and growth. Take some time out to reflect on your past romantic experiences with men and then write them a small note explaining your gratitude. What can they teach you about who you are and what you know about dating and relationships?

So... how can you thank your ex-boyfriends? Leave your thanks in the comments section below.

—◊—

Made in the USA
Lexington, KY
11 January 2017